Renegade Hero
or Faux Rogue

Renegade Hero or Faux Rogue

The Secret Traditionalism of Television Bad Boys

ASHLEY M. DONNELLY

McFarland & Company, Inc., Publishers
Jefferson, North Carolina

LIBRARY OF CONGRESS CATALOGUING-IN-PUBLICATION DATA

Donnelly, Ashley M., 1978–
    Renegade hero or faux rogue : the secret traditionalism of television bad boys / Ashley M. Donnelly.
    p.   cm.
    Includes bibliographical references and index.

    ISBN 978-0-7864-7144-7 (softcover : acid free paper) ∞
    ISBN 978-1-4766-1463-2 (ebook)

    1. Antiheroes on television.   2. Men on television.   3. Sex role on television.   4. Television—Social aspects—United States. I. Title.
PN1992.8.A65D66 2014
791.45'652—dc23   2014009410

BRITISH LIBRARY CATALOGUING DATA ARE AVAILABLE

© 2014 Ashley M. Donnelly. All rights reserved

No part of this book may be reproduced or transmitted in any form or by any means, electronic or mechanical, including photocopying or recording, or by any information storage and retrieval system, without permission in writing from the publisher.

Front cover image: *Dexter* TV Series Season 6, 2011 (Showtime Networks/Photofest)

Printed in the United States of America

McFarland & Company, Inc., Publishers
   Box 611, Jefferson, North Carolina 28640
   www.mcfarlandpub.com

For Mike and Aine.

Thanks for the noise-cancelling headphones,
the space to create, and the hugs
that got me through the process.
I love you both.

Acknowledgments

This book would not have been possible without the support of the Telecommunications Department and the College of Communication, Information, and Media at Ball State University. I would also like to thank Lee Davidson, my personal copy editor, and Alysia Sawchyn who helped me with some last-minute reading and insights. Thanks to Dr. Bob Batchelor for his insistence that this book not only could be written, but should be, and to Dr. Gregg Bachman who offered to read and critique random pieces of this puzzle to get me back on track when I was banging my head on my desk. Jason Smith, Julia Largent, and Jacob Zubler all helped keep me moving along with their research assistance even when I scowled at them or made strange noises and for that I am grateful.

Table of Contents

Acknowledgments	vi
Preface	1
Introduction: How Did We Get from There to Here and What Is a Faux Rogue?	5
1. Why Showtime's *Dexter* Is Truly Terrifying	33
2. *Sons of Anarchy*: Power, the Justification of Violence and Reform Through Capitalism	53
3. *True Blood*: Subverting the Myth of American Inclusion	70
4. *Breaking Bad*: Privilege and the Power of Choice	91
5. *Boardwalk Empire*: The Romantic Side of Crime and Capitalism	109
6. The Woman and the Faux Rogue	125
Conclusion	157
Chapter Notes	175
Bibliography	183
Index	189

Preface

The following book is my attempt to understand the power of television narratives in a time of confusion, blatant public hate, and ideological contradictions in America's public sphere of discourse. New media have exploded, the need for information and entertainment has become insatiable, and a demand for immediacy dominates consumption. One would imagine that freedom of choice and audience autonomy should be increasing through new avenues of communication like Web-based shows and independent direction and production in all media industries, thus ensuring a growing power of democracy and discourse in our media sphere. Yet in my years of teaching and researching popular culture and media studies, what I have seen suggests the opposite.

I've become fascinated by the vise-grip the Big 6 has on American (and international) media and how little energy is expended on exploring the fictional narratives produced by the major corporations—and how little anyone seems to be able to do about it. My students come into my courses already jaded by news bias and political discourse. A callous awareness of media manipulation has become an uncomfortable norm in discussions of critical social issues with both undergraduates and graduate students who aim to become a part of the culture industry. Yet they, like most of my colleagues and friends, still happily absorb the messages sold to them through American television fiction even though these fictions are mediated through the same factors as the news and infotainment that they dismiss.

Having studied trends in interest in pop culture studies and in my attempts to stay current with what America is watching, in 2007 I started

Preface

to notice the growing presence of what I would have initially called the anti-hero in mainstream fictional dramas. The more I watched shows like *Dexter* and *Sons of Anarchy*, the more I realized that these "anti-heroes" were simply reincarnations of every pro–Capitalist, ethnocentric, conservative hero to have thrived on television before. These guys just happened to be bloodier. And slightly more sociopathic. Thus I began my investigation of such characters with verve.

What follows is a study of the cumulative messaging that comes from a selection of mainstream serial dramas. The overall book attempts to explore them contextually, identifying how the sociopolitical issues of the early 2000s are present in their latent messages and how the fictional narratives might affect audiences within the same contextual position. This is not a book interrogating each series in depth. I do not talk at any length about production or narrative quality, nor am I attempting to give a thorough analysis of each individual show. What I'm offering is an analysis of what Frankfurt School critics like Adorno and Benjamin would call "dialectical images" produced and reproduced throughout the various programs. I am situating the shows in a particular time period, discussing the particular economic, social, and historical issues of which they are a part. Though fictional narratives tend to be somewhat cyclical and some might argue that we have seen these ideas before (characters like Dexter reflecting certain characteristics present in early film noir, for example), the point of my argument is not to say that any of the issues I address are new or unheard of, but that, within their particular sociohistorical situation, the messages of the shows I examine are particularly powerful for very particular reasons.

I am most concerned about the main heroes of mainstream serial dramas masquerading as rogue heroes doing "what's right" regardless of U.S. law or typically accepted moral codes. Such "faux rogues," as I've named them, are seemingly leading a revolution against established leadership, challenging entrenched ideas of "right" and "wrong," and redefining what it means to be a true hero. Initially I had hoped this was true, excited by the idea that audiences are digesting narratives of change, optimism, and empowerment through popular culture. However what I'm seeing and what I hope to prove through my discussion of five popular dramas is that these faux rogues are simply re-teaching outdated

Preface

ideals of white, masculine power, Capitalist supremacy, labor exploitation, class-based prejudice, and ethnocentrism.

Doing this under the guise of a new kind of kickass hero to be emulated is a powerful tool of audience manipulation and a threat to our nation's ideological construction. Popular television, though often overlooked or dismissed as simple entertainment, is an extremely powerful voice in mainstream culture. A voice that shapes our national identity, our acceptance of social norms, and our ideas of what it means to be powerful. I want this book to draw awareness to the power of cumulative messaging in television serials. I want to help create awareness of the impact that television fictions have on our collective ideologies. By first identifying how popular television narratives are being manipulated by those with media power, it is my hope that we can then begin to understand how to use dramatic television as a means for positive change. I also want to stress the importance of bringing politics and popular culture together in academia. The following book, though referencing critics and theorists and using notable works as support beams, is written to be accessible to both academics and non-academics. Ideally, scholars, students, and fans of television will all find something in here to connect with and something to inspire their own critical work.

The political fight in cultural and critical studies seems dimmer now than it ever has before and I, along with several of my contemporaries, am concerned by this. I hope I can make enough connections for readers between U.S. political and social issues and the entertainment of popular television to spark questions, reconsiderations, and, ideally, action.

Introduction:
How Did We Get from
There to Here and
What Is a Faux Rogue?

The television has been a staple of the U.S. home since its widespread production at the end of World War II. According to the U.S. Department Bureau of Labor's 2009 survey, "Watching TV was the leisure activity that occupied the most time [in the U.S. home] (2.8 hours per day), accounting for about half of leisure time, on average, for those age 15 and over."[1] According to the Nielsen Company, during the week of May 23, 2011, the top five rated shows in the country[2] drew between 10,364,000 and 29,288,000 viewers.[3] Over 99 percent of U.S. homes include at least one television set.[4] Despite an increasingly loud argument that TV is dying in mainstream culture, the number of viewers and faithful followers of TV shows consistently challenges this noise of discontent. The "voice from the box" pervades the U.S. subconscious in a way that no other form of media can quite match. More than books, more than websites, more than radio, and more than independent media, television serves as a constant in the U.S. home. Whether we record "our" shows, stream them through Netflix, or tune in live to whatever derivative reality show is popular at the moment, the vast majority of the enfranchised[5] population is able to focus on serialized television for several seasons in a row. And such dedication is why I argue that the television, more than films or books, or any other form of media, has the largest influence over American ideological construction.

Introduction

The study of television, unlike the study of film or literature, forces one to explore the context and historicity of the stories being presented. Not that film or literature or any other form of art must ever be divorced from such study, of course, but texts that stand alone as works of a particular novelist, director, sculptor, architect, or poet are, arguably, easier to examine singularly, from a variety of viewpoints, without necessarily situating them within a particular political context. And though television is changing and its audience has more freedom of choice, more flexibility in the mode through which they consume shows, and more autonomy from traditional television advertisement, television shows as a whole present a body of work that is fleeting, derivative, and ultimately tied to the historical and political period in which they are produced.

> Granted, in years gone by, particular *programs* may have held greater sway, as when 82.6 percent of American television-owning households turned to *The Ed Sullivan Show* in 1956 to watch Elvis, when 32.3 million Britons tuned in to watch England defeat Germany in the World Cup Final in 1966, or when the *M*A*S*H* finale played to 125 million Americans in 1983. But just as we could hardly announce that sports are dead simply because not everyone is playing football, so too does television remain a force to be reckoned with. Television can still regularly command a nightly broadcast viewing audience of over 100 million in the United States, and while ratings-topping shows such as *American Idol* in the U.S. or *The X Factor* in the UK may "only" have garnered audiences of 20 million (65 percent of the U.S. population) in 2010 and 13 million (20.1 percent of the UK population) in 2009 respectively, such numbers are still amazing.... Thus, while patterns of use and the screens we use are changing, the need to understand the relationship of television as a business, cultural storyteller, and object of considerable popular interest remains as crucial as ever.[6]

The following chapters by no means attempt a universal explanation of television or American culture as a whole. Obviously no culture is entirely hegemonic. There are exceptions to my arguments, as there would be to any cultural analysis. And one must remember the context of my arguments is particular to the early 2000s timeframe. I am attempting to use "snapshots" from popular programming to identify the cumulative messages present in mainstream U.S. television. As Gray and Lotz argue above, the need to understand what is happening in

Introduction

mainstream television remains as important as ever, and through my discussion of the following shows, I hope to present a cogent analysis of what these narratives actually are saying. Looking at them as cultural artifacts, signs of popular, collective enjoyment, I hope to expose their ideological messages. I do not argue that x affects y exactly one way or another, but I instead suggest how the repetition of ideas and arguments that are the building blocks of an ideological system may formulate a potential worldview for viewers. Though I understand that there are multiple audiences receiving such stories through very different filters, my argument is that, if absorbed enough, the hegemonic narratives of mainstream television will reach a multitude of audiences with their often dangerous, oppressive messages.

Thus, the following book, to borrow a colorful phrase from Žižek,[7] "mercilessly exploits" television as a means of breaking through the façade of American mythology that is continually perpetuated at home and abroad to get to the meat of the social, cultural, and economic issues of the early 2000s.

A Brief Overview of the Hero in U.S. Television

The following book examines the nature of the male "anti-hero" of contemporary U.S. television and explores whether or not his presence is a genuine movement away from ideological absolutes on television or something less grandiose and possibly more detrimental to our current cultural climate. We begin with a simple discussion of the male hero in U.S. TV and his role in American culture. It follows both the mainstays of the character archetype through the decades and the seeming metamorphosis of this figure over the past fifteen years. What then follows is my argument that the "new" American anti-hero is nothing more than an antiquated figure of limited depth posing as a leader of change.

In 2011 PBS released four episodes of a series called *America in Primetime* through which four archetypal characters in American TV are examined: "Independent Woman," "Man of the House," "The Outsider," and "The Crusader."[8] All of the episodes feature current writers,

Introduction

directors, producers, and actors from popular television shows. "The Crusader" was particularly interesting to me, as I was garnering material for the following chapters of this book. It begins with Michael C. Hall, the actor who plays Dexter on HBO's hit series and who also starred in the wonderful *Six Feet Under* series, saying one thing: "We're drawn to heroic characters, whether they're more traditional or otherwise, because there is a fundamental appetite for a savior."[9] A savior. To many, the hero can be summarized with this one singular word, a man (in this book I speak about male heroes only, saving female heroes for a project with the depth and focus they deserve) who does what's right for the good of the cause, who keeps humankind safe, and who sacrifices himself or a part of himself in order to save others. As "The Crusader" unfolds, it is striking how many writers, directors, and actors connect their hero character with a kind of Christ figure, yet one who does not simply sacrifice his life for the good of the many, but, more specifically, one who sacrifices part of his soul with each act of heroism he performs. Alan Alda's Hawkeye from *M*A*S*H* is referred to frequently, as are Jack Bauer from *24*, Detective Frank Pembleton from *Homicide: Life on the Streets*, Dexter, and even Sgt. Andy Sipowicz from *NYPD Blue*. These men's moments of weakness, selfishness, and hostility and their criminal acts are discussed as necessary for someone who takes the world's evil upon himself in an attempt to eradicate it.

Though their individual acts are called into question by some of the professionals in the show, each time this interrogation into the potentially villainous behavior of "good characters" occurs, the hero ultimately is defended. The all-encompassing argument is that heroes such as these, even if they do terrible things, will give all of themselves to avenge, protect, or save the innocent, even if they themselves come close to losing their humanity. It is a beautiful tale, truly poetic. But is it true?

Robert Cochran, co-creator of *24*, says in "The Crusader" that when there is much going on in the world that we, as humans, cannot understand, we make sense of such things by telling stories about them. And this is true; Greek and Roman gods interfered with our lives in ancient times, weather and illness were blamed on witches, and religions across the world use parables to teach and explain that which is intangible. After 9/11 Cochran and the *24* team wondered if it was appropriate to

Introduction

continue airing the show. They decided not only to continue airing the show but also to send Bauer deeper into a world of terror, torture, and other forms of violence that made so little sense to the general populace, they believed they were helping viewers cope and understand the world around them. Even after Abu Ghraib, when U.S. citizens were forced to see images of *our* soldiers torturing prisoners of war, and when Guantanamo Bay was in the forefront of many politically focused minds, Jack Bauer tortured and terrorized subjects on primetime television. By this logic, the horror of the fictional world in which Bauer not only participated but *defended* was the show's way of helping us understand the abominable practice of torturing a human being for "good reason." So, in essence, yes, these stories help us understand, perhaps, motivation and rationalization, but my concern is that mainstreaming narratives of torture and violence against humanity does not simply explain things to us as simple-minded people unable to grasp the complexities of warfare; it justifies them, making us complicit in the atrocities committed by a few and desensitizing viewing audiences to these acts. It plants these seeds of an ideological worldview that should scare us, not strengthen us.

The complexities of narratives such as *24* were not always present in mainstream television. However heroes and ideology are forever intertwined. Studying American folklore, Roger D. Abrahams argues that "legendary heroes arise because values guiding action exist within a certain group and individuals appear or are imagined who act in line with these values to a superlative degree."[10] In essence, the hero of any group not only will embody its norms and expectations but will exceed in the qualities or areas deemed valuable or laudable. Heroes encompass and represent a social construct. This social construct is one that gives valor to those it sees excel in traits that are important but often rare, such as bravery or extreme strength. Notably, many of the qualities associated with heroes from the Greeks on can be labeled as "masculine" in the heteronormative dichotomy. According to Holt and Thompson, co-authors of "Man-of-Action Heroes: The Pursuit of Heroic Masculinity in Everyday Consumption," in the "man-of-action" hero tale, tales of figures such as James Bond, Dirty Harry, and Rambo, "the same happy ending is forever repeated: The heroic superman vanquishes the diabolical foe, proves his manhood with panache, restores moral order,

Introduction

saves society ... gets the girl, and then takes his well-deserved seat at the pinnacle of a patriarchal status hierarchy."[11] The "man-of-action" serves a purpose: He is a leader, a role model, and someone to trust. He brings simplicity in times of chaos and comfort in times of fear. Regardless of culture, time period, or ideological belief, a hero is someone central to the narratives who helps create and preserve the worldview of social groups. The first "mainstreaming" of heroes happened through the small screen of television.

TV came of age, if you will, in 1948, '49, and '50—the years following World War II. Marshall Herskovitz, co-creator of *Thirtysomething*, believes this "accident of history," as he calls it, these fifteen years after World War II, were a cultural backwash of what happened during the war, and that a lot of things were taken as a given that needed to be questioned. One of these was the depiction of male heroism.[12] In the early days of television, Westerns quickly became a staple of the medium. Shows such as *The Lone Ranger*, *Gunsmoke*, and *Bonanza* are simple examples of a genre of massive proportions. In early Westerns, set during the time of America's conquest of the West, issues related to codes of morality—clear lines between "good" and "evil" (white cowboy hats versus black cowboy hats), the need for law in what was still an abstract situation of order, and the idea of bringing honor to a land of chaos—were the key themes repeated again and again. These tales of cowboys were by no means new: They recalled ancient tales of knights, the Japanese ronin, and so on. TV Westerns featured good men, men of honor, roaming the Wild West rescuing women, defeating villains, and subduing the everpresent threat of "Indians."

Herskovitz, as stated above, believes these shows were about a form of male heroism that needs to be interrogated. As many of the older writers, producers, and actors in "The Crusader" who watched such shows in their youth remember the kinds of men they saw, week after week, they discuss men who were brave and strong and stood up for what was right, men who knew everything, who always won, and men who were rough, tough, and unemotional. The heroes of early television represent a very particular kind of masculinity that limits and dictates what a man *should be*. And what is most interesting about the discussion of the men talking about these shows is that they are very candid in

Introduction

their admissions that they were most certainly not "these men" and that the men they saw and interacted with in real life were not Western heroes. They were not immersed in a world of John Waynes outside the world of television.

Tom Fontana, co-creator of *Homicide: Life on the Streets,* offers a suggestion as to why such characters dominated television narratives. He suggests that America was feeling very "muscular after World War II in the '50s" and high on the notion that "the American way of life was the only way of life and the best way of life."[13] Dominant cowboy characters had a certain swagger, a righteous toughness that, according to Fontana, America needed. At the apex of a new period in history, though there had always been the American Adam and the revolutionaries who forged our young nation, in the era after World War II we "wanted our folk heroes, our TV heroes, to be reflective of our own image of ourself as a country,"[14] which meant a nation that could take on Hitler and win, that could send its young men into an atrocious war and come out victorious. Though history has taught us that the scars of that war would haunt a generation of men, our TV heroes made them supernatural, larger-than-life strongmen, like Superman, who fought for "truth, justice, and the American way." We did not need complex characters or moral ambiguity, particularly as a country that had just deployed the atomic bomb, the most horrific, devastating, and feared weapon in the history of the world. Shawn Ryan, creator of *The Shield,* argued that America did not tune in to *Gunsmoke* each week wondering if the heroes were going to make the right decision. They did not tune in "wondering, 'Are these guys going to make the wrong choice and maybe steal some cattle today?'" Viewers knew the white hats would always make the right decisions.

The Lone Ranger, ABC's first true hit, epitomizes the form of hero as savior. He "helped anyone in need, never accepted payment for his services, and always defeated the bad guys."[15] The Lone Ranger never failed, and when viewers saw him riding in, they knew all would be right in the world again. In his article "Beowulf to Batman: The Epic Hero and Pop Culture," Roger B. Rollin suggests that it is

> possible that the messianic overtones of the formula which *The Lone Ranger* so obviously played upon were partly responsible for its wide

Introduction

appeal: in times of crisis we look for a deliverer; a Beowulf or a Lone Ranger. The vague origins and the sudden departure of such heroes also serve to enhance their legends. These legends in time take on almost religious status, becoming myths which provide the communities not only with models for conduct but with the kind of heightened shared experiences which inspire and unify their members.[16]

Recalling Michael C. Hall's early comments in "The Crusader" about audiences craving a savior, as in the cowboys of the frontier in the 1950s and the early cop dramas that followed in suit, it is easy to see how that need was met by television heroes and how what seem like simple narratives of good guys versus bad guys create a longer narrative of justice, rules of behavior, and an ideological system in which American ideals of masculinity, heroism, and codes of ethics dominated the messages beamed into the living rooms of an ever-increasing audience.

It's Always About Cowboys!

Anecdotally, as I worked my way through this book, I begrudgingly accepted a graduate assistant from a program outside of my department. He needed work hours to get his stipend, and because of his course load, he had nowhere to fit in terms of teaching or TA-ing. So I took him on as a research assistant. My reluctance had nothing to do with this smart young man as a person; it was that he was in the Computer, Information, and Communication Science master's program, which meant he had a future in, well, "computer stuff." But we got along and he was a fantastic worker. The best part of our two-semester collaboration, however, was the day he came into my office beaming and extraordinarily excited to discuss his database research. This, in my experience, is very rare. Before he even sat down, he declared, "They're all cowboys! Even the cops!"[17] It took me a minute before I could figure out what he was talking about. All I had asked him to do was pull some articles for me on heroes, American heroes, and so forth. But he got interested the more he worked and started reading everything quite closely until he realized that, from the beginnings of TV to today, in terms of male heroes, "They're all cowboys!" Of course we discussed the differences and subtleties, but this

Introduction

young guy with a future in "computer stuff" now has a fascination with American heroes and their connections to our bizarre history with the Wild West.

The best part of his insight is that, of course, he is right. Scholars have been talking about this for decades, but Jake's enthusiasm was catching. Though I knew the purpose of my book and my interest in how our heroes have become mutated, the fact that they all possess aspects of the archetypal cowboy suddenly became important to me again. My anti-heroes are cowboys, too—and rather than take that as a given, I needed to really understand the significance of the archetypal holdover while understanding that now on TV the hats are gray and the same day as they ride in to town to rid it of an evil sheriff, our cowboys may in fact do some cattle rustling.

In "The Crusader," the directors make an interesting jump from Westerns to M*A*S*H. How, Judd Apatow asks, could U.S. television possibly screen an incredibly popular show about a vicious war in Korea right in the middle of the Vietnam War? He does not know, and I definitely do not, but listening to Apatow's discussion touched home as he described watching M*A*S*H reruns from the time he was five or six years old; he argues that this simple act of watching reruns shaped his moral and ethical understanding of the world through the lens of Larry Gelbart. Apatow hit on something that those coming of age in the 1980s "got" as they were immersed in it and that those raised on *Gunsmoke* and *The Lone Ranger* would eventually have to wrestle with: their responsibility in understanding and decoding the moral ambiguity of complicated heroes. Though Hawkeye is no Dexter, the seeds of hero complexity were sown in the M*A*S*H era of television.

Alan Alda, when looking back on his time on M*A*S*H, says, yes, Hawkeye is a maverick, but at the same time, he is quite conservative: He wants nothing more than the government to leave him alone so he can get properly drunk and have some uninterrupted sex.[18] What Alda does go into great detail about on camera are the ethical issues he and the other M*A*S*H cast members were forced to deal with. He discusses in detail the episode in which he wants to perform an unnecessary appendectomy on Colonel Lacy because Lacy persists (recklessly, in Hawkeye's opinion) in sending his soldiers into unnecessary and deadly

Introduction

battles. Alda discusses the "real-life" fight he had with Mike Farrell (who played B.J.) over the script and how they ended up, nearly verbatim, including that argument in the scene, as they both felt the ethical dilemma needed to be voiced to the U.S. population.[19]

1950s

Television has presented viewers with narratives and characters that could shape their worldview since it first began. As stated above, in the late 1940s and early '50s, television had heroes who matched the American ideology the nation wanted to present to the world: a rough, tough, masculine image full of justice and earnest goodness. After Westerns dominated the small screen, cop dramas followed, moving the focus from the western frontier to an urban one. According to Hal Hemmelstein in his book *Television Myth and the American Mind*, as television evolved throughout the '50s and the post–World War II convivial attitude of success waned in the face of rising tensions with Russia, the McCarthy trials, and the space race, what TV dramas

> gave us during this period of global uncertainty was a predictably highly simplistic ideological frame in which petty criminals were quickly and easily apprehended by the authorities—law-and-order cops whose crime-solving methods, often excessively violent, went unquestioned. From the realistic routine of police work so effectively portrayed in *Dragnet* (1952–59), the melodrama of the urban frontier moved to the excesses of *M Squad* to the ultraviolent *The Untouchables*, men who fought the violence of organized crime with a retribution unparalleled in television history and backed by the authority of our federal government.[20]

Television, many scholars argue, did increase in violence quickly, yet the violence of Westerns and cop dramas had the benefit of being easy to rationalize, particularly as their narratives neatly ended with good conquering bad.

1960s

According to Hemmelstein, "the 1960s were ushered in by the optimism of John F. Kennedy's New Frontier. A mood of youthful exuberance,

Introduction

expansionism, and, however briefly, of compassion swept the nation."[21] Kennedy offered the hope of equality to minorities. The "Kennedy-Khrushchev missile showdown, itself, interestingly, conjuring images from the opening of *Gunsmoke*," offered a glimpse of a nation once again feeling strong and just, and television dramas were "reinforcing this decidedly upbeat, if self-delusory, mood."[22] Television dramas were firmly exploring the urban frontier of courtrooms, the justice system, and the medical field, all areas in which humanity was the focus and an interworking of systems overcoming injustice and human agony.

"While the family Western of the early 1960s, *à la Bonanza*, was providing views with a mythic psychic geography similar to that of the suburban-middle-landscape comedies of the period," in which adults perhaps wanted to believe was the new order of pecuniary security and family love and warmth, argues Hemmelstein, the romantic motif of the Western "journey" was now being perpetuated by the suburb and exurb hero, "our contemporary, 'one of us.'"[23] Another scholar argues, however, that

> by the mid–1960s, the dream of a harmonious, middle-class America was fraying visibly at the edges. Latent schisms of class, race, gender, and generation erupted into open conflict in the world outside television entertainment. But programming executives in the 1960s, for all their declared sensitivity to changes in public mood, continued to produce mild, consensual series like *The Donna Reed Show* and *My Three Sons*. If television news was preoccupied with urban unrest, an unstable economy, the escalating Vietnam War and a generation of college students rebelling against their parents' values, the episodic series blithely suggested that nothing uncomfortable was happening.[24]

The 1960s seemed to end with conflicting ideological images on screen, between the reality of rising crises and escalating movements in American social systems and the traditional family comedies and dramas and vindicated heroes of the more gritty dramas.

1970s

Though '60s television, generally speaking, tended to conflict with the real-world issues of the country at the time, *All in the Family* made

Introduction

its debut in 1971, articulating the social, ideological, and generational clashes discussed previously. The spin-off shows that followed remained in the vein of socially responsible or at least socially open programming. At the same time, police dramas flourished, among them *Barnaby Jones, Columbo, Kojak,* and *Hawaii Five-O.* Though their streets were grittier than ever and their backstories often more painful and difficult than their predecessors, the fine men (and women) on the side of jurisprudence always won and left Americans with safe (television) streets at the end of each episode. In addition to safe streets, America could look to its medical professionals for a new source of primetime heroes, such as *Marcus Welby, M.D.* and *Quincy, M.E.* The 1970s also saw the rise of *M*A*S*H,* and it is here, I argue, that one can truly begin to see the complexities of social issues and ideological constructions played with through dramatic characters, most notably anti-heroes such as Hawkeye.

Ironically, the new face of the Humanist hero arrived around the same time as a shift in television organization and marketing tactics leaned towards audience study and commercialism. A new policy in the 1970s made "demographics" the official new ratings strategy, breaking audiences down by age, sex, income, and other variables to isolate the most profitable television markets. "Scheduling now became an elaborate strategic exercise no longer designed merely to reach the widest possible audience with any given show, but to group programs and commercials in various time slots to target specific audiences."[25] This new shift in focus firmly bound network shows and advertisers, restricting not just time slots and schedules, but content as well. Advertisers wanted to attract viewers who would buy their products, and producers needed to please advertisers for their financial support. Thus the symbiotic relationship, seen through the new lens of demographics, was forged.

1980s

As TV came of age, so did the people's fight for diverse media ownership.

Introduction

In 1964, the Local TV Multiple Ownership Rule was written into law. This law prevented owning multiple television stations in any given market, unless there are more than eight stations within the market. In 1970, the Radio/TV Cross Ownership Rule was founded, which prevented big media from owning a television and radio station in the same market jurisdiction. Similarly, owning both a broadcast television station and a newspaper was barred in 1975.[26]

However, as the Reagan administration pursued a policy of deregulation, the television industry was able to capitalize on this chance to garner its power.

President Ronald Reagan began reversing regulation laws and systematically demolishing media restraints. First, Reagan rescinded the rules that ensured that non-entertainment programming would be broadcast. Reagan then initiated the major overturn of media regulation policy in 1987, when the Bush administration sought to put an end to the Fairness Doctrine. In the court case *Meredith Corp. v. FCC*, the courts ruled that the FCC was no longer responsible for regulating the Fairness Doctrine because Congress did not mandate it.[27]

Later I discuss what has become known as "The Big 6," the conglomeration of six mega-corporations that own and operate 90 percent of mainstream media in America. Television and the narratives it offered would be forever changed after 1980. This is embodied by the popularity of the show *Dallas*, which ran from 1978 until 1991. The show featured J.R. Ewing, played by Larry Hagman, a wealthy Texan involved with oil and cattle. It was an evening soap opera drama whose lead player was a greedy, scheming, diabolical oil tycoon. It was a show dedicated to making money and the lifestyle that went along with that goal. It was followed in 1981 by *Dynasty*, which took the glitz and glamour of the nouveau riche to extremes. In this decade in American TV, though it did have its heroes, preserving the cop and medical dramas on shows such as *Hill Street Blues, Miami Vice, The A-Team, CHiPs, MacGyver*, and even *Doogie Howser, M.D.*, it is difficult to pinpoint, exactly, a new hero outside of the cowboy archetype. Lives were saved, moral order restored, and a clear box of reality was presented in most '80s narratives. Though there were some changes, such as the inclusion of more characters of color and more complex roles for women, the real shift in hero formation did not begin until the 1990s, with the exception of Detective

Introduction

Frank Pembleton, played by Andre Braugher, of *Homicide: Life on the Streets*. In this gritty cop drama, Pembleton first resembles the kind of character that many of the participants of "The Crusader" labeled a kind of Christ figure. Deeply religious, Pembleton genuinely wants to help people, but his job slowly and deeply changes him as he is immersed in the worst of what the world has to offer. His shoulders heavily burdened, he begins to buckle. Some rides are too rough for this cop, and the reality and violence and soul-destroying nature of police work is bared for audiences to see. Pembleton is relatable and very, very human.

1990s

In the '90s, the cop drama genre flourished, notably *NYPD Blue*, which ran from 1993 to 2005. Similar to *Homicide*, the show is gritty, exposing the ugly side of both criminals and the workings of jurisprudence. Detective Andy Sipowicz is a drunk, is gruff, and is willing to beat suspects if he feels like it. A modern-day cowboy, Sipowicz is difficult to bond with but is a man who truly does seem to want to be on the side of justice. In 1994, the medical drama *E.R.* emerged; it was the first medical drama to win a series Emmy since *Marcus Welby, M.D.* Though it did not veer too far from the trail earlier medical dramas had blazed, it featured significantly more human characters, doctors who made mistakes (in both their personal and professional lives), and patients who died. The show emphasized the flaws of all its characters even as it featured them as medical heroes saving lives

The *X-Files* first aired in 1993. Billed as a "science fiction horror drama," the show portrays a secret office of the FBI that explores unexplained phenomena. The partner combination of Agent Fox Mulder, a profiler and avid believer in extraterrestrials, and Agent Dana Scully, a medical doctor and innate skeptic, the tension and back-and-forth banter between the two created a believable, human component to a show full of conspiracy and supernatural plotlines. The *X-Files*, though it came from a long tradition of shows such as *The Twilight Zone* and *Tales from the Darkside*, aired at a time when the children of those raised during Watergate and Vietnam, and tragedies such as the Iran Hostage Crisis

Introduction

and the economic troubles of the 1980s, were coming of age. Many had gone through Cold War drills in school and knew from a young age about nuclear threat. The world of "Gen-Xers" was tainted by an inborn mistrust of government and a relatively bleak outlook toward their futures. Shows such as *The X-Files* tapped into this distrust and disaffection and offered an outlet in the form of conspiracy entertainment.

The 2000s

Toward the end of the 1990s and the beginning of the 2000s, more and more heroes were emerging who no longer looked like the cowboys of years past or like Superman. In fact, even Superman himself got a kind of make-over. *Smallville*, which ran from 2001 to 2011 on the CW network, focused on a teenage Clark Kent, emphasizing his weaknesses, his doubts, and his very human growing pains. Though he remained a superhero fighting for truth, justice, and the American way, the show made him much more dynamic, exposing his doubts and his dark side. In 1997 *Buffy the Vampire Slayer* first aired, creator Joss Whedon having invented a character who was part cheerleader, part vampire-killing machine. It was a formula that worked: The series ran until 2003, spawning the spin-off *Angel*, about a vampire determined to make up for his past and the world of other dangerous monsters. The sci-fi–fantasy genre was ripe for offering complex heroes and heroines if simply because plotlines and expectations are more malleable in the genre. Regardless, complex, sometimes downright heinous characters became heroes, and the seeds of the anti-hero as protagonist were about to bloom.

The first major character I connect with those of this book is Tony Soprano of *The Sopranos*, which aired on HBO from 1999 to 2007. A family mob drama, the show was something special, as the simple one-liners from traditional Mafia films were replaced by Soprano's monologues in his psychiatrist's office. The cowed wife was now a very loud voice of dissent, and Soprano struggles in the series to maintain control over both his "family" and his literal family. Murders, strip-club fronts, and affairs all remained, as well as many of the other tropes of

Introduction

gangland fiction, but the complexity and dynamic components of Soprano make him easy to root for.

Debuting in 2004, *House M.D.* featured one of the most offensive, unpleasant anti-hero protagonists to grace the small screen. A world-renowned diagnostician, Gregory House is god-like in his field. He is also an antisocial drug addict with very little capability for empathy. He is Sherlock Holmes on a really, really bad day looking for clues to a seemingly unsolvable case. Though he is easy to despise, his desire for understanding and his relentless pursuit of life-saving treatments redeem him, and he becomes a beloved lead in the eight years of the show's running. He is a cowboy on the medical frontier, forging blindly ahead, often with a stupid level of bravery. He may act like a man in a black hat, but his underlying motivation is as pure and straightforward as that of the heroes of early Westerns. He wants to save people and solve problems. House was one of the characters who first piqued my interest in the anti-hero lead of contemporary U.S. television. I left him out because the show is too neat and too clear-cut in contrast to the bloody, confusing arenas of those I engage in the following chapters. Overall I feel it safe to say that the very late 1990s and early 2000s began to offer TV shows and characters that set the stage for the anti-hero leads who exploded onto the set in the mid–2000s.

A Guide to Understanding the Shape of the Following Book

When I first began my exploration into television show characters including Dexter, Jax Teller from *Sons of Anarchy*, the vampires of *True Blood*, and Walter White from *Breaking Bad,* I thought, perhaps, that mainstream fictional narratives were beginning to focus on a new kind of humanist ethic in American culture. Though these characters' acts are often brutal, manipulative, and cruel, their motives and rationalizations are deeply rooted in their beliefs of what's right not just for a particular situation (as is the trend for traditional anti-heroes), but also for humanity as a whole. They seem to be striving for autonomy, justice, equality, and an intangible kind of "rightness" for their fellow citizens,

Introduction

even when (sometimes especially when) their behavior comes into conflict with the ideologies of the U.S. government, any kind of law enforcement, and even the ideals of dominant religious doctrines. I had begun to hope that, as a nation, Americans[28] were beginning to establish a new kind of tolerance for gray areas, a new understanding of Others, and a new appreciation for an inherent "goodness" of humankind.

As the 2000s roll on and the polarity of American politics reaches new levels of absurdity, holes in the nation's economic, structural, social, and cultural foundations are being exposed. The surge in cultural paranoia that was produced post–9/11 has not gone away. Heated debates over issues such as gay marriage and illegal immigration dominate the headlines. As a nation, we seem divided, intolerant, and generally angry. The idea that television and its heroes could produce a kind of panacea for division and prejudice was intoxicating.

Yet, the more I considered this potential paradigm shift from the black-and-white ideals of law and moral codes that permeate mainstream popular narratives to a deeper consideration for the complexity of all human beings, the more I realized I was completely wrong. "New" heroes (or anti-heroes, as some might perhaps call them) such as Dexter, for example, avengers of innocence and vigilantes brave enough to take on the faceless forces of bureaucracy that allow criminals to go free, are, contradictorily, nothing more than enforcers of pre-established ideologies that illuminate the privileged and serve as a means of presenting a face of a united, thriving nation, contentedly engaged in global politics.

What else could one really expect from TV shows produced by and bound financially to large corporations determined to maintain their own wealth and power? As M. Keith Booker argues in the conclusion of his *Superpower: Heroes, Ghosts, and the Paranormal in American Culture,* "most popular culture is produced not from below but from above, by huge corporate media giants that have no interest in challenging the status quo other than perhaps to insinuate consumerist ideas further into the popular consciousness."[29] American mainstream television overwhelmingly produces repetitive, consistent stories that underscore populist ideals of exploitative power, patriarchy, and a limited vision of national identity. Notions of justice, equality, and perseverance, some of the cornerstones of the mythology of the United States, form the basis

Introduction

of the majority of popular television and film crime dramas of postmodern America. Beyond their similarities in theme, U.S. newscasts, magazines, TV shows, and movies are bonded together not only by their repetitive tales of celebrity, polarized, biased versions of political and economic information, and complete and total obsession with materialism and consumerism, but also by the large conglomerate corporations that own and control them. Currently, six large conglomerates control the vast majority of cable television networks: GE, News-Corp, Disney, Viacom, Time-Warner, and CBS own 90 percent of media in America.[30] With each passing decade, the notion of "free press" in U.S. culture loses more ground to the large, faceless powers of corporations. The entertainment and news industries have become nearly inseparable, which limits the democratic media sphere, effectively destroying the "public space" of airwaves, press, television, and film. When such public space is destroyed within a democratic society, so too is the arena in which people can gather to educate one another, articulate multidimensional sociopolitical views and ideas, and protest against that which violates their rights as citizens. To exemplify the impact of privatized media, the following shows us the potential power of television's voice. What is left is privatized, industrial-owned media, whose voice is louder and more accessible than any other.[32] On August 27, 2012, Joe Biden (or, rather, his social networking committee, submitting on his behalf) sent out a fundraising e-mail stating the following:

> Three months in a row, Mitt Romney and the Republican Party have trounced our fundraising totals. And, along with allied outside groups, they're using that cash to try to obliterate our side on the airwaves, outspending us in some battleground states by margins of up to three to one. The pundits are saying this is how we could lose the election.[31]

This is, of course, a generalized, somewhat one-dimensional analysis of the current state of for-profit television. And in his article "TV, Ideology, and Emancipatory Popular Culture," Douglas Kellner warns of approaching popular culture from such a negative perspective: "[C]ultural criticism that works within this perspective is often able to state little more than the obvious: that television, and other media, is now dominated by various forms of capitalist ideology."[33] Such an approach, he argues, "yields analyses of popular culture productions

Introduction

that are banal and repetitive, and provides no way of taking seriously the rebellious, oppositional, and subversive moments in almost all forms of popular culture."[34] Thus, one might be concerned that a book exploring the fallout of the domination of a nation's ideology by conservative, Late Capitalist forces may lead to simply a generalized argument against the underlying ideals of political conservatism and Late Capitalism. And it may be easy to fall into that trap, especially as the optimism of Kellner's work with regard to the emancipatory power of television is so hard to garner over thirty-five years after his call for action. But the goal of this book is to explore how mainstream media has managed to integrate the *illusion* of emancipatory ideals into a very decisive framework of conservative ideologies and to consider what impact, nationally and internationally, this might have on millennial audiences. In my conclusion I address the idea of emancipatory possibilities in millennial media, exploring the idea with the goal of identifying how such a positive notion could be conceived and put into practice.

The theoretical framework of the following chapters is grounded in traditional critical theory and post–Marxism, with a strong focus on the postmodern nature of the current U.S. culture industry. Though many critics argue that critical theory, with its staunch modernist roots, searches for individuality, and dedication to the metanarrative of Marxist thought is incompatible with postmodernism—the destruction of metanarratives, the deconstruction of the independent subject, and the domination of the culture industry by commercial interest, my argument is that the two, within the context of the following chapters, support one another and help clarify the situation of contemporary U.S. culture. I refer to critics such as Fredric Jameson, Žižek, and Baudrillard, all of whom examine the postmodern with the strength of their Marxist backgrounds as support.

For example, Jean Baudrillard in *Simulacra et Simulation* contends that the "only weapon of power, its only strategy against [its] defection, is to reinject realness and referentiality everywhere."[35] Baudrillard argues that Western culture has moved into an age when nature is truly dead and all we are left with are simulacra, symbols of reality (without the originals) and signs, rather than the objects they represent. He believes "experience everywhere is now derivative and literally superficial, and it has achieved its final 'utopian' form in the instantaneous abundance

Introduction

and banality of the 'cultureless' society of the United States, quintessentially in Disneyland."[36] Realness, truth, and notions of power are therefore illusions; his argument about referentiality and power suggests that *true* power, a kind of all-encompassing form of social control, does not exist; only simulacra of power does. Baudrillard's argument is grounded in Jean-François Lyotard's theory of the demise of the metanarrative in postmodernism. Lyotard, though he frequently argued that he was not a "postmodernist," suggests that the metanarratives of modernism are no longer functional in the postmodern condition. If one looks at the metanarratives of Christianity or Marxism, for example, "true" power—the power of God in the former and the Capitalist in the latter—exists unquestionably for that particular narrative to function. As such structural belief systems lose strength in the postmodern world, so too do the powers at their center. This is not to say that narratives of Christianity or Capitalism or other systems of understanding do not exist. Of course they do. But the conceptualization of a global Grand Narrative—one firm construction of a particular belief—with the shift from modernism to postmodernism has ceased to be a central focus in most theoretical and artistic pursuits.[37] The idea that there can be only one source of power or that one power must dominate all others has been proven erroneous time and again. Yet, universally, certain people or groups of people have historically attempted to identify and propose one idea or person or characteristic they see as omnipotent.

As Baudrillard argues, the only way to maintain the image of power in postmodern culture is to continually reinforce symbols of power and simulacra of that power. An ideal way to reinforce these symbols is through mainstream American media, with its enormous domestic and international audiences. There is no shortage of shows that present audiences with a protagonist who has been plucked from a long history of villainy—vampires, serial killers, gangsters, drug dealers, and addicts, to name a few. Yet such shows with new "faux rogue" heroes, such as Dexter, or Vampire Bill from *True Blood*, consistently interject symbols of historically dominant ideals of control (heteronormative, white, and masculine, for example), thus undermining the superficial theme of rogue heroism. This plays with narratives of moral ambiguity as a way to create the illusion of a new kind of hero while at the same time

Introduction

continually reinforcing images and concepts that form the basis for power structures dependent on a particular form of masculinity and a particular form of race relations. I've chosen a handful of shows to examine with the goal of understanding how their seemingly unique antihero protagonist is actually a faux rogue. Though it was most definitely not my intention, as I worked through the text I found repetition in my results. Many of the traits of the faux rogues are the same, despite seeming so different from one another on the surface.

Though no culture, audience, industry, or medium can be described as entirely hegemonic, mainstream television in the United States is so uniquely produced within the confines of corporate control that, under close examination, the ideological messages within its fictional narratives are overwhelmingly similar. Though the audiences to which these narratives are presented are diverse and complex, I am concerned about the power such consistent stories hold over the ideological construction of these audience members despite their own understanding of their independent system of beliefs. That stories of the faux rogue may come to symbolize rebellion or produce a sense of emancipation is destructive to an entire audience body, as it masks oppression under carefully controlled discussions of power.

Jameson argues that "even overtly political interventions like those of The Clash are all somehow secretly disarmed and reabsorbed by a system of which they themselves might well be considered a part, since they can achieve no distance from it."[38] If so, how can a system dominated by ideologues of a particular form of power, encapsulated by the hyperreality that is television, supported by a loss of historicity, produce anything but simulacra of metanarratives that support its power structure? It is a challenge. In the hyperreality of television, it is impossible. Television is fiction and not reality. It is always a reproduction. Thus, "true" metanarratives are not possible to create; the metanarratives in TV are always simulacra.

Theoretically, some might argue that I cannot use Jamesonian theory simultaneously with Lyotard's assertion of the death of the metanarrative. Adam Roberts, in his precise, articulate *Routledge Guide to Fredric Jameson*, asserts that Lyotard and his "incredulity" toward the metanarrative[39] in postmodern culture is essentially opposed to

Introduction

Jameson's use of Marxism as a kind of metanarrative (particularly in Jameson's *The Political Unconscious*) as a way of understanding culture.[40] Yet Slavoj Žižek is able to reconcile this apparent dichotomy in the vision of the two theorists. In his essay "Jameson as a Theorist of Revolutionary Philately" he asks, referring to Jameson's "supple description of the deadlock of the dialogue between the Western New Left and the Easter European dissidents"[41]

> are there two Jamesons: one postmodern, the theorist of the irreducibile multiplicity of the narratives, the other, the more traditional partisan of the Marxist universal hermeneutics? The only way to save Jameson from this predicament is to insist that Marxism is here not the all-encompassing interpretive horizon, but the matrix which enables us to account for (to generate) the multiplicity of narratives and/or interpretations.[42]

I argue that Žižek's reconciliation of the "two Jamesons" is not simply applicable to Jameson's discussion of the East/West dialogue issue but can also be applied to the majority of his work from *Postmodernism, or the Culture of Late Capitalism* onward. As I am using critical theory and postmodern theory as lenses through which to examine television narratives, I prefer to think of Jameson's Marxist theoretical foundations as a lens through which he examines postmodern culture, rather than as a restrictive metanarrative. Through this framework I am able to reconcile Lyotard and Jameson and use them in a synchronistical way to discuss mainstream postmodern culture and metanarratives of power.

The domination of the masses by the few is not by any means a new problem. Marx's philosophical influences identified it in antiquity, but to re-evaluate the situation in the early 2000s America is crucial for understanding how the U.S. population is dealing with swiftly changing economic, social, political, and cultural ideologies.[43] Entering this investigation via the TV is to strike at the heart of mainstream propaganda, exploring this largely hegemonic system of production with an aim to identify how the voice of a few can come to dominate millions.

By centering the argument of this book on the contemporary protagonist, the faux rogue character who seems so new and daring, I hope to dispel the myth of a new rhetoric of autonomous, beneficent heroism in contemporary U.S. culture and expose the continuous corporate push for conformity, oppression, and continued subservience to antiquated

Introduction

metanarratives. I present this argument through a series of chapters that develop the idea of an American TV hero and analyze specific serial dramas during a five-year span (roughly 2008 to 2012). I then offer a conclusive discussion of the potential cultural ramifications of the use of this false anti-hero as a major figure in contemporary U.S. television.

In this introduction, I have begun by exploring the idea of the American hero on television. TV, historically, economically, socially, and politically, differs in its situation within contemporary American culture from other forms of media such as film and popular novels, so it is important to identify how television has established particular *kinds* of heroes who have become templates for the medium. Focusing on the dramatic serial, I discuss who has triumphed, who has been vilified, and how both the heroes and the villains have been manipulated for corporate gain, leading us to a point in which our villains are our heroes.

In Chapter 1 I begin an analysis of the Showtime series *Dexter*. Dexter, a "good" serial killer, works by day as a forensic expert for the Miami-Dade police force and by night attempts to rid the streets of the South Florida city from truly monstrous Others as a vigilante butcher. I explore the new cultural implications of the *Dexter* series, and how the re-creation of metanarratives within the series might guide the postmodern subject toward the continued passive acceptance of white, male dominance. I also examine how *Dexter* fits in with the serial-killer narrative history of American popular culture and how the representations of women and race within the show, working with the figure of the vigilante serial killer, create a systematic oppressive narrative of power in contemporary U.S. culture, influencing audience ideological construction and self-identity.

In Chapter 2 I examine *Sons of Anarchy*, an FX Original series about the inner workings of a motorcycle gang in California. U.S. popular media has a long tradition of biker gang fiction, most notably the works of the late 1960s that surround the Hell's Angels. Bill Osgerby argues in his 2003 article "Sleazy Rider: Exploitation, 'Otherness,' and Transgression in the 1960s Biker Movie" that fighting, deviant sex, and all-out debauchery dominated many of the films featuring bikers from the '50s to the late '60s, but by the mid–1970s, "the image of the outlaw biker was increasingly configured as a signifier for the sturdy independence

Introduction

and healthy egalitarianism of the 'American Way.'"[44] *Sons of Anarchy* does an excellent job of combining these two mystiques of the biker gang. The gang members are clearly Other in the sense that their behavior (violence, drugs, sexual exploits) pushes the moral boundaries of normal expectations, yet their symbiotic relationship with the town of Charming (a symbol of small-town America)—their role as peacekeepers and gatekeepers in charge of keeping hard drugs, rapists, and white supremacists out of the town—allows audiences to view them as the "good guys," the traditional outsiders with hearts of gold and good intentions. Jax Teller, the protagonist of the series, personifies this paradigm.

Yet Jax, the player cast as an independent outsider, a true rogue among rogues, presents audiences with a narrative of non-identity. He rebels against an established system of control within an organization "outside" of both the commercial market and martial law, thus he searches to establish an identity that has collapsed in upon itself. His rebellion is an acceptance of mainstream Late Capitalist systems of politics and economics.

In Chapter 3 I move from motorcycles to vampires, focusing on the HBO series *True Blood*. At the beginning of the series, vampires have recently "outed" themselves across the globe, as a successful blood substitute had been patented, allowing them to live without relying on human blood. As the series progresses, characters of various supernatural natures are introduced, some "good," some "evil." The "supes" are all revealed to have intrinsic and complicated political orders and strict regulations among themselves, and their entrance into the "world arena" (though the show is nearly completely focused on the United States) is presented as fraught with difficulties; some fundamentalist religious organizations are intent on destroying the "demons," legal issues such as marriage and business ownership come under scrutiny, and a general social reorganization that includes so many Others presents itself on both global and interpersonal levels. The show emerges from Charlaine Harris's novels, all of which handle the metaphors of homophobia and racism in a candid and direct manner. The show, however, has taken a different direction as the vampire-as-ally figure is morphed into a more ambiguous representative of something that is not simply a traditional Other.

Introduction

The vampire has been a ubiquitous figure in popular culture for well over a century. Folktales and legends have discussed the creature in nearly every culture worldwide for centuries, if not thousands of years. Yet in the past five years, the vampire-as-ally has become a trope in popular U.S. fiction, film, and television. What this chapter discusses is how U.S. mainstream television, *True Blood* in particular, uses the figure of the "friendly" vampire to perpetuate the rhetoric of Western capitalism and the myth of inclusion in our national ideology.

With the economic crisis of the past few years viewed by many as a result of the weakness of a capitalist system, the rhetoric of pro-capitalists has increasingly focused on the idea of positive "globalization" versus imperialist domination. The benevolent vampire on industry-owned network television serves as a way of fascinating audiences with young, attractive, powerful, typically white, extraordinarily wealthy "Others," focusing on all they have to offer rather than on their traditional manifestation of bloodlust-fueled monsters. What is produced is an image of inclusion that is vastly limited and ideologically irresponsible.

Chapter 4 moves from the mythology of monsters and issues of globalization to very specific U.S. economic and class issues as seen in *Breaking Bad*. Though *Sons of Anarchy* offers some crossover in focus in terms of race identity and class identity, *Breaking Bad* allows class, a conversational taboo within a cultural mythology that subscribes to a sense of utopian classlessness, to open up. The Arizona world of foreclosed suburban homes and families destroyed by issues such as medical debt is presented as an arena for the growth of chemist-cum-high school teacher-cum-meth king Walter White. White is presented as a traditional American everyman who initially enters the dangerous and deadly world of the methamphetamine trade to try to save his family. The timeliness of the show, emerging in line with the housing crisis and recession that hit America, presents yet another character who shifts his identity and alignment with mainstream law and morality due to forces beyond his control to become what some identify as an anti-hero. Yet the violent excess of the show and the extreme character arc through which White progresses offers a very different ideological message more in line with traditional Late Capitalism and stringent class relations than it would first appear.

Introduction

Chapter 5 analyzes *Boardwalk Empire*, a nostalgia drama based in Atlantic City during Prohibition. Like *Sons*, *True Blood*, and *Breaking Bad*, the focus on illegal substance dealing provides fodder for an examination of the way in which capitalism and the black market are intertwined in Late Capitalism. Such a relationship could be examined to explore the rampant political and economic corruption in contemporary U.S. culture. However, in *Boardwalk Empire*, as with many contemporary television shows and films, this trope is romanticized and mutated in such a way that, rather than sparking outrage or investigation, it allows for a systematic reveling in the rebellion of the corrupt. Using Jameson's discussion of the loss of historicity, I examine how *Boardwalk Empire* exploits corruption and glorifies violence as a means of perpetuating the power of the few and the exploitation of the oppressed.

In Chapter 6, each of the above shows is revisited, this time with a focus specifically on the women of the series. Few truly remarkable examples of female-dominated faux rogue series exist, so rather than pick an arbitrary single show, I explore the lives of the women of *Dexter*, *Sons of Anarchy*, *True Blood*, *Breaking Bad*, and *Boardwalk Empire*. Female television archetypes remain as embedded in U.S. culture as the male hero-villain archetypes identified in this introduction. What Chapter 6 addresses is how current discourses of feminism are presented through and alongside the complex representation of the faux rogue. Like the would-be humanist anti-hero male, the strong female leads of many of these shows appear to be new kinds of characters, challenging traditionally oppressive stereotypes, but the thin veneer of rebellion and change with which they have been painted is easily stripped away with an analysis of their characters. Chapter 6 offers an accessible exploration of how contemporary U.S. culture identifies that which is feminist.

This book's conclusion shows that series such as those detailed above culminate to affect not only national audience ideological construction, but the global consciousness as well. The faux rogue, a strategically dissimulative new primetime hero, is a much bigger threat than he seems. Scarier than a serial killer and sneakier than a hungry vampire, the faux rogue sneaks into the mainstream system, darkening and oppressing the postmodern audience, undermining any attempt at emancipatory usage of the television medium. Yet as I summarize and defend my

Introduction

argument, I offer examples of shows or episodes of a particular series that, in some way, contradict my argument, identifying a counter-argument in the hopes of exploring how shows can be effective tools for education, reform, and audience empowerment. There must be a way to get beyond a dismissal of corporate control of television as inevitable and reignite, through new formats and systems of reception and delivery, the flame of the emancipatory power of mainstream television.

1

Why Showtime's *Dexter* Is Truly Terrifying

> DEXTER [VOICEOVER]: *Everyone hides who they are at least some of the time. Sometimes you bury that part of yourself so deeply, you have to be reminded it's even there at all. And sometimes you just want to forget who you are altogether.... I'm not the monster he wants me to be so I'm neither man nor beast. I'm something new entirely, with my own set of rules. I'm Dexter. Boo.*
> —From season 1, episode 4

Many of the characters I discuss throughout this book can be considered, to some degree, vigilantes. These are protagonists who take the law into their own hands with the intent of righting a wrong or defending those they consider innocent and/or vulnerable. And so I have chosen the show *Dexter* to begin my discussion of the faux rogue as a way of introducing some of the key themes of this text: vigilantism, violence, power, justice, and heroism. Showtime's *Dexter*,[1] based on the novels of the same name written by Jeff Lindsay, premiered in October of 2006, introducing audiences to Dexter Morgan, a Miami-Dade Police blood-spatter analyst by day and vigilante serial killer by night. The series, scheduled to end during its eighth season in 2014, has become popular both nationally and internationally and was even briefly syndicated (with significant editing) on CBS in 2008 for primetime viewing. Award-winning and critically acclaimed, *Dexter* has become a ubiquitous reference in U.S. popular culture. And though he soldiers through the series as a champion of "good," and fans and critics alike continue to engage with him as a lovable anti-hero, his threat is not confined to the criminals of a fictitious Miami. I argue that Dexter, and the seemingly new breed of similar anti-heroes so popular in contemporary U.S. television, poses a threat to audiences' ideological constructs of power.

Power, rather than Dexter's acts of violence, is the true focus of the following chapter. I want to examine how putting lives into the hands of rogue heroes to do with what they will could potentially affect the ideological construction of a national audience. As discussed in my introduction, identifying this effect is not simple: The receiving audience is varied by race, class, ethnicity, gender, age, sexual preference, and so on. Millions of different people with different core beliefs watch this show. So it's not that I am arguing that *Dexter*, or any show for that matter, will somehow magically create some kind of hegemonic ideological narrative among its viewing audience. What I am arguing is that the fictitious metanarratives created within the series and its signs and symbols of power, when shown over and over again both within the show and within the body of television narratives featuring lone anti-heroes, work together to create a cohesive narrative that, cumulatively and over time, does have the power to shape a collective worldview. By normalizing specific ideas, empowering some and demeaning others, a disturbingly hegemonic narrative of oppressive powers emerges that, when watched passively, can foster acceptance of these restrictive ideals.

Power

The study of power is crucial to understanding the importance of television narratives in contemporary U.S. culture. "Power" is a complicated term with endless connotations. For the purpose of this book, I refer to power as that which implies the possession of ability to wield force, authority, or substantial influence. To have power means to have the ability to control. This control, however, need not necessarily be negative or oppressive. As Michel Foucault argues in *The History of Sexuality*, power is as productive as it is repressive; it is multi-faceted and omnipresent. Power is everywhere and working in all directions.[2] He criticizes the "juridico-discursive" conception of power, arguing that

1. Why Showtime's Dexter Is Truly Terrifying

not all power is intended to restrict or repress. Power is not necessarily always restrictive; it also can be creative. As my discussion of ideological discourse owes a great deal to Foucault's conception of the discourse of sexuality, it is from his definition of power that I draw my own. What is most important to understand about power in relation to the study of contemporary forms of cultural expression is the relationship between power and ideology.

Karl Marx's basic model for understanding societal structures and human relations is the base and superstructure model. Fundamentally, the base represents the economic platform on which a society is structured. The superstructure consists of laws, politics, and other ruling ideals that deal with maintaining the basic economic structure. The superstructure also consists of concepts such as religion, morals, ethics, and culture. Marx calls the formations within the superstructure "ideology." According to Adam Roberts, ideology for Marx is defined as

> "false consciousness," a set of beliefs that obscured the truth of the economic basis of society and the violent oppression that capitalism necessarily entails. Various people believe various things: for instance that the fact that some people are rich and some people are poor is "natural and inevitable"; or that black people are inferior. The purpose of these beliefs, according to Marx, is to obscure the truth. People who believe these things are not going to challenge or even recognize the inequalities of wealth in society, and so are not going to want to change them.[3]

Ideology, as it is defined for the purpose of this work, is a set of beliefs, or "way of seeing," that appears to us to be "universal" or "natural" but that is in fact the product of the specific power structures that constitute our society. It is a collection of beliefs held by a group that shapes their actions. Ideological beliefs can be moral, ethical, political, philosophical, or religious. Marx's concept of ideology has shaped many critical thinkers' understanding of cultural ideology. This basic hypothesis has been refined and developed by critics over time, but understanding the fundamental definition is crucial to the reading of other critics including Louis Althusser, Theodor Adorno, Frederic Jameson, and Jean Baudrillard.

French critic Althusser's contribution to the concept of ideology and power informs my own critical response to the ideology of popular culture in general. Althusser recognizes what he calls "Ideological State Apparatuses," or "ISAs," the types of ideals ingrained in subjects' consciousness from birth and the types of ideals such as laws, that infiltrate schools, politics, and cultural representations that reinforce the power of those controlling the economic structural base. The foundational concept of ISAs relate to the works of critics like Theodor Adorno, who attacked mass culture on the grounds that it was used to control the ideology of the masses. Jazz and Hollywood cinema, for example, products of the "culture industry," held for Adorno the threat of escapist fantasy, which distracted citizens from recognizing their realities and working toward a better system. These escapist fantasies are filled, arguably, with Althusser's ISAs.

Fredric Jameson, whose work on the "waning of affect" and "loss of historicity" helps inform a large portion of this book, is "usually seen as a Hegelian Marxist, an inheritor of the traditions of Lukacs and Adorno and more or less hostile to an Althusserian approach."[4] However, Jameson does follow Althusser's concepts on seeing "ideology not just as 'false-consciousness,' but as the structures of thought and feeling that define us as citizens of late capitalist society."[5] Jameson, though typically hostile to the totalizing aspects of Althusserian Marxism, argues in his 1992 *The Geopolitical Aesthetic* that as citizens of late-capitalist society, our own concept of our ideological system is "already soaked and saturated in ideology."[6] Jameson's belief that as products of a system we are unable to fully act against it informs his theories of a lack of critical distance and the waning of affect. As stated in my introduction, Jameson argues that it is impossible to function outside the realm of the ideological from which we have developed, implying a systematic acceptance of Althusser's ISAs. Ideally, a diverse, empowered citizenry can change this, a concept I address in my conclusion. However, as stated above, passive acceptance of cultural narratives ensures it.

In my introduction I discuss French critic Jean Baudrillard's work and how it is in many ways aligned with Jameson's, in that Baudrillard's work on the simulacrum is incorporated in Jameson's theory of the logic of postmodernism. Baudrillard's concept of hyperreality is clearly echoed in Jameson's 1991 text. While Marx believed that production was the basis of social order, sticking closely to Marx's original argument, Bau-

1. Why Showtime's Dexter *Is Truly Terrifying*

drillard, in the 1960s, proposed the argument that *consumption* was actually the basis of social order. He argues, "[T]oday it's not just about controlling the code—the process of signification. The elite are not separated from the rabble by purchasing power alone, but by their exclusive access to signs—and by being at the top end."[7] This argument suggests that the initial base-superstructure model is outdated. It also suggests that Jameson's "branch" model could be updated as well. The branch model implies a reliance on an economic base for modes and relations of production but a semi-autonomous relationship with aspects such as "culture" and "law" is, to the degree that it depends on production, not consumption. I believe that, though the economic is foundational to the structure of a culture's ideology, signs of power are not necessarily controlled by modes of production but can in fact be manipulated by products of culture, including mainstream cinema and television.

I argue, drawing on Baudrillard's theory that power is related not simply to the use of signs but to those who control and manipulate them, that the model we should now assume in late-capitalist society is a cyclical model. Basing my concept on Marx's initial model and on Althusser's concept of ISAs, I argue that whoever has control of the production of signs of power is able to influence an overall superstructure of ideology. If, as Adorno suggests, the images on Hollywood screens of wealth and privilege are there to distract and to reinforce the image of power held by few, and if, as Baudrillard suggests, being able to consume is not enough for true power, then who holds the power? The power lies in the production of signs; thus a medium such as television, which is constructed entirely of signs, has an immense ability to articulate ideals of power, and those with the money and influence to control which narratives appear on mainstream television wield an enormous amount of influence.

Power and Violence

Violence in contemporary society is ubiquitous: From images of war to the vehemence in political rhetoric, an undercurrent of violence is all around us. And television offers us continuous, consistent exposure to this phenomenon. The controlling power of violence has transformed over thousands of years from a divine-right mandate of rule by the likes of emperors or kings over the life and/or death of those they ruled to a systematic necessity of prolonging the life of the many and dictating the death of few. Foucault argues that the West has undergone, since the classical age, a profound transformation of mechanisms of power from a sovereign's power over life and death to a new system of power over a "right to death."[8] "This death," he suggests, "that was based on the right of the sovereign is now manifested as simply the reverse right of the social body to ensure, maintain, or develop its life."[9] He applies his concept of "right to death" using examples of the state's ideas of warfare, the death penalty, and suicide. This "bio-power was without a question an indispensable element in the development of capitalism; the latter would not have been possible without the controlled insertion of bodies into the machinery of production and the adjustment of the phenomena of population to economic processes."[10]

The binding between power and control over death, much like the power associated with society's development and the discourse of sexuality, creates a structure in which the ultimately personal human experience of death becomes a part of a collective ideology. This collective ideology suggests control over death by those in power, which suggests that submission to such powers will make death both logical and potentially unavoidable. By claiming responsibility for the preservation of life, the implication is then that there is some control over death. In terms of ISAs, from childhood, those in contemporary American culture are taught ways to avoid accident, avoid illness, and avoid trauma. Our culture is obsessed with prevention, certain that diseases, criminal threats, and accidents can be avoided or obliterated through law, order, and other forms of socially controlling power. Thus, popular depictions of violence in culture become increasingly important.

Media and Violence

The omnipresence of violence in contemporary culture serves as a messenger for reinforcing a collective ideology of the importance of life

1. Why Showtime's Dexter *Is Truly Terrifying*

over death. Images of violence, in a culture in which those in power seemingly have the ability to control death and preserve life, become further-sharpened tools of didacticism. When the popular news media, which has become increasingly sensationalized and graphic, presents news of violence, the questions are always, "Why did this happen?" "Who is responsible?" "How could this be prevented?" Killers are profiled and their reasons for murdering explained. Accidents are investigated to assign blame or identify mistakes. Images of war are, as they have always been, presented with bias and rationalization. Horror films become clichés, the victims are easily identified, the perpetrators explored, deconstructed, and explained. Public reaction to crime and disaster is captured in sound bites, and Baudrillard's theory of hyperreality—a reality in which the "unreal" of production replaces the "reality" of existence—seems unavoidable, as the world becomes more media-saturated and we standardize our reactions to and rationalizations for death. The mediation of disaster, for example, transfers the emotional and psychological experience of those intimately involved in a tragedy to the masses. Though we may not have been present at a school shooting or at Ground Zero, the saturation of media images in our lives molds our response in a way that we would not have constructed it ten, twenty, or a hundred years ago. Seeing the reaction of those who were there, for example, may also, arguably, contribute to the way we construct our own responses to tragedy, even if this occurs only on a subconscious level. The hyperreality of depictions of violence affects our most basic, emotional responses to trauma.

Human interest in understanding violence is universal. Theorists within the humanities, policy makers in governments around the world, and social scientists, for example, all attempt to explore the causality of violence, its attraction, and its impact on different members of their society. To attempt to produce a new exploration of violence and culture is to enter into an already crowded academic arena, one in which great minds like Gandhi, Freud, and Foucault have already contributed groundbreaking ideas. The study of violence, however, is one that can continuously evolve and develop, and therefore new explorations of violence and culture must be produced. As I conclude the chapters that follow, most of which deal with high levels of violence on television, I hope

I will have added to this discussion in a small but timely way. The discourse surrounding violence, like, according to Foucault, that surrounding sexuality, is one that represents the shifting power structures of mainstream society. The way violence is presented within a culture shows us what is acceptable, what is Other, what is threatening, and what is expected.

Dexter, Power and Violence

So, then, what is *Dexter* teaching us about Otherness, normality, or what is expected? What does the representation of a lovable serial killer offer audiences? Is his presence, his status as a "good" killer and a vigilante hero so important to us that we are willing to overlook the traditional issue typically espoused by such dark figures—that fear that challenges us, as humans, to confront our fears of our own darkness? It is this difference, this lack of judgment by popular and critical response that I argue makes *Dexter* so important and so dangerous: The *Dexter* series perpetuates the ideal of a patriarchal power doing whatever it must to protect the innocent, even if it means bloodying just hands. Dexter veers away from the gothic and horror tradition, as I discuss in detail below, from which he was born in that he does not force the question of his "good" side conquering his "dark"; he feels secure in his darkness. In season 6 the antagonist Travis Marshall tells Dexter that he's going to hell for interfering with Marshall's plan. Dexter responds:

> No. I think I belong right here. Because maybe there's a place for me in this world. Just as I am. Light cannot exist without darkness. Each has its purpose. And if there's a purpose to my darkness, maybe it's to bring some balance to the world [season 6, episode 12].

The didactic tradition of the Other and the struggle to overcome "deviance" is not a challenge for viewers of *Dexter*. We, as an audience, are allowed to revel in the darkness of darling Dex. Dexter is taught from a young age, by his father, that he can—and should—embrace his murderous tendencies:

1. Why Showtime's Dexter *Is Truly Terrifying*

HARRY: Okay, so we can't stop this. But maybe ... we can do something ... to channel it. Use it for good.
TEENAGE DEXTER: How could it ever be good?
HARRY: Son, there are people out there who do really bad things. Terrible people. And the police can't catch them all. Do you understand what I'm saying?
TEENAGE DEXTER: You're saying ... they deserve it [season 1, episode 1].

Dexter uses the serial killer figure politically, but not to simply challenge or support the status quo of a particular political system. *Dexter* validates a much larger worldview, one of patriarchal control, whiteness, violence, vigilantism, and the use of human darkness to achieve personal goals.

In her essay "Neoliberal *Dexter*?" Michele Byers also addresses the argument that the show serves as a means of extolling white masculine power, yet her argument positions *Dexter* as a part of a clear, sociopolitical narrative. Though I agree with her stance that Dexter reiterates the notion of whiteness as "normative," as is discussed further, below, and that his violent behavior perpetuates the idea that "taking the law into one's own hands is—as the Bush government so often demonstrated—the prerogative of privileged white masculinity,"[11] I argue that positioning him as a "neoconservative hero"[12] assumes the existence of a particular, precise metanarrative of neoliberalism and neoconservatism that, in reality, no longer stands in twenty-first century America. This is evidenced through the lack of a clear ideological center among those on the right of U.S. politics—most recently seen through the infighting, false posturing, and backtracking of conservative presidential primary candidates in the pre–2012 election melee.

Dexter's character certainly echoes aspects of both neoliberalism and neoconservatism—his need for autonomy and his "services" that support an ineffective governmental judicial structure, for example. Yet his character is not static. His moral ideals and conceptualization of himself change throughout the narrative arc of the series, just as the narratives of particular sociopolitical platforms morph depending on external stimuli and interparty clashes. Such shifts and changes in a central character that many critics and fans identify as a stable protagonist with codified ideals of "right" and "wrong" and "good" and "bad" are particularly detrimental to the audience's understanding of these ideals, their acceptance of these meanings, and, thus, their ideological construction about power and violence. Dexter cannot simply lead toward a particular political philosophy. The serial killer hero instead creates a simulacrum of an entire metanarrative of white, masculine power that goes beyond the boundaries and fluctuating ideals of political parties, religious doctrine, and basic governmental systematic rules.

Dexter Morgan spends the majority of his nights immersed in vigilante-based serial killing. He also has had a wife, children, and the devotion of friends. He is respected at work. In short, this violent criminal has been welcomed into the sphere of civility. Not only is he embraced within the world he inhabits, he has the attention and devotion of the masses in mainstream American culture. He's cute. We root for him. We like his kids. We want him to find love even as he wipes the blood of his victims from his face and hands. Ratings, fan websites, merchandise, and the casual acceptance[13] in popular culture narratives support the argument of the national consumption and enjoyment of the series.

David Schmid argues in his essay "The Devil You Know: *Dexter* and the 'Goodness' of American Serial Killing" that the "show is merely the latest episode in a long history of American engagement with criminality and violence, an engagement that has helped to define what it means to be American."[14] And though I do concur that the United States has a long and relatively happy relationship with violence and national identity, I confidently argue that American popular culture typically struggles with the idea of a lack of a moral center. The deviant protagonists of anti-hero–based films and television are typically offered with a foil,[15] someone following the traditional Judeo-Christian moral order with whom the audience might compare themselves in order to assure themselves that the anti-hero is, in some way, ethically or morally wanting. I argue that audiences unconsciously look for ways to confirm this ideology. We watch horror films or television shows on which those who commit crimes are referred to as "perpetrators," "criminals," and various other labels that reinforce the concept that these beings are Others, not everyday citizens. Watching TV shows such as *CSI, Law and Order, The Mentalist, Lie to Me,* and *Criminal Minds* that repress or exterminate

1. Why Showtime's *Dexter* Is Truly Terrifying

the murderous Other not only justifies this system of beliefs but also makes audiences feel distanced from that which we perceive as a threat. As Philip L. Simpson writes in his remarkable book on the serial killer in American fiction and film, *Psycho Paths*, the "horror genre can best be defined as that which depicts monsters for the purpose of disturbing, unsettling, and disorientating its consumers, often for the seemingly paradoxical purpose of reinforcing community identity."[16] The Other serves, in all forms of fiction and film universally, as that which both deviates from and defines the "norm."

Within the culture industry, we expect and reward—through popular response, revenue, and marketing—the conformity of commercial entertainment that meets such aesthetic expectations. Typically, gothic or horror films fulfill these expectations, offering easily distinguishable Others. In her article "Parodied to Death: The Postmodern Gothic of *American Psycho*," Ruth Helyer argues that

> classic examples of Gothic literature deal with characters' fears of the forbidden and their repression of unauthorized urges. They warn against extremes of pleasure and stimulation, which are seen to dull the capacity to reason, and encourage the transgression of social proprieties and moral laws. Archetypes of "civilized" society are used in the narrative to justify the condemnation of unacceptable acts, and likewise feed into our conception of reality.[17]

Though in the gothic tradition the main character may be one struggling to contain both his[18] "good" and "evil" sides, the didacticism of traditional gothic literature ensures that outside of the struggling protagonist exists a culture of jurisprudence and clearly expressed social and moral ideologies to which the "good" inside the man should aspire, allowing the good to triumph over the deviant Other. Dexter allows us to root for the deviant Other.

Though Dexter has the potential to alienate audiences because he does have a definite problem (he's a serial killer), he is a "good" guy, or as many fans exclaim when trying to explain the show, a "good serial killer"—he's a vigilante, a killer of bad guys, a man seemingly bound very strictly by a code of ethics. Dexter joins the ranks of such killers as Henry in John McNaughton's *Henry: Portrait of a Serial Killer* and Patrick Bateman from *American Psycho* in that his ability to engage the audience and rouse support as a sole protagonist starkly contrasts the role of monstrous Others played by most serial killers in mainstream popular culture.

Henry and Bateman are presented without the foil of jurisprudence in their wake, making them protagonists by default, yet they are, unmistakably, murderous Others. Dexter, however, though presented alongside positive images of jurisprudence, lacks a clear foil in the form of a traditional hero. He, instead, becomes the true protagonist for whom the audience is to cheer. It is this transition of the serial killer from a social deviant to a *true* protagonist that makes the show so ideologically important.

The Role of the Father

Dexter devotes himself to the adherence of "Harry's Code," a system of ethics instilled in the beloved murderer by his adoptive father. Harry was the police officer who discovered young Dexter soaked in his mother's blood at the crime scene of her murder. He took in young Dexter and raised him along with his own, biological daughter, Debra. When he noticed Dexter's burgeoning homicidal tendencies, Harry took it upon himself to put the damaged Dexter on the "right" path, focusing his murderous tendencies on those who "deserved" them, teaching him how to research, how to kill, and how not to get caught. In the premiere episode "Dexter," Dexter tells us, "Harry was a great cop here in Miami. He taught me how to think like one; he taught me how to cover my tracks. I'm a very neat monster." Dex is deeply devoted to his foster parents and does all he can to keep the burden of his antisocial behaviors far from their shoulders. He explains: "I don't blame my foster parents for that. Harry and Doris Morgan did a wonderful job raising me. But, they're both dead now. I didn't kill them. Honest."

Dexter's life is dominated by the voice of his deceased father, perpetuating a narrative of patriarchal justice and a presence of the "voice of the father" that pervades the entire series.

According to Byers, "[t]he father's code is thus delivered in the first season as the anchor, the moral language through which Dexter can tell

1. Why Showtime's Dexter *Is Truly Terrifying*

his story and take responsibility for his actions, a feat set against his brother's inability."[19] In season 1, Dexter finds himself entangled in a web of murders committed by a brother he never knew he had, Brian. Brian was also a victim of trauma (he too witnessed his mother's murder). Harry, however, determined that Brian was too old to save, too damaged. Brian's path diverged from Dexter's the moment the Rule of Harry was established. Brian then became an out-of-control homicidal maniac, victimizing "innocents," in contrast to the vigilante machine Dexter was to become. The importance and stress of patriarchal guidance and dominance within the series begins as Dexter chooses to murder his errant sibling.

The "father" arc of the series is particularly important. Not only does it explicitly establish the need for patriarchal guidance and control, it further justifies Dexter's actions as his relationship with fatherhood develops. In season 1, the voice of the father is established. The audience is bombarded with scenes from Dexter's adolescence as he learns various life lessons from Harry. Harry, though deceased, appears to Dexter frequently in the flesh. He's not a hallucination, however, but the visual metaphor for the "code" that moves Dexter through his daily life. In season 2, we see Dexter's first struggles with the shackles of Harry's Code. Dexter blurs the lines of the code, pushing boundaries and breaking out of his incognito existence. It presents an almost adolescent challenge to the voice of the father: Dexter begins to break a variety of codes by having an affair with the incredibly bizarre Lila. The new sexual passion he discovers within himself parallels the hormones and emotions of a teenage rebellion. This continues into season 3 as Dexter engages a potential ally, a slightly older male friend. Though it was never overtly stated, the audience could easily assume that Dexter was not encouraged to make strong friendships as he grew, should he divulge any of his secrets. But as season 3 progresses, the rebellious killer realizes he has made a mistake by ignoring the wisdom of Harry; the decision to murder the out-of-control Miguel Prado, a clearly monstrous Other, pushes Dexter back into the fold of Harry's Code, reestablishing the dominance of patriarchy. In season 4, after his marriage to Rita, Dexter becomes a father with the birth of his son, Harrison, and the adoption of his stepchildren. He also spends season 4 exploring the ideals of fatherhood, from neighborhood fathers and from someone he hopes he can truly learn from and connect with: another serial killer. Dexter learns of Arthur Mitchell, a.k.a. the Trinity Killer, who has gone uncaptured for decades. He discovers that not only is Mitchell a successful killer, he also has a wife and children. Dexter engages Mitchell not only to potentially destroy him, but also to learn how he manages to balance fatherhood and serial murder. At first there is hope that Dexter may have found some answers beyond Harry's Code, but, alas, the Trinity Killer turns out to be a truly monstrous Other, abusive to his family and psychotic. He murders Rita at the end of season 4, and Dexter exacts his final revenge, leaving him once again alone with only Harry's Code to guide him. As season 5 progresses, Dexter, now a single father, returns to his vigilantism with verve, declaring it to be the only way he can heal and truly be a good father. "If I wanna be around for my son, I have to do this right. I'm killing for two now."[20] He also helps the beautiful, young Lumen, the lone surviving victim of a "rape club," not only helping to even the score with those who have hurt her, but also helping to train her in Harry's Code. In season 5, episode 12, Dexter tells the audience in a voice-over:

> Lumen said I gave her her life back ... a reversal of my usual role. Well, the fact is, she gave me mine back too. And I'm left not with what she took from me, but with what she brought. Eyes that saw me, finally, for who I really am. And a certainty that nothing ... nothing is set in stone. Not even darkness. While she was here, she made me think for the briefest moment I might even have a chance to be human. But wishes, of course, are for children.

The voice of the father and the role of Dexter have officially become one at the end of season 5.

Season 6 is dominated by the presence of the Doomsday Killer. The season revolves around Professor James Gellar (Edward James Olmos) and his student Travis Marshall (Colin Hanks), who seek to bring about the end of the world through killings based on the Book of Revelation. The entire season is dominated with images of Christianity. Even in his personal life, Dexter is faced with questions of religion. His decision to enroll Harrison in a Catholic nursery school results in questions from one of the school's nuns about his belief system. Dexter declares he

1. Why Showtime's Dexter *Is Truly Terrifying*

believes in nothing. Parallel to this is the storyline of Brother Sam (Mos Def), a piously religious ex-con who devotes himself to the salvation of lost souls and the ideological rehabilitation of the toughest of cases. He befriends Dexter, and Sam's devotion triggers obvious questions within the enigma of Dexter's conscience about issues of faith and belief. When Harrison falls ill, Sam prays for Dexter, and Dexter addresses the possibility of a higher power for the first time. Yet, ultimately, the vision of a higher being is destroyed. Brother Sam is murdered, and Dexter kills Sam's killer despite Sam's protests that he merely forgive. Travis, the willing apprentice of mastermind Professor Gellar, turns out to have killed Gellar three years earlier and has been besting Dexter on his own. Eventually Dexter is able to destroy Travis, putting to rest any questions of a higher, stronger power that may exist beyond his control. Dexter has become the dominant male, the patriarch, a god-like figure of power.

Remaining the Unexamined

Beyond the voice of the father and beyond the justification for violence that the show so cleverly allows, Dexter creates a world defined by the "rightness" of whiteness and masculinity cleverly disguised beyond a veil of inclusion. In his article "The Unexamined," Ross Chambers explores the unexamined nature of whiteness and the fact that its nature is "unparadigmatic" compared with all that is considered "non-white." The focus of his essay is on the power whiteness possesses because it remains unexamined, in contrast to the paradigmatic nature of the non-white categories that invite exploration and scrutiny because of their very difference. "Whiteness," he says, "is not a classificatory identity but just the unexamined norm against which such identities are defined, compared, and examined.... Whereas others may have group identities, white people as a group are just the unexamined. But there is more political strength in that than in all the identity politics in the world."[21]

The unexamined quality of whiteness and its alignment with power in Western cultures generally means that a void exists in art and popular culture where stereotypes or other figures intended for representational criticism should be. What Chambers seems to be suggesting is that, if a culture treats white men in power as individuals, dissent against their actions will generally be specific to the man. Whereas culturally we have had a traditionally easier time creating stereotyped bogeymen of various races and ethnicities, what America had been lacking was a figure in art and culture that served as a means to criticize this "unexamined" group as a whole. In her article "Everyman and No Man: White Heterosexual Masculinity in Contemporary Serial Killer Movies," Nicola Rehling argues that white masculinity has had

> the privilege of functioning as the universal, unmarked, neutral term, a positioning dependent on the burden of excess signification carried by those bodies that are marked. Writing of African Americans, for instance, Michael Rogin argues that oppressed people are awarded a "surplus" of symbolic value (417), according to which negative representations of an individual indict an entire social group. The maleness and whiteness of serial killing, conversely, both on and off screen, can remain obscured in discourses of individual pathology or more generalized discussions about the violence endemic to U.S. society.[22]

The white, unmarked serial killer—that is, one who is heterosexual, middle-class, and not otherworldly or supernaturally monstrous—can be used as a general metaphor for violence or for any issue beyond its attachment to the violence of whiteness, while, still, identifying an ethnic killer brings with it the necessity to discuss the ethnicity. In the U.S. cultural structure of the early 2000s, for example, if a white, unmarked male committed a shooting spree after losing his job, the social discussions that followed would center on issues like gun control, the economy, or violence in general. If a Muslim gunman had committed the same crime for the same reason, however, the social conversation would undoubtedly address issues of religion, ethnic difference, or even terrorism. Nearly always the second lone gunman's actions affect an entire group, while the first gunman's would not. The *Dexter* series follows in this same vein, which I find disappointing. Dexter's actions are rationalized through early childhood trauma. The culture of violent white masculinity is not problematized. Dexter seems painfully aware of this even if he never addresses his race when discussing his carefully con-

1. Why Showtime's Dexter Is Truly Terrifying

structed public persona. He speaks of this persona often, as he does on season 6, episode 2:

> DEXTER [VOICEOVER]: Wolves come in many forms. Some have big eyes; the better to see you with. Others huff and puff. Or others hide in the plain sight. I should know because, like it or not, I am one, too!

He also notes carefully how he dresses, what he drives, how he smiles—but he never speaks aloud the most obvious sign that helps him seem "normal" and that is his white masculinity.

Dexter works in a multiracial environment surrounded by both powerful men and women. At first, the diversity of the cast suggests a narrative of equality, but as the episodes pass, this narrative unravels. Situated in Miami, *Dexter* features many Cuban-Latino characters. His nemesis in seasons 1 and 2, Sergeant James Doakes, is an African American dedicated to the pursuit of truth and justice. Dexter's fellow "lab geek" is Asian American Vince Masuka, a charmingly perverted yet unquestionably talented forensics expert. Dexter's boss, Lieutenant Maria LaGuerta, and his sister Debra are both dedicated, aggressive, successful women in a largely male-dominated field. Dexter's victims, those he chooses to slaughter in the name of good, come from all backgrounds, are of varying races and ethnicity, men as well as women. No sexual violence occurs in Dexter's slaughter of women, a refreshing change from most mainstream fictions. Yet the undermining of equality and the perpetuation of the ideal of a dominant, righteous white male appear from the very beginning of the show.

In the pilot episode, we see Debra, a devoted and ambitious policewoman, introduced to the audience dressed as a scantily clad prostitute during her vice-squad duties. Her desire to be moved to the homicide division has been thwarted by a tense relationship with her lieutenant, Maria LaGuerta. Immediately, Debra is sexually objectified despite her extremely masculine demeanor. Her way of identifying herself as powerful is to mimic—through her gait, her dress, and her notably foul mouth—the successful men in her life, most importantly her father. For example, in season 3, episode 3, "The Lion Sleeps Tonight," the performative Debra offers the following exchange with Dexter:

Renegade Hero or Faux Rogue

> DEXTER: Rita's pregnant.
> DEBRA: You're lying.
> DEXTER: I'm not lying.
> DEBRA: A baby? A motherfucking roly-poly, chubby-cheeked, shit machine? Are you kidding me?
> DEXTER: I've never heard it described in quite those words before, but yeah.

Though she is powerful, smart, and independent, we see her *first* as a sexual object in a power struggle with another woman, undermining her power and the role of women in a professional setting. This damaging image of women being unable to co-exist professionally has become ubiquitous in mainstream dramas. Debra, season to season, continuously falls victim to her emotional attachments to men and her general naiveté. Her professional prowess and intelligence are frequently undermined by these "feminine" traits.

LaGuerta, a powerful Cuban woman in a predominately white, male field, plays a vital role in the show, but in the second season we see her use her sexuality and powers of manipulation to regain the title she lost in season 1 because of poor judgment. She sleeps with her lieutenant's fiancé and successfully drives the new female lieutenant mad, forcing her to be expelled from the office. This sequence of events relies on the stereotypes of women as manipulative (particularly through sex) and emotionally unstable. Dexter's wife Rita is introduced first as a victim of severe domestic violence, rescued and "rehabilitated" by Dexter himself. Rita, though sympathetic and a generally innocuous character, is consistently presented as needy, nagging, demanding, dragging Dexter away from himself and shackling him to a life of domestic servitude. The women in Dexter's life help develop a clear narrative of the need for patriarchal guidance and dominance, including his alignment with Lumen in season 5.

To some extent, the issues I've raised in relation to gender and those below in regard to race could simply be dismissed as the series trying to present all of its characters as inherently flawed, like the main antihero himself. Yet, though their flaws make them realistic characters, these flaws always lead to a downfall or some kind of pain and turmoil. Never are the supporting characters able to trump Dexter as the clear

1. Why Showtime's Dexter *Is Truly Terrifying*

protagonist in the series. For example, the first main character to die in the series is Sergeant Doakes, the only main African American character to last more than one season in the show. Though he died attempting to bring Dexter to justice, he took the fall for Dexter's previous crimes and was branded a serial killer. Doakes is portrayed as exceptionally intuitive and powerful. He is the only lead character in Dexter's world to suspect his monstrosity. And although race plays no actual role in his demise, the fact that he is the first main character to die is important in terms of what it could potentially signify: his lack of tactical abilities to outsmart his target, his emotion and obsessions obscuring his rationale, and so on, all of which demarcate him as less powerful than the white male he pursues. He is caricatured as an "angry black man," going further and further into his own madness as he pursues Dexter. A particularly problematic exchange takes place between Dexter and Doakes in season 2, episode 7, "That Night a Forest Grew":

> DEXTER: No matter what you try, no matter when, no matter how hard you work, I'll always be a step ahead of you for one simple reason.
> DOAKES: And what's that?
> DEXTER: I own you.

Contextually within the narrative this makes sense, of course, but its uncomfortable reminder of slavery underscores and problematizes the entire exchange and the entire power struggle between the two men.

Vince Masuka, the only Asian American character, though gifted as a lab scientist, is socially awkward, sexually perverse (or so he presents himself), and persistently lonely and excluded. He's brilliant, but he does not fit in with the culture of his work, a stereotypical and outdated presentation of Asians and Asian Americans. The Cuban characters in the show, Miguel Prado (and his brothers), Lt. LaGuerta, and Sgt. Batista, are systematically undermined because of their passions. Miguel loses control of his own system of vigilantism, and LaGuerta, as discussed above, is not only manipulative and flippant with her sexuality, but she, a successful, powerful woman, allows her passion for Batista to threaten her career. Angel Batista is first shown as innately Other when he tries to proposition a prostitute and we are told this has been a regular habit. He also places his career in jeopardy because of his passion for LaGuerta.

Renegade Hero or Faux Rogue

Though the white characters give in to their passions frequently as well, to use this fatal flaw for *all* of the Latino characters of the show relies, again, on a racial stereotype and, again, presents Dexter, the white male figure, as the triumphant hero, even after his many mistakes. Throughout *Dexter*, we are presented with a clear narrative of triumphant, righteous whiteness.

Though each individual issue presented in the above discussion of *Dexter* with regard to race, gender, and patriarchal control could possibly be explained away separately as simply plot points or narrative creativity, when viewed as parts of a whole, not just for the series itself but within the realm of popular U.S. television, one can begin to understand the types of metanarratives being created (as simulacra of historical metanarratives) and the ideological implications with regard to power that such stories perpetuate. White, masculine power underscored by vigilantism creates the new hero of American culture. For a culture finding itself threatened by both external Otherness and internal corruption and lacking any kind of true outlet for democratic discourse, the simulacra of these metanarratives in the fictional world of television serves to support the wealthy, mostly white males who maintain a grip on "power" in U.S. society. And Dexter Morgan, a rogue and supposed champion of the people, is simply one example of this false ideal of a new kind of hero: a faux rogue. And it is into his hands that viewers are passively placing the "right to death."

2

Sons of Anarchy

Power, the Justification of Violence and Reform Through Capitalism

U.S. popular media has a long tradition of biker-gang fiction, most notably the works of the late 1960s that surround the Hell's Angels. The fascination began in the '40s and '50s both tangibly and in film. And in the late 1960s, the Hell's Angels' "mounting notoriety made them the bane of conventional society, but within the developing counterculture, they were eulogized as rebellious outsiders."[1] While writers Ken Kesey, Alan Ginsberg, and Hunter S. Thompson and artist Jerry Garcia propagated the image of the bikers as noble outlaws, the "outlaw biker culture of the 1960s was a repository of reactionary chauvinism. Violent, racist, homophobic misogynists, the Hell's Angels held the civil rights movement in contempt and brutally attacked antiwar activists."[2] Bill Osgerby argues in his 2003 article "Sleazy Rider: Exploitation, 'Otherness,' and Transgression in the 1960s Biker Movie" that fighting, deviant sex, and all-out debauchery dominated many of the films featuring bikers from the '40s to the late '60s, but by the mid–1970s, "the image of the outlaw biker was increasingly configured as a signifier for the sturdy independence and healthy egalitarianism of the 'American Way.'"[3]

Sons of Anarchy, an FX original series, does an excellent job of combining these two mystiques of the biker gang. However, it is logical to assume that potential viewers may have pre-conceived notions of the show *Sons of Anarchy*, notions colored by the later images of bikers in U.S. popular culture: an image of aggression, villainy, and uncontrollable, almost feral men and women.

In contrast, the members of the fictional Sons of Anarchy, regardless of how rough around the edges they may be, initially appear to operate much more within the realm of civility. They hunt down rapists, they are diligent about keeping most drugs out of the town of Charming, and they play a kind of philanthropic role. The show's protagonist, Jax Teller, is a new father and a young up-and-comer with somewhat idealistic dreams of his future and the down-to-earth attitude of a much-loved son. However humanized the show makes Jax and his fellow gang members appear, their motorcycle "club" is actually representative of what has become known as a "one percent club."[4] These clubs are "the most dedicated and antisocial" of biking associations, the most connected with extreme criminality, and typically the larger and more connected organizations in a web of gangs and clubs internationally. Early in the show, the Sons appear to be a small club, but as the series progresses, it reveals that they are an international organization with ties to a rogue branch of the IRA and other international associations related to gun and drug trafficking.

The club consists of predominantly white males. Racial hegemony is not addressed in the show until season 4, but critics and fans alike seem to suggest that such hegemony within gangs is "realistic." However, the fact that the only other gang of white men featured in the show happens to be a group of white supremacists (the "Nordics") and the other gangs are composed of solely Mexicans ("The Mayans") or African Americans ("The One-Niners"), these groupings perpetuate a narrative of racial division.

Identity Issues

This racial division further complicates the identity formation of the men of the show, most notably Jax. For the gang members, certain attributes are assumed as part of their identity: They are hypermasculine, heterosexual, capable of extreme violence, limited in their expression of emotion, and dominant in their intimate relationships. Thus Jax, even as he internally struggles with his identity formation, as is discussed later, outwardly conforms to his role as white, hypermasculine patriarch.

2. Sons of Anarchy

His inner conflict and many of the show's conflicts come from his efforts to exist outside of this code of behavior. This inner conflict and desire to break out of a life of crime and blood are what identify Jax as the show's anti-hero protagonist. He is Othered by his association with a gang but longs to be a part of the more normalized civilian world. His rebellion against a system of constraint, expectation, and oppression (he begins the series being groomed for leadership as vice-president of the club) and his attempts to undermine it are ironic in that the system he wants to be a part of is just as conformist, corrupt, and oppressive. Jax wants to be a cog in the late capitalist machine, working within a pre-established infrastructure that many see as restrictive, corrupt, and antiquated. Jax's search for identity is a search for a life of normality in middle-class America. Our "anti-hero" wants to live in the suburbs, abide by the law, and make money legitimately. Jax's desire for a normative existence is all blatantly stated at various points in the show, yet in its fifth year *Sons of Anarchy* maintains its "badass" reputation as a raw, edgy show for men.[5] But this is a very good disguise for a show that perpetuates patriarchy, established power hierarchies, order, and capitalism. The show glorifies violence as a means of both attaining and maintaining power through a narrative of anti-intellectualism. Few problems are solved by clever planning alone; nearly all involve bloodshed.

Outlaws, Others and Outsiders

In this chapter I use both the term "Other" and the term "outsider." The two terms overlap and at times will do so within this chapter, and some critics use the two interchangeably. But for clarification, I define Other as that which is completely outside the realm of the norm for a social group (or culture), something (or someone) so removed from that which is identified as normal that it could never be included in the social group in any way. It must conflict directly with the ideological system of the group or culture from which it is shunned. But the "outsider"

> has the possibility of being accepted by and incorporated into the group; [its] offspring are very likely to be accepted into the group. The Other,

however, is perceived as different in kind, as lacking in some essential trait or traits that the group has; [its] offspring will inherit the same deficient nature and be the Other also.[6]

Motorcycle gang members are typically outsiders who engage in behaviors that mark them as Other. Murder, rape, and acts of brutality are not acts of simple rebellion that are outside of the norm, but acts that cannot coexist with the ideology of a nation that deems these as offenses worthy of prison time and sometimes even execution. Vaguely and often contestably, as a group, U.S. culture has defined its boundaries against that which is Other from an ideology that supports the sanctity of human life and the rights of the individual to live without the threat of physical harm. In and of themselves, gang members are not Other; they are human with the potential for reform and the potential to produce non-outsider offspring. Yet many become so mired in behaviors that represent Otherness that they themselves become essentially Other. In *Sons of Anarchy*, Clay's transition from president and solid leader of the club to tyrant exemplifies this. He becomes someone so removed even from his own ideological foundations that he becomes monstrous. He begins the series as domineering, controlling, and violent, but his humanity is still intact as he interacts with his wife Gemma and his club "family." Yet he devolves, his greed and desire for power overcoming him to the point where he alienates even the most deviant of the Sons members. He loses his ability for remorse and his goal of unity for his gang.

Jax, though he changes and becomes *more* Other through his actions, maintains his status of outsider through his children and his ultimate goal of leaving his life of crime and violence. Eventually, his search for identity and desire to escape the violence and criminality of the Sons core morph him, ironically, into one who fits within the realm of civility. He is not Other, nor truly an outsider, as his search for legitimacy leads him to capitalism and cooperation with figures of jurisprudence at the end of season 4.

The Dream

As discussed previously, Jax's identity crisis at the beginning of the series sets him up as anti-hero and potential humanist hero. He is a new

2. Sons of Anarchy

father to a premature baby boy, Abel, born to his ex-wife Wendy, a drug addict whose continued drug abuse leads to Abel's early arrival. In the pilot episode, as he is scouring his family's storage unit for baby gear, Jax stumbles upon his deceased father's journal and photos of the early members of the club. Jax's father, John, formed the club in 1967 with eight other men, including Clay and Piney, who are main cast members in the series. As Jax reads the journal, he begins to understand the mission of the early days of the Sons of Anarchy—currently a gun-running, outlaw biker gang with chapters throughout the world. It's a far cry from what John had envisioned; he had imagined a kind of commune—"real hippie shit," as Jax calls it.

Unspoken yet implied through photos, the Original Nine were veterans returning from Vietnam, searching for belonging and finding camaraderie in the club they formed. Jax begins to understand his father's true nature and his dreams for the original club through John's words:

> JOHN [voiceover]: First time I read Emma Goldman wasn't in a book. I was sixteen, hiking near the Nevada border. The quote was painted on a wall in red. When I saw those words, it was like someone ripped them from the inside of my head.
>
> JAX [reading his father's words out loud]: Anarchism ... stands for liberation of the human mind from the dominion of religion; the liberation of the human body from the dominion of property; liberation from shackles and restraint of government. It stands for social order based on the free grouping of individuals.
>
> JOHN [voiceover]: The concept was pure, simple, true. It inspired me. Lit a rebellious fire, but ultimately I learned the lesson that Goldman, Prudot and the others learned. That true freedom requires sacrifice and pain. Most human beings only think they want freedom. In truth they yearn for the bondage of social order, rigid laws, materialism. The only freedom man really wants, is the freedom to become comfortable.

Jax's unearthing of John's mission, as well as his words of warning about the new direction in which the club was headed at the time of his death and the loss of its original goals, gives Jax pause and he reflects on his current lifestyle, his new son, the future of his club, and the desires of his father.

Renegade Hero or Faux Rogue

A Real Family

Like *Dexter*, *Sons of Anarchy* is tethered to the voice of the father, most notably in the early episodes, when John Teller is heard in a voiceover monologue as Jax reads his journal. His letters and other writings become central to the plot as the series moves on. His looming presence, though not as dominant or visual as Harry Morgan in *Dexter*, is a reminder of the patriarchal hierarchy that guides Jax's conscience. Jax's interpretation of his father's writing and various moments in the series that show him masterminding complex strategies offer a glimpse of a clever man, one not shaped by traditional education but someone innately intelligent, quick-witted, and self-reflexive. After Abel's birth, Jax appears to rely more and more on his mental abilities than his physical ones, looking for ways for the Sons, a.k.a. SAMCRO (Sons of Anarchy Motorcycle Club, Redwood Original Division), to earn money legally and ways to avoid bloodshed, such as buying and selling land and, of course, his brilliant plan to invest in a porn studio. Yet he is frequently overruled or dismissed by Clay's desire for violence and a club that goes to the gun first.

Though the club runs guns and gets involved in a variety of other illegal activities, the members play a peacekeeping role and maintain a mostly respectable citizenship within Charming. They also appear to be a very family-friendly club. In a scene during season 1, episode 5, Jax, concerned about his best friend Opie (who is recently out of jail), confronts Opie's wife Donna:

> JAX: I love that guy more than anyone, but I also see what's happening to him and it scares the shit outta me. Opie can't be half in, half out. It'll get him killed, Donna.
> DONNA: Then I want him out. That other guy got out. Kyle.
> JAX: Kyle was kicked out. You know why? 'Cause the night Opie got arrested for blowing up that truck yard, Kyle was supposed to be his getaway ride. Only the asshole panicked when he heard sirens, left Opie behind.
> DONNA: Opie never said anything....
> JAX: 'Cause Opie's not a rat. Brothers don't turn on each other. He did the time. It's what we do. Opie will never walk away from the club. We both know that. He's like me; it's all we know. It's in our DNA, and if you

2. Sons of Anarchy

keep pulling him in the other direction ... we're not the glue, Donna. You are.

The kids play at family gatherings, Jax's baby son is welcomed home by a full-on club party, and wives and girlfriends play a central role in the daily lives of the members. Although this family-centered façade further endears them to audiences and aids in the image of the men as "good guys," it also ensures that the narrative of patriarchal power persists throughout the series. The club works as a patriarchal power protecting the town; the hierarchy of the club and the consistent references to men "providing" for their families and keeping "club business" just among the men as well as the dominate presence of heteronormative pair-bonding (only sexual images of the men and their "old ladies" or their female hooker-stripper-porn star dalliances are shown) ensures consistent articulation of masculine power. But not just masculine power; hyper-masculine power. The peace is kept by brawn, force, guns, and intimidation. The heroes are physically hypermasculine, and their sexual exploits highlight their virility. Heteronormative, hypermasculine patriarchy is presented as the only form of successful masculinity. This is reinforced by the club's insistence on an ability to fight and kill without remorse. This emotionless violence was not always a part of SAMCRO's legacy, however. In season 1, episode 2, Jax reads in John's journal,

> Most of us were not violent by nature. We all had our problems with authority, but none of us were sociopaths. We came to realize that when you move your life off the social grid, you give up the safety that society provides. On the fringe, blood and bullets are the rule of law and if you're a man with convictions, violence is inevitable.

As mentioned above, in season 1 Jax is vice-president of the club, being groomed for leadership by his stepfather Clay. From the very beginning of the show, images of Clay's weakening, arthritic hands are emphasized. As the pain and swelling increases, his ability to ride his motorcycle decreases, as does his ability to lead. Ceasing to ride means a cessation to his presidency, further emphasizing physical prowess as equating to hierarchy power. When the show began, many critics and fans latched onto the parallels between the show and Shakespeare's *Hamlet*—Jax as the wronged prince, his stepfather the interloper. Creator

Curt Sutter has acknowledged the themes in his show, and Ron Perlman, who plays Clay, suggested in an interview that the motif would run throughout the entire series.[7] These parallels are dominant enough to create an entirely secondary chapter on the show, one best suited to a Shakespearean scholar. For brevity and concision I will not offer any kind of analysis on these matters. Regardless, the use of the play's themes, particularly the tension between Clay and Jax, sparks Jax's journey into himself, and it is this journey upon which I focus to articulate how his initial appearance of a humanist hero morphs into that of a faux rogue by the end of season 4.

Nature vs. Nurture

Season 1 begins Jax's struggle with his identity. He was born into club life. His parents have always been reigning queen and king. Jax knows no other lifestyle. From the pilot episode we see him play his role as Prince Charming, with schoolgirls and shop girls twirling their hair and gazing at him with desire that they might one day play the role of his old lady. (Yes, he gets to be "prince" and they get the moniker "old lady"—I didn't make the rules.) His life seems mapped out for him, his identity fixed and his path certain. He proudly hangs his first mug shot on the wall of the "clubhouse" along with his fellow members, and his kutte or "cut," the cut-off sleeved jacket worn by male bikers, already features both the vice-president and "Men of Mayhem" patch, the second meaning he has killed for the club. His body is adorned with club tattoos, including a full back tattoo of the club's logo. The blood of the lifestyle runs in his veins. In season 2, episode 8, Jax attempts to explain this to Tara:

> TARA: You keep saying you want to change things, but you keep repeating old behavior. You can't have it both ways.
> JAX: Is there anything you love so much, you'd protect it, no matter the cost, the damage it did to you?
> TARA: Yeah. Yeah, a child.
> JAX: Yeah. That's how I feel about this club. Since I was five, Tara, all I've ever wanted was a Harley and a cut. Change won't happen quick, or without blood, but it'll happen. It has to.

2. Sons of Anarchy

Thus the internal struggle he first encounters in season 1 is more powerful for him than for some of the other characters presented in this book.

Along with the discovery of his late father's words and the birth of his son, the return of Tara, his teenage sweetheart, to Charming also brings emotional turmoil to the surface for Jax. Near the end of the pilot episode, Jax goes to the hospital to see Abel for the first time. He encounters Tara, now a skilled physician, and the passion and emotion between them is palpable until Tara sees blood on Jax's clothes from his earlier exploits with the gang. In a disappointed rather than disgusted voice, she tells him to clean himself up and go see his son. It is obvious that Tara had hoped that Jax had changed but is reminded of how deeply mired he is in the gang.

Throughout the first season, Jax is still searching for meaning within his life and within the Sons, falling back on violence only in reaction to violence. Yet he, like the other faux rogues of this book, gradually changes as the series progresses. Every time he tries to leave the club and reform his identity, he is pulled back in and it seems as though his life is designed beyond his control. Ironically, a major trigger for this is Tara. She, unbeknownst to anyone, has fled back to Charming to escape her psychotic ex-boyfriend-stalker, who happens to be an ATF agent. She tells everyone she returned to mark her father's passing and to give something back to the community by working in its hospital.

Gemma's outrage at seeing Tara again is explained when the audience learns that Tara left Jax after high school, breaking his heart. Gemma lifts Tara's shirt and exposes her lower back tattoo, a mark of the club from her time with Jax. Tara says she kept it to remind her of what she left behind, yet she ran back to Charming for the protection of those she left behind. At the end of season 1, when she is nearly raped and killed by her ex, Josh Kohn, Jax saves her, murders Kohn, hides the body, and reunites with Tara. Still working through his issues with the club, Jax turns to his father's words. John's journal states,

> Inside the club, there had to be truth. Our word was our honor. But outside, it was all about deception. Lies were our defense, our default. To survive, you had to master the art of perjury. The lie and the truth had to feel the same. But once you learned that skill, nobody knows the truth in or outside the club; especially you.

Renegade Hero or Faux Rogue

This quote resonates with Jax, encouraging the part of him that wants to help the club by engaging in more legal activities.

Good intentions aside, however, the disappearance of Kohn means that Jax attracts extra attention from ATF agent June Stahl, in town because Deputy Chief Hale attempts to bring down SAMCRO. Hale's boss, Chief Wayne Unser, who has been in league with the club for some time, did not retire, and Hale resents that he is being held back. He also doesn't understand Unser's relationship with SAMCRO. Unser uses them not only to help keep the peace in Charming, a symbiotic relationship, but also for some underworld dealings of his own. He doesn't retire, despite his progressing cancer, under pressure from Clay. Hale sees himself as hero, a straight-laced law enforcement officer with no tolerance for the Sons of Anarchy. But bringing in Stahl, a sociopath in her own right, brings nothing but tragedy.

Stahl is doggedly determined to undermine the club. She frames Opie, Jax's best friend and Piney's son, as a "rat," putting him and his family in jeopardy. As a result, Clay arranges his assassination, only failing to realize his mistake when Tig, the club's enforcer, has already made his kill—killing Donna, Opie's wife and the mother of his two children, by mistake. John's journal, Abel's birth, Tara's return, the crooked presence of two representatives of jurisprudence, and Donna's death all force Jax to ponder his life's trajectory in a way he never could have imaged. For the audience, Jax is a tragic hero and a potential savior.

However, Jax, more so than any of the other faux rogues of this book, is trapped in a system determined to shape his identity and his future. Jax's autonomy is limited not only by his current responsibilities, but by the life he was born into. Jax, like Abel, was born into the Sons culture and, particularly as a male figure, his identity was constructed for him before he could even speak. Abel, ten weeks premature, lies in the NICU with a tiny, baby blue SAMCRO stocking cap on his head, a small but very important reminder of the gender and club roles he will be expected to perform. In their article on the symbols and values of the motorcycle club, James F. Quinn and Craig J. Forsyth confirm the persistence of the "macho demeanor" of biker culture in both behavior and appearance. "Riding remains a predominantly masculine activity. This sort of macho demeanor combines with an appearance and wariness shaped by the demands of riding, to create an imagery that is evocative of the one percenter."[8]

Manly Men

In addition to the perils associated with the actual act of riding a motorcycle, for the men associated with one-percenter clubs, the "constant risks engendered by interclub warfare, criminal activities, and bold, if not reckless, motorcycle operation are thus interrelated as methods by which powerful bonds between club members are developed."[9] The notion of brotherhood, the masculine bond formed by collective risk taking, instability, and the consistent presence of physical threats are what many non-initiated civilians associate with gangs in general. *Sons of Anarchy* represents and reinforces this hypermasculine, homosocial lifestyle (particularly prominent, according to Quinn and Forsyth, in one-percenter gangs) as the men engage in and perpetuate a particularly violent and dangerous way of life. Not only does this set the stage for an exploration of Jax's identity formation, in general it is an ideal background for a masculine soap opera, an ironic yet somewhat dismissive term critics have used to discuss the show as a whole.

The image of the violent homosocial bond underscores every episode as the men fight other gangs, outside threats, and one another. In the pilot episode there is a huge party at the clubhouse, complete with scantily clad, easily available women, beer, weed, and fire—all the tropes of a "man's party." There is also a scene of bare-knuckle boxing between Juice and Tig, bloody and intense until it's broken up and the men hug each other, laughing and trading compliments. The world that Jax was born into is exclusively hypermasculine, with violence as the glue that binds the club itself together. To exist and compete in this world means a consistent engagement with danger and violence. To earn patches and office, the more bodies one needs in his wake. This formulation of masculine power dominates much of human history. As gender lines blur and the diversity of types of masculinity becomes more progressive, more accepted, and more prominent in mainstream American culture, shows like *Sons* and other mainstays of popular culture, such as the mainstream action film, serve as reminders of the history of violent, primitive masculinity.

In Hegel's 1807 *Phenomenology of Spirit*, he "envisioned life-and-death struggle as a precondition of full self-consciousness."[10] Entertainment in the form of television shows such as *Sons*, violent sports, video games, and gory films recall Hegel's ideal of "personhood."

> As Hegel only saw males as being truly capable of "self-consciousness," we might reformulate his statement in less abstract terms: unless a male has risked his life struggling on equal terms with another male, he has not really actualized his masculine potential. In this scenario only the male who is willing to risk it all emerges as the "master," while the one who yields by choosing life over death is placed in the subordinate, implicitly "feminized" position of slave or bondsman.[11]

This battle for the position of "master" has been a part of Jax's psychological make-up since infancy, and at the very beginning of the *Sons* series we see him battling between his desire to maintain life (and thus risk being not only feminized but ostracized by his family) and the desire to take his place as master within the hierarchy of the club, as he had been raised to do. Thus his hypermasculine identity is in part innate, as it is all he has known, and part performance as he wrestles with his desires for a different kind of life—a life free from violence and within the realm of civility. Yet the more he struggles with this conflict, the more he is provoked to become what Hegel would call a "fully self-conscious man."

This provocation back into a world of viciousness and hypermasculine performance begins with Tara's need for rescue and Jax's murder of Agent Kohn, followed quickly by the presence of Agent Stahl, Donna's death, Jax's re-commitment to Tara and the need to protect her, and finally the rape of his mother Gemma.[12] The presence of the various women in the show often serves to provoke masculine response, such as women needing rescue or women needing to be avenged. But they also push Jax to act out, such as when he makes various attempts to free himself from Tara. During these periods, Jax's hypermasculine performance has him sleeping with numerous women and returning to his room at the clubhouse, the center of masculine domination. Stahl repeatedly provokes primitive responses from the men of Sons, always with disastrous, bloody results.

2. Sons of Anarchy

It is not always the women in the show who force Jax back into his performative role of masculine killer. When Abel is kidnapped, Jax is helpless at the loss of his son, and he loses what grasp he had on the man he had hoped to become outside of the narrowly prescribed role he was to inherit. Abel was key to Jax's role as "outsider" rather than Other, but when his son is threatened, Jax becomes an Other, lost to his primitive role as protector and vigilante.

Following leads as they search for his son, Jax and several other members of the club leave for Ireland, involving themselves with the inner workings of the "True IRA Council." In this situation in season 3, the men are truly Other. They now exist outside of U.S. law and engage with a group detested nearly universally, a group with no regard for the innocent civilians they kill or the damage they do to the very cause they are trying to support. Jax recognizes this as he is finally reunited with his son; Abel had been handed off by his kidnapper to an illegal adoption mill. He is already placed with a new family by the time Jax finds out about the situation. Once he does locate Abel, he is approached by a priest who suggests that Jax leave Abel with the loving, stable family who "adopted" him, allowing the young child an escape from the life of crime, death, and pain that would surround him should he grow up instead with SAMCRO. Jax agrees. Though he cannot seem to gain control of his own life or his own identity, he sees the opportunity to offer his son that very thing. However, even in this moment of self-sacrifice, Jax's club engagement interferes and Abel's adoptive parents are killed by an enemy of SAMCRO. Abel is once again abducted until Father Ashby, the priest who encouraged Jax to let go of his son, trades his life for Abel's, and the child is returned to his father's arms.

After Gemma finally reveals her rape to Jax and Clay near the end of season 2 (she had withheld the information, fearing that retaliation on the part of her husband and his club would damage SAMCRO), the two men put aside their differences and bond once again against a common enemy, reuniting their families and their ideological worldviews. Jax, who had decided to become a "nomad" and distance himself from the club, changes his mind and he is once again a dedicated vice-president and ally to Clay. He discounts his father's writings and internal conflicts with which he had been dealing throughout seasons 1 and 2 seem to dissipate. This pattern becomes cyclical in the show, and with each setback, Jax has to start over in his identity reformation. In season 3, however, as discussed earlier, when Jax finds himself in the world of the rogue IRA and is offered a chance to spare his son a life of blood and fear, the inner conflicts slowly resurface.

Reassessing Family

    Upon their return from Ireland, the SAMCRO men are incarcerated for fourteen months. Season 4 begins with their release. Jax comes back into the free world to the waiting arms of Tara, their new son Thomas, and Abel. Jax proposes to Tara, once again with the promise that he will leave club life and move on with her and their young family. It is in season 4 that Jax's identity crisis truly reaches a fever pitch and the world of his youth, his family, and all he had valued thus far in his life is challenged to a point at which he cannot ignore his discontent any longer. In the first episode he even says, "The bond that holds this club together isn't about love or brotherhood any more. We lost that a long time ago. It's just fear and greed now."

    Jax confides in Clay that he wants to leave the club. What Jax does not realize is that Clay is desperate for money, as he recognizes his own ailing health and esteem within the club are rendering him vulnerable. He and Gemma are also faced with the threat of Jax discovering a secret they've hidden from him since he was a teenager: When Jax went to Ireland, his father's ex-mistress slipped a large packet of letters his father had written her into Jax's luggage without his knowledge. These letters reveal Clay and Gemma's affair as well as the fact that they set Jax's father up, arranging for the road accident that ended his life. Clay then took over his presidency, steering the club toward guns and international criminal engagement. Obviously, neither Clay nor Gemma wants this secret to come out. Clay knows he will be banned from SAMCRO and Gemma will lose both her son and her status as matriarch. Gemma approaches Tara directly, able to remove the letters that incriminate her and get Tara to agree to hide the secret from Jax for his own sake. Tara

2. Sons of Anarchy

agrees, hoping to keep Jax from becoming once again deeply involved in the club that they are so close to leaving. Clay, however, decides the situation is more urgent and more potentially destructive and subsequently puts a hit out on Tara. He also kills Piney, a fellow member of the Original Nine and the only living member of the club who shares the secret.

Clay's mental state deteriorates as he becomes more paranoid about the letters and his future. He becomes obsessed with money, making a deal with a Mexican drug cartel to mule for them for a substantial compensation. This level of criminal involvement is new even for SAMCRO, and it divides the club. Turmoil bubbles to the surface, once again ensnaring Jax.

Jax agrees to go along with Clay's plan if he is allowed to walk away from the club after one run. Jax's agreement and Clay's erratic behavior split alliances, and the club's involvement with the cartel brings carnage to Charming. In the face of danger to both his club and his family, Jax decides that Tara should go ahead of him to Oregon to interview for a job there, and asks her to take the boys with her. He offers to follow his family up the road. Along the way, Jax experiences a kind of hyperreal moment of what his life could potentially be when he is finally free of the club. He makes small talk at a gas station with an older, middle-class man, an everyman figure there to symbolize normativity and civilian order. The two men discuss bikes, rolling their eyes at the need for family cars, and the thrills of both. Further up the road at a rest stop picnic, Jax and Tara enjoy a carefree lunch with their sons, and it is clear the two are imagining the life that awaits them, the one that feels almost within reach. It is an idyllic scene full of sunlight and green grass, pastoral and pleasant, symbolizing a life Jax knows nothing about and can only imagine. And though it is, as stated previously, a hyperreal moment in time, it fills both Jax and Tara with hope.

But, as the life of a one percenter tends to go, Jax's illusive moment of peace is shattered as Tara is nearly abducted, violently injuring her hand as she barely escapes. The failed abduction, part of Clay's plan to eliminate Tara, brings the entire young family back to Charming and Jax back into the world of the club. But the damage of this particular moment of violence does not simply destroy the peace or re-engage Jax in SAMCRO politics. His identity issues, of course, resurface as he begins to suspect Clay's involvement and as he learns more about the cartel for which they are working (which is discussed further, later in this chapter). Tara's life is also changed. The damage to her hand and arm is severe and she fears she will no longer be able to continue as a surgeon—the center of stability and control in her life. In her hospital bed her entire worldview is shattered and she resigns herself to a life in Charming, with SAMCRO, as Jax's old lady—a far cry from the upper-middle-class life of civility they had been headed to days before. Without Tara's stability and strength of character, Jax is more lost than ever.

There is a ridiculous amount of interclub politics in the final acts of season 4, involving Russians, the Irish, Mexican cartels, and the One-Niners from Oakland. Politically and socially the club is a disaster. Opie discovers that Clay killed his father. Jax discovers that Clay arranged for John's death. The CIA and the U.S. Attorney's office are everywhere, one working on a RICO[13] case that indicts the Sons and one that needs the Sons to help close a case on the cartel. It is truly an epic showdown and there is collateral damage everywhere. When Gemma realizes that Clay put the hit out on Tara, she confronts him. The two fight, and he beats her badly. At this point, Clay becomes truly Other. Even Tig, the club's sergeant-at-arms (essentially its "enforcer") is disgusted by Clay's actions and he removes his patch, signaling an end to his alliance to Clay. Opie, distraught over Piney's death, storms into the clubhouse gunning for Clay. He manages to wound him, but not fatally, as he is stopped by Jax. Jax is forced to keep Clay alive because he needs him to finish a deal with the Irish. At this point it is revealed that Jax is in bed with the CIA, who need SAMCRO muling for the cartel in order to close their case. If Jax doesn't cooperate, the CIA threatens to turn the club over to the Feds and their RICO case. Working for the CIA ensures their immediate safety. Jax's actions, however, deepen the schisms in the club, estrange him from his best friend, and preclude his escape from Charming and from SAMCRO.

Jax unseats Clay as president and, though he knows he can't actually kill him (because he can't work with the Irish without him), makes it clear that he will die soon and by someone in the club. Despite all their plans for the future, the finale of season 4 highlights Jax at the head of

2. Sons of Anarchy

the Sons table with Tara by his side, an exact duplicate image of an old photograph of John Teller and Gemma in the early years of the Sons. Jax's identity is once again in flux as are his alliances and his sense of self-awareness. With all that came to light throughout season 4, Jax's sense of past and purpose are challenged. And though he is not quite the villain that the other faux rogues in this book truly are, he is an outsider verging on being an Other. His passion for an idealized middle-class life and the struggles he continuously goes through to achieve the dream of what is actually a simulacrum of normalized existence are what make him a faux rogue. He is an anti-hero and possesses many heroic qualities. Yet he cannot escape his past and cannot formulate a new identity for himself, highlighting the powers of established hierarchies and the shackles of tradition. He also consistently falls back on hypermasculine, patriarchal power and violence when he has an intellect that would allow him to succeed in other ways, which renders him a poor example of a rogue hero. His desire for a normative life dependent on material wealth and prescribed middle-class ideals make him a conduit for the perpetuation of a traditional ideology of class difference, capitalist power, and anti-intellectualism. And his status as president of SAMCRO places him as a leader of a club ensconced in violence, hypermasculinity, and a deeply rooted hierarchy of patriarchy.

3

True Blood: Subverting the Myth of American Inclusion

> *Contemporary criticism has forced students and teachers to see that there are no innocent texts, that all artifacts of the established culture and society are laden with meaning, values, biases, and messages that advance relations of power and subordination.*
> —Kellner and Durham[1]

> *[I]t's a show about vampires, it's not meant to be taken that seriously. It's supposed to be fun.*
> —*True Blood* producer Alan Ball

The two quotes above offer insight into the battle of writing about popular culture. As an academic who sees the power that mainstream media has over millions of people, I am drawn to exploring and analyzing what so many dismiss as mere entertainment. Shows such as *True Blood*, HBO's adaptation of the Sookie Stackhouse novels written by Charlaine Harris, are easy to overlook or dismiss as simply escapist entertainment. The series is by no means exceptionally well-written or even well-produced in comparison with some of HBO's other, more cinematic dramatic series. Yet it is this kind of series, a drama full of supernatural creatures, sex, and ridiculous plot lines that I find most fascinating. *True Blood* and shows like it enthrall millions of viewers. According to the Nielsen report for the week of June 11, 2012, the show (in the second week of its fifth season) netted 4.4 million viewers, making the "top ten" list of cable shows that week. That's 4.4 million people

3. True Blood

engaging with a dramatic series that, though it seems to be innocuous, frivolous, escapist entertainment, offers a very clear narrative of capitalist power and the role of the Other in contemporary U.S. culture. This chapter highlights the impact of hegemonic narratives on audience ideological construction and discusses how *True Blood* subverts the American myth of inclusion with regard to sexuality and religion. Using the vampire as my key anti-hero-faux rogue, I highlight how a fantasy show so seemingly diverse and postmodern actually presents a very narrow, potentially dangerous narrative.

Television as a whole, as I've discussed thus far, is uniquely situated in postmodern culture. Surprisingly, it can easily be explored and examined using the theoretical tools of modernist critics, such as Theodore Adorno and his conceptualization of the American culture industry. Yet using such theories can be dangerous when examining contemporary U.S. culture.

> The Frankfurt school described a mass society and culture that sought to incorporate individuals into a more homogenized culture, controlled by big corporations, the state, and centralized media. By contrast, the current form of consumer capitalism is more fragmented, specialized, aestheticized and eroticized, and celebratory of difference, choice, and individual freedom than the previous stage.[2]

For example, when watching *True Blood*, one might be quick to argue that it is, in fact, a very progressive show, removed from the shackles of antiquated ideologies, celebrating difference and promoting tolerance and equality—a prime example of diversity and multiple viewpoints. Superficially it is a diverse program, complex in its discussions of power and representations of Otherness. There are a multitude of various kinds of supernatural beings who learn to cooperate with one another, several characters representing the GLBTQ community, characters of color, and inter-species, inter-racial relationships. Yet the show's progression and its attempts at deconstructing traditional ideas of power are consistently undermined, as is discussed in detail later in this chapter.

Subversive Beginnings

From the very beginning of the series, audiences are bombarded with contradictory messages. Its award-winning title sequence epitomizes this state of contradiction. This title sequence does a precise job of presenting the audience with the themes of the series and the complexity of very human issues presented throughout each episode. Its images of sex, religion, death, violence, rebirth (in the form of a baptism), the KKK, and predatory animals are supported by the song "Bad Things" by Jace Everett. The chorus articulates the complex messages that pervade the series: a lack or confusion about subject identity, deviant behavior, and a willingness to engage in acts that have been traditionally labeled as "bad." The subversive nature of the show's narrative is presented at the beginning of every episode. And though this title sequence could be presented as a mini-film of difference, diversity, and the multifaceted, multi-voiced nature of the postmodern audience, its convoluted images serve, in tandem with the narratives of the series, to present confusion over "right" and "wrong," power hierarchies, and how one might deal with the supernatural.

Occasionally it can be easy to forget or dismiss the abundant voices of difference permeating mainstream media. According to Meenakshi Gigi Durham and Douglas Kellner, "it is true that media culture overwhelmingly supports capitalist values, but it is also a site of intense conflict between different races, classes, gender, and social groups."[3] And while this is correct on a grand scale—difference is abundant across a variety of mediums and across the global realm of entertainment—American-produced television is so uniquely controlled that hegemonic narratives are everywhere, as discussed previously in this book. So when I argue about the power of the narrative of the *True Blood* series, I must stress that I am speaking contextually, within the realm of U.S. corporately controlled television in the socioeconomic and political situation of the early 2000s.

Vampires and Capitalism

In his 2002 book *Consuming Youth: Vampires, Cyborgs, and the Culture of Consumption*, Rob Latham discusses the

> always fraught and uneasy compromise of social interests, forged in spheres of politics and culture, that ensures the ongoing rule of a dominant

3. True Blood

class. This hegemony is neither automatic nor guaranteed, but must itself be reproduced: The consent of the dominated classes has continually to be won, and while the resulting consensus may last for decades, it remains exposed to the social fallout of economic crisis and other historical contingencies, which may lead to cultural-political crises of legitimation that can fatally undermine the entire system. What all this means, in other words, is that it is crucial to grasp the contextual specificity of how a regime of accumulation and a mode of regulation are dialectically articulated at any given moment rather than assuming a purely formal, serenely functional homeostasis.[4]

The dominant class of any culture is essentially a house of cards, one that must be meticulously maintained and reinforced. America does this most effectively through its popular mainstream media. Consuming audiences of mainstream media are being inundated with messages intent on maintaining oppressive ideologies in order to support the socially dominant class—the reconstructed or simulacrum of metanarratives, as I discuss with *Dexter* and *Sons of Anarchy*. My concern with all of the shows including and similar to the ones discussed in this book is that their narratives are creating ideologies that perpetuate capitalist hegemony and American conceptualizations of Otherness under the guise of difference, rebellion, and progress. *True Blood*, an excellent example of this, initially appears to be a metaphor for the American myth of inclusion and the triumph of difference.

> Hegemony can only be maintained so long as the dominant classes "succeed in framing all competing definitions within their range" (Hall, 1997), so that subordinate groups are, if not controlled, then at least contained within an ideological space that does not seem "ideological": which appears instead to be permanent and "natural," to lie outside history, to be beyond particular interests.[5]

Globally, the prospect of "hegemony" of any kind is impossible. But most popular media in the United States, regardless of how it is framed or argued, often leads to an attitude that assumes the hegemony of late capitalism as a universal necessity. In the midst of a crisis of capitalism, a push to conceptualize this economic form as "natural" or as a logical end is crucial for those who garner the most wealth and power from its current manifestation. This is being done in the States by equating democracy with capitalism, illogically demonizing socialism, and destroying public space in media for open discourse, thereby silencing the voices of contradiction. Rather than garnering the power of the diversity of the nation's population and progressing toward a new ideology of inclusion, compromise, and dynamic relationships worldwide, shows like *True Blood* are made, undermining the very voices and people that could produce true change.

Altering the Abject

Superficially, as stated previously, *True Blood* is a diverse program, complex in its discussions of power and representations of Otherness. Specifically, the repurposing of the vampire figure from an abject figure of horror to a desirable hero figure is problematic due to the centuries of stories and archetypal expectations associated with the vampire character. These expectations and associations frequently complicate the idea of a "new" kind of vampire hero throughout the show.

The vampire character, a cultural icon across the globe for centuries, has a variety of connotative meanings in various legends. Regardless of when and where the vampire legend has been told, it has traditionally been used to frighten audiences. Vampires are typically abject figures. As identified by Julia Kristeva, the abject is something we face that is outside of our symbolic order and induces horror as we recognize its Otherness. Kristeva identifies the corpse as a prime example of that which is abject: We face it only to recognize that which should be alive (within our sphere of symbolic order and understanding) but is not.[6] The vampire, then, a creature that is dead yet animate and sentient, is absolutely abject and serves as a tool for scary stories across the globe.

The vampire in popular culture has served to horrify, titillate, and fascinate audiences for centuries. Though it is difficult to pinpoint an exact time at which the narrative of the vampire began to morph into a different, more human monster in mainstream U.S. popular culture, it appears that something which served as an archetype for fear has turned into something with which to empathize. The vampire has become more a Byronic hero than a boogeyman. There have always been exceptions to the role of vampire as villain, but a growing trend seems to be leaving

3. True Blood

the gore and horror behind in favor of the tortured anti-hero. Anne Rice's vampire series exploded in the late 1980s with its puffy shirts and sexy, captivating heroes, and *Buffy the Vampire Slayer* shifted the study of vampires in popular fictions to the forefront of pop culture studies in the 1990s. In the early 2000s, even young-adult fictions such as the *Twilight* series and *The Vampire Diaries* feature vampires as heroes attempting to cohabitate with humans rather than simply drink them. *True Blood*, which first aired on HBO in 2008, offers an adult drama that focuses on the human nature of the vampire, producing interesting, complex characters dealing with their place in the world as both abject and non-abject. They are, arguably, fighting to be included in the normative symbolic order.

On a basic level, the abject figure of the vampire has been commodified, simply repurposed as a tool (a narrative hero) for scriptwriters and thus better able to fulfill a role within the U.S. understanding of a particular symbolic order. And though one might argue that figures such as the vampire or the zombie or any other creature of nightmare is simply an easily malleable tool for authors of fictions to recycle to the tastes of populist entertainment, I am concerned that the manipulation of such a figure of abjection has social, economic, and political repercussions.

Television, unlike other forms of popular media, has a way of engaging audiences because of its serial, long-running nature. Characters become more familiar than, for example, heroes of Hollywood films, in that they have time to develop and become more complex, well-rounded figures. Fans address them by their first names, sharing the latest show gossip, and conjectures and personal judgments of their actions on screen as though the characters exist on our same plane of reality. Though obviously we, as audience members, know they are not "real," our consistent engagement with them changes our relationship with them. They become household names, work gossip topics, and tabloid figures. Yet they are, at their most basic level, commodities. They are objects of corporate control. As commodities the characters in television serials can be "symbolically 'repossessed' in everyday life, and endowed with implicitly oppositional meanings, by the very groups who originally produced them. The symbiosis in which ideology and social order, production and reproduction, are linked is then neither fixed nor guaranteed."[7] The repurposing of villains, particularly villains with centuries of connection to evil and darkness, is especially disturbing, as is the case of vampires under the guiding hand of corporate television.

Life Blood

Vampires as a metaphor in early Marxism drained the lifeblood from the alienated workers in the form of capitalist overlords. They commodified the working class. The vampire was an abject figure for Marx; it was a dark, evil power draining the life of others for its own benefit. Yet in *True Blood*, the relationship between commodification and capitalist gain is complicated. Within the series, the vampires are commodified in the sense that their blood is used as a commodity, but they also commodify humans and other supernatural beings in both a literal sense (they feed on them) and a metaphorical sense—they use them, objectify them, and alienate them just as the Capitalist figures in Marx's work alienated their labor forces. In the show, as with most fantasy fictions, the vampires are the most wealthy and empowered creatures (both physically and in a socioeconomic sense), in contrast with the other supernatural characters such as the werewolves, shapeshifters, and telepaths who lead lives that are more human and noticeably less powerful. These creatures' powers are tied to the physical, whereas vampires have physical strength and the ability to manipulate minds, giving them both sociopolitical leverage and physical power.

Depicted in a fantasy series, this characterization makes sense; it appeals to the human desire for control and lends to the escapist enjoyment one expects from such a series. Yet the cumulative message of how the vampires wield their wealth and might undermines the idea of such notions as innocuous. The vampires of *True Blood*, though they can exist on synthetic blood, often choose to feed on humans; their wealth and attraction allows them to buy people, commodifying them and fetishizing blood. This has been a longstanding trope of vampire fictions, of course—the enthralled Renfield, the powerlessness of the first bitten (such as Mina in *Dracula*), and the desperate human servants who appear in most vampire-based pulp fiction. But in *True Blood,* through

3. True Blood

the idea of blood donation (the paid, willing humans are politely called "donors"), blood becomes a complicated fetishized object. Not only is human blood a commodity, but vampire blood is as well. It can be used to heal; it can be bought and sold as a dangerous, addictive illegal drug; and it is a key part of most of the show's sex scenes. Blood becomes a global commodity. "Brewers" of Tru Blood (the faux blood drink) are capitalizing on the need for synthetic blood, vampires are paying willing human donors, and humans are paying for vampire blood. The capitalist playing field seems oddly even, and the vampire metaphor of early Marx seems outdated. Yet the repurposing of the capitalist vampire is still frightening.

Nothing has changed in the power hierarchy of late capitalism. Though more may have entered the field of play in global capitalism, few players actually hold the most money. This is exemplified in the narrative of *True Blood*. In keeping with the traditional presentation of vampires, in addition to their super strength, super sex, and super speed, the *True Blood* vampires are also super rich. Hundreds of years of extended life have left them extraordinarily wealthy and powerful—their power being physical, economic, and social. The vampires, with mansions, teams of protective services, car services, jewels, and other physical demarcations of wealth, stand in stark contrast with the humans, shifters, and other supernatural creatures, most of whom are landless and working-class, a point made more precisely as they are situated in small, mostly rural hometowns in Louisiana. For example, Sam Merlotte, though he is a business owner and landlord, lives in a small trailer adjacent to his bar. His tiny cottages have housed many of the show's characters including Arlene and Terry and their family of five and Holly and her two teenage sons, and even his own shifter family is packed into one of the small homes in seasons 3 and 4. The dark side of the shifter world is introduced through Sam's younger brother and their mother along with Tommy's father Joe Lee. The two parents make their money in illegal dogfights, forcing young Tommy to shift and fight. Their life is brutal and ugly and their livelihood, which depends upon the abuse of their bodies, is mired in poverty.

In addition to presenting viewers with a narrative that superficially perpetuates the myth of inclusion, *True Blood* also presents an image of power that is tied to brutality and vast wealth. This is effectively exemplified through the character of Russell Edgington, the 2,800-year-old vampire king of Mississippi. The oldest vampire in the series, and the key antagonist of series 3 and 5, Russell was originally of Celtic origin, but now lives the life of a spoiled Southern Dandy. Openly homosexual, Russell revels in materialism and collectables. His mansion is a parody of itself, with shelves and cases of ill-gotten gains lining the walls of gilded wallpaper and velvet draperies. Russell's grasp on his sanity is slippery at best, but his "consort" Talbot seems to keep him somewhat tied to reality. When Eric kills Talbot as retribution for Russell's murder of his family, that grasp is lost. After rampaging blindly, he bursts into a news station, interrupting a broadcast:

> NEWSCASTER: Oregon has rallied in anticipation of the state's upcoming ratification vote on the Vampire Rights Amendment. Polls show the measure gaining support in recent months although nearly twenty percent of the country remains undecided.
> [*Suddenly Russell appears behind Jerry. His fist comes through Jerry's chest and then rips out Jerry's spine. People in the studio are heard screaming.*]
> RUSSELL: Does that help you decide, America? Do not turn off the camera! You've seen how quickly I can kill. Ladies and gentlemen, my name is Russell Edgington, and I have been a vampire for nearly three thousand years. Now, the American Vampire League wishes to perpetuate the idea that we are just like you. I suppose in a few small ways, we are. We're narcissists. We care only about getting what we want no matter what the cost, just like you. Global warming, perpetual war, toxic waste, child labor, torture, genocide … that's a small price to pay for your SUVs and your flat screen TVs, your blood diamonds, your designer jeans, your absurd garish McMansions! Futile symbols of pertinence to quell your quivering, spineless souls. But no, in the end we are nothing like you. We are immortal. Because we drink the true blood. Blood that is living, organic and human. And that is the truce the AVL wishes to conceal from you because, let's face it, eating people is a tough sale these days so they put on their friendly faces to pass their beloved VRA but make no mistake. Mine is the true face of vampire! Why would we seek equal rights? You are not our equals. We will eat you after we eat your children. Now time for the weather. Tiffany?

Russell's outrageous display not only underscores the Otherness of vampires but further monstrocizes his already Othered character, as is discussed later as I analyze the show's treatment of gay and lesbian characters.

Money and Might

Combining the two ideals of might and money that the vampires are so reliant upon, I am reminded of the power of imperialism and control rather than assimilation. "Cultural imperialism" is discussed further later on, and my argument is not that *True Blood* is in and of itself somehow affecting anything on a global scale; it is that, though the image of Marx's vampire seems antiquated, in the popular, contemporary series the very idea of the vampire as a wealthy being living off of the lifeblood of others remains exactly the same. Many of the show's vampires resemble traditional capitalists and behave with an attitude of entitlement bolstered by their strength and wealth.

Vampires Will Be Boys

Vampire Bill, William Compton as he is formally known, is the first "hero" introduced in the series. Bill was a member of the Confederate Army, headed home to his young family when he was turned, against his will, by his maker Lorena. Lorena and Bill lived as truly monstrous creatures of the night until Bill became resentful of being forced to live by her whims and had Lorena release him. When vampires "came out" and Bill showed up at Merlotte's, he was a Southern gentleman, refined in his manner and polite, full of the kinds of humility and respect he'd grown up with as a Compton in Bon Temps before the Civil War. Though lethal and possessive, he and Sookie develop a passionate relationship and Bill seems like a genuinely good "guy," particularly in comparison to Eric Northman, the ruling vampire sheriff of the area and Bill's immediate ruler. The following exchange between Bill and Sookie is a typical one of their early relationship and offers insight into Bill's character:

> SOOKIE *[while driving home with Bill]*: I use to get so mad when people judged vampires just for being different. It's like they were judging me

Renegade Hero or Faux Rogue

too. I told myself their fear was nothing but small-mindedness. But maybe that's what I wanted to believe. 'Cause the more open my mind gets, the more evil I see.
BILL: Sookie, most of us, vampire, human or otherwise, are capable of both good and evil. Often simultaneously.
SOOKIE: You can't expect me to believe that Eric is capable of anything good. Not after how he tortured Lafayette.
BILL: I have had worse sheriffs.
SOOKIE: I don't understand how you can defend him.
BILL: He saved your life.
SOOKIE: I can still hate him.
BILL: I hate that he may be putting you in harm's way once again, for his own selfish reasons. And I hate that he has shown you the barbarousness we call justice. If I could glamour it away for you, I would.
SOOKIE: I'm glad you can't. I'm sick of things sneakin' up on me. Rene and whatever the hell that was that attacked me last night. If I'm never gonna be safe, I'd rather know what to be afraid of.
BILL: Well, after last night, I hope that doesn't include me.
SOOKIE: I know there is evil in you. I know there is and it scares the hell outta me. But you're right. There's goodness in you, too, and when I look in your eyes, that's what I see.

While Bill wants to "mainstream," that is, to live among humans and consume synthetic blood, Eric flaunts his vampirism, lording over his nightclub Fangtasia as every fangirl (and boy's) dream of what a vampire should be. He sits on a throne in his club, calling subservient fans to him, ordering his staff about, and playing the role of the dark lord. A large, impressively built Viking, Eric is blond and striking in comparison to Bill's more human appearance. Eric also enjoys his power, ordering humans around and wielding his power as sheriff strictly and with frequent lethal force. The following exchange between Eric and Bill highlights not only Eric's attitudes toward humans but the initial difference between the two vampires early in the series:

Eric: And it goes without saying he needs to be found.... Which is where Sookie comes in.
Bill: No.
Eric: She's yours and I'm asking your permission to take her with me to Dallas.
Bill: Eric, you can do whatever you want with me but I am not putting her in this position any more. I cannot and I will not allow you to bring her into these matters.

3. True Blood

>ERIC: We made a deal, your human and I. That if I didn't kill anyone, she would work for me as often as I like. You remember that, don't you? You were there.
>BILL: Taking her across state lines is a far cry from taking her to Fangtasia for the evening.
>ERIC: I'm only asking your permission out of respect. If I want her, I can simply take her. Is no your final answer?
>BILL: It is.
>ERIC: Poorly played, Bill.

Eric's attitude toward humans is ambivalent and amusing. The following exchange with a fellow vampire serves as an example of his attitude:

>ERIC: Tell me, what is it that you find so fulfilling about human companionship?
>ISABELLA: They feel much more strongly than we do. Everything is urgent, exciting. Maybe because their lives are so temporary.
>ERIC: Yes, they certainly don't keep well. Do you crave the prospect of him growing old, sickly, crippled, somewhat repulsive?
>ISABELLA: No, I find it curious, like a science project

His response to humans is not always so negative, of course. In response to the terror of Edgington's public act of aggression, Eric argues, "I enjoy a good head-ripping as much as any vampire, but in this case it might be wise to consider the value of the heads in question." Eric also appears to have a soft spot for children. After rescuing Arlene's children while their mother was under the influence of Maryann, Pam's patience runs thin:

>PAM [miffed]: You make me so happy I never had any of you.
>ERIC: Oh, come on, Pam. They're funny. They're like humans, but miniature. Teacup humans.

Regardless of Eric's humor and his often surprising moments of humanity, Bill remains the more humane of the two in the first few seasons of the series. Yet this slowly begins to change.

When Bill becomes king of Louisiana, he begins to change, moving from his family home in Bon Temps to a modern mansion complete with human protectors, blood servants, and exorbitant luxury. Not quite as gawdy or comic as Edgington's home, Bill's is reminiscent of the insane vampire's home, perhaps a foreshadowing metaphor for what is to come as the series progresses. His mild temper slowly simmers to a boiling one as the use of brute force becomes easier for him. With the wealth and power he summons as king, he lays waste to his enemies, first dispatching Queen Sophie-Anne Leclerq and claiming his position as monarch, followed by his destruction of Nan Flannigan, the voice of the mainstreaming movement. When Bill is betrayed and captured by the Sanguanistas, those who believe that vampires should rule as a master race, feeding on humans as though they are cattle, he is enraptured by the mistress of the Sanguanistas, Lilith, the supposed mother of all vampires. Overwhelmed by his desire for her powers, he betrays everyone he loves at the end of season 5 for the sake of Lillith's blood.

Eric, on the other hand, loses his memory after being cursed by the witch Marnie Stonebrook. He is taken in by Sookie, and his personality is suddenly completely different. He is almost childlike in his vulnerability. No longer haughty or arrogant, he is tender and honest, seducing and then falling in love with Sookie. He hears tales of his nearly one thousand years of bloody deeds and is shocked and sickened by them. Sookie falls deeply for him in return. When Eric's memory comes back, he is no longer the Eric he was in earlier episodes, but a more dynamic, complex, and emotional character. In contrast to Bill, Eric grows more compassionate and concerned with humanity throughout season 5.

As different as the two vampires are, they serve as the two main heroes of the series, the two protagonists I label as faux rogues. Though their characterizations are complicated and problematized by outside sources and the two change so drastically, both succeed in their trials through brute strength, masculine authority, and wealth. They have the means to wage wars and the capacity for both good and evil. They are one and the same, neither truly good nor evil, but tools of the beasts that lurk within them. They are almost more human than humans in their appetites and desires and the depth of their lust for power, which knows no end. They perform heroic deeds and prove to be the antiheroes of the series in a practical sense, succeeding over those more evil than they throughout each season and saving both humans and weaker supernaturals. But their essence is made of want, and it is only through power and force that they are able to feel whole. They perpetuate a narrative of warmongering and insatiable want.

3. True Blood

What Is It with Americans and Vampires?

True Blood and the new vampire narratives of the past several years have simply changed the abject figure into an attractive, sympathetic being able to fit within the social order, making the notion of a capitalist "monster" less threatening and more something to emulate. At a time when late capitalism is in crisis, as it has been at the start of the new millennium (beginning most noticeably with the housing crash of 2008), making it sexy in popular culture can only help maintain its place within the American mythology. For audiences, "TV plays a strong role in the polity, and therefore in assigning symbolic or cultural/narrative citizenship to various types of subjectivity."[8] Although its consuming audience is not hegemonic and the show is, of course, filtered through the lens of the consuming subject, the narrative of what constitutes "normal" citizenship has the power to shape a diverse consumer group's ideological construction about a particular issue.

In their discussion of "Television and Consumer Societies," Lyn Gorman and David Mclean identify the work in communication studies beginning in the 1980s that negated the power of cultural imperialism, yet they also discuss Richard Kuisel's arguments of what might instead be called "cultural transfer" rather than "cultural imperialism." Kuisel argues that while cultural transfer (in popular culture) "may be a two-way street," most "of the traffic has been one direction—from the United States."[9] It is this bombardment of choices being exported that speaks to the international power of American popular culture, television in particular. What we export are programs that depict

> a variety of images of the United States. They [include] images of crime, violence, poverty, and urban decay—one reason why the global preeminence of American popular culture does not inevitably translate into the "soft power" by which the attractions of a culture can supplement the hard power of military or economic might. Yet American programs (as well as non–American versions of U.S. genres and formats) have typically presented a good life that extols "an aggressive contemporaneity" and the accumulation of wealth,[10]

a message inundating *True Blood*. The power and might in the series lie in the accumulation of wealth and the notion of the "good life" associated with excessive means. The more a nation exports a particular ideology, the more it has a propaganda-like effect on its citizens. It supports a national mythology and reinforces a particular ideology that, though it seems to exist in a vacuum, forms the idealistic construction of a nation-state.

In the United States, our national mythology, as much as it can be discerned, is one of inclusion. And as fraught with pain, ignorance, hatred, and intolerance as the struggle for GLBTQ rights continues to suffer, it does appear that as a nation we are making strides toward a system that does not vilify a person because of his or her sexual orientation or identification.

Initially the show seems remarkable in its attitudes toward difference and its constant shifting of power among various characters.

> Author Charlaine Harris—who wrote the best-selling Sookie Stackhouse mystery novels that the TV show is based on—hoped fans would pick up on the link between vampire rights and gay rights when she published the first book in 2001. "When I began framing how I was going to represent the vampires, it suddenly occurred to me that it would be interesting if they were a minority that was trying to get equal rights," Harris says. "It just seemed to fit with what was happening in the world right then."[11]

The show, though it superficially correlates equal rights and supernatural beings, consistently undermines the idea of equality. It does allow for a broad range of sexual exploits with limited repercussions, and the small, rural town of Bon Temps is, with very few exceptions, inclusive of the GLBTQ community.

Yet the issue of vampire sexuality brings with it the most Otherness and the notion of deviance in the series. On the show, sex with vampires involves blood and a clear hierarchy of power. For example, when a vampire gives a human or shifter his or her blood, the receiver is uncontrollably drawn to the donor sexually despite his or her own sexuality. The blood can serve as a form of sexual control, not a loving commitment. The fluidity of sexuality within the vampire community is heavily emphasized. Unfortunately, when it is highlighted, this "difference" is often monstrocized, particularly for the female vampires. For example, Nan, Pam, and Queen Sophie Anne are portrayed as powerful but extraordinarily dominating, bitchy, unfeeling, and even crazy, and it is

3. True Blood

their sex acts with other women that are most frequently portrayed awkwardly—in moving vehicles during conference calls or with donors chained up in Fangtasia's basement, versus Sookie's sex scenes that are featured, not intruded upon or interrupted like novelty scenes or jokes. The idea that these are not "regular" women or that only women who eschew traditionally feminine traits can be powerful is a very strong message perpetuating a heteronormative system. Though Tara's (human) relationship with Naomi is shown as loving and positive, it is brief, less explicit, and overshadowed by the Otherness of the many images of sexual difference. Tara's enviable inner strength as a person diminishes after her break-up with Naomi (episode 42, season 4). When Tara joins forces with Antonia/Marni in her vindictive campaign against vampires, she becomes a pawn, confused and blinded by hate. She finally realizes her mistake and regains her own inner power, and offers herself as a kind of sacrifice when she takes a lethal bullet for Sookie. The result of her self-sacrifice is her re-birth as a vampire in season 5. Tara morphs from the main symbol of human endurance and power into a monstrous Other when her rage and self-hatred run rampant.

Though I struggle to see positive presentations of GLBTQ characters in the show, I argue that, initially, the series stood out in its excellent characterization of Lafayette. Though first presented as an extreme example of a gay male stereotype and a drug-dealing pornographer, his character becomes three-dimensional and fully developed as the show progresses. But it is only after his torture and captivity in season 2 that we see his true humanity.[12] When he is imprisoned in Fangtasia's basement, his makeup and performative flamboyance are gone, and he is shackled along with Royce, the character who taunted him about his sexuality in season 1. The two talk and attempt to work together as people. As the series progresses, Lafayette develops a relationship with Jesús Velásquez, a witch, also called a *brujo*. He and Lafayette develop a loving, committed, and very human relationship. In their scenes together, Lafayette is usually bare-faced and less performative. His humanity and vulnerability are emphasized, and the love and trust he and his partner share forms one of the most functional relationships in the series.

Yet Jesús, out of necessity, introduces Lafayette to the depths of his brujo powers through which Lafayette discovers that he is an exceptionally powerful medium. In season 5, the extent of his powers grows, showing darkness in its essence. These powers are given to him by Jesús's murderous, seemingly insane native Mexican grandfather, a reminder that the darkness that forms in Lafayette's magic is the product of a non-white man with supernatural powers underscoring some of the show's more negative presentations of people of color. In a sense, though he is still a complex character who loves and grieves, he is monstrocized as an Other, undermining the positive portrayal of a "normal" gay man. Though *True Blood* appears to embrace an attitude of inclusion and acceptance of homosexual or bisexual men and women, in the end, each character, as exemplified above by Lafayette, is in some way monstrocized. Even Ball is quoted as saying, "If you get really serious about it, well, then the show could be seen to be very homophobic because vampires are dangerous: They kill, they're amoral."[13] This has not gone unnoticed by queer theory scholars. "The 'good vampires' are those that are able to contain their appetite for blood and sex and the 'bad vampires' are those who kill people, drink their blood and are hyper-sexual," says Lauren Gutterman, coordinator of OutHistory.org, a project of CUNY's Center for Lesbian and Gay Studies.[14]

Although the show seems to attempt to normalize and address global inclusion of the GLBTQ community, it is obvious that the writers and director struggle with breaking out of the conceptualization of homosexuality as both deviant and dangerous. There is not a single homosexual character in the series who does not possess some kind of "dark" power. The initial epitome of the scary gay monster is, of course, Russell Edgington. Absolute lunatics aside, though the other characters may be friends, lovers, heroes, or begrudgingly helpful anti-heroes, the fact remains that they are clearly Other.

In addition to a show that constructs an ideology of capitalist dominance and the subversion of the GLBTQ fight for equality, *True Blood* also undermines the American mythos of inclusion with its increasingly frequent allusions to Christianity and its place of power in a belief hierarchy as it pertains to the "heroes" of the show. In its fifth season, the show's central narrative centers on religion, that of the vampire "Authority" in particular. The season, which coincided with the fever pitch of the U.S. presidential campaign, focusing on the fight between the main-

3. True Blood

streaming Authority, the political group of leaders that wishes to coexist with humans, and the violent Sanguinistas who believe in vampire superiority, viewing humans only as food. According to creator Alan Ball, he and his team

> wanted to play with the politics-religion angle, since that seems to be something that never stops.... Some of the things being said by some people during the Republican primary were so horrifying to me and I thought, "What if vampires wanted a theocracy? What would that look like?" Whenever anybody thinks they know what God wants and wants that to apply to government, whether Americans or the Taliban, it's kind of a terrifying thing.[15]

Any time the men and women at the production level of a show attempt to engage with a political issue within their series narrative, I find it admirable. The problem, however, is that though the motivation is positive, the message is all too often lost. And such is the case with *True Blood*'s tangle with religion. Season 5 does spell out the human cost of theocracy and in the beginning draws a clear line between the "good" vampire Authority attempting to unite with humanity and "mainstream" by living peacefully among them; but it presents this not as a democratic decision, but as a dictatorial decree. As the narrative progresses, the violence and intolerance one would expect from the Sanguinistas, the theocratic vampires bent on dominating and destroying mankind, is seen in the eyes and actions of Roman, the Authority leader. Disagreement and dissent in his ranks is dealt with through death and torture. The line between positive and negative governmental action is blurred, undermining Ball's attempt at referencing the negative side of religion and politics. In season 5, there are no winners and no good guys on either side—with the exception of Eric.

When the Sanguinistas conquer the Authority and begin their bloody rule, Bill and Eric are initially drawn in. These followers of Lilith and their belief in vampire superiority have a preserved vial of what they believe is the blood of Lilith. As they indulge, hallucinations ensue, and the first of many bloody rampages begins with Bill and Eric in tow. After a wedding party massacre, Lilith appears to the new Authority members, mesmerizing them and ensuring that the bloodshed will continue. Yet as Eric watches his vampire sister held, enraptured by the blood-soaked figure of Lilith, his maker Godric appears to him, and the spell is broken for the Viking vampire. He decides then to save his sister and his friend and stop the forthcoming "religious" terror. Eric becomes the key rogue hero of the season as Bill is lost and enthralled by Lilith. The season ends with no satisfactory conclusion of the Lilith-based reign of terror.

Oh No, Not Religion Too

Season 5, however focused the narrative is on religion, is by no means a stand-alone story about religion for the show. Throughout the entire story arc of the series, a narrative about religion has been created. For a show that deals with supernatural creatures, one could imagine that, like symbols for the GLBTQ fight, the *True Blood* characters could use their difference to emphasize equality or at least tolerance of a variety of religions. Unfortunately, just as the U.S. mythology of religious freedom is consistently buried beneath the dominance of Christianity in mainstream media, *True Blood*'s inclusion of various religions actually supports a hierarchy of religions in which a patriarchal God reigns supreme.

From the beginning of the series, the show does a good job of demonizing the fanatical, hateful church the Fellowship of the Sun. Much like Ball's concern about the tyranny of religion and politics in 2012, from its beginnings *True Blood* was vocal in its narrative against intolerance, which is to be admired. However its portrayal of all religions beyond patriarchal Christianity is skewed, undermining its message of inclusion and equality.

In season 2, Maryann Forrester, a maenad, is intertwined with Tara and eventually turns Bon Temps into an orgy-hosting, blood-eating, murderous mob of lunacy with the absence of its local hero vampire, Bill. Upon his return, Bill, with help from Sam Merlotte (a shapeshifter), is able to destroy the false god. Her destruction, according to the legend developed in the show, rests on her belief in herself and her ability to draw forth the god of her past (presumably Bacchus). When she realizes she has been tricked by Sam and that Bacchus did not come for her, her

3. True Blood

self-belief wavers and she perishes. Belief is shown as weak and unimportant if the god in whom one believes is not "true."

In season 3, we are introduced to Holly, a new barmaid at Merlotte's. She and a newly pregnant Arlene become friends, and Holly reveals that she is a practicing Wiccan. Arlene, believing that the baby she is carrying is her murderous ex-partner Rene's and not the child of Terry Bellefleur, her new boyfriend, confides in Holly. Holly offers Arlene a "natural" solution that could terminate her pregnancy, performing a full Wiccan ceremony in the woods with Arlene. Ultimately the spell fails and Arlene carries to term. Yet the message of this first introduction to Wiccans on the show is powerful. It is seen as a feminine religion, evoking a goddess and the power of nature, all of which are positive, relatively correct attributes. However, what *True Blood* shows us is the destructive power of the religion and its potential to kill. The ceremony, performed secretly, reflects negatively on Holly and women in general, recalling tropes in literature and other fictions that connect women and nature and women and secrecy.

Season 3 introduces a Wiccan group that accidentally starts a war with the vampires. Their leader, Marnie, channels a witch from the sixteenth century, one who had managed to raise vampires from their lairs and compel them to walk into the daylight, self-immolating. Antonia, the witch channeled, was beaten, raped, and burned at the stake for her "crime" of being a witch in Catholic Spain. What one might consider a sympathetic character, she turns into a tyrant, killing innocents and losing control in her desire for revenge against vampires. Witches and Wiccans are not the same, but in the series their powers are aligned, connecting a peaceful religion to an out-of-control spirit who is, again, a woman.

Among the rise of Wiccans and witches, Jesús, Lafayette's boyfriend, reveals his brujo powers, returning to his childhood home, coming into contact with the powers of his ancestors. The scenes in which ancestral powers, both his and Lafayette's, are featured are disturbing, dark, and menacing. The brujo powers, the show suggests, are very close to the powers of darkness. Yet Jesús proves himself as a source of good. He frees two souls in a blaze of bright light, helping to free Terry and Arlene of a haunting. He is killed in season 4, but his presence is felt numerous times after when he comforts or warns Lafayette.

Renegade Hero or Faux Rogue

Another character, one featured only briefly in season 2, also makes ghostly appearances at crucial times. Godric, Eric's maker, is the oldest vampire known. Having grown tired of the evil he has seen in his thousands of years on Earth, he becomes a passive, peaceful vampire willing to martyr himself to protect his progeny. In a touching scene, a troubled Godric is portrayed only at peace when he faces his "true death" as Sookie prays to her Christian God. His ghostly visits afterward are to warn Eric of the dangers of following the false god Lilith. Though never expressly stated, a theme emerges in the show very much grounded in Christian theology. The fact that the two spiritual characters are named Jesús and Godric does not detract from this. Christianity, however, in its nondenominational, southern devout form, casts a holy glow across the show. Seen in Sookie's crosses and prayers and in the praying of others, this is expressed verbally by Jason Stackhouse's best friend, Hoyt, in season 2 when he tells Jason that the only church he needs is the Baptist church up the street that teaches him only to love and to be a good person, when Jason says he's off to fight with the Fellowship. In an understated and subtle way, the show again and again denounces religions other than Christianity, excluding an enormous portion of its viewing audience from the myth of inclusivity.

In *True Blood*, our rogue heroes turn out to once again be white, male figures, both only ever shown in heterosexual sex scenes and both ensconced in a world of supernaturals where, ironically, Christianity reigns supreme. Bill is American and Eric, though Scandinavian in origin, develops a more and more American twang to his voice as the seasons progress and the more "heroic" he becomes. Both are staunch capitalists, dependent on wealth and might for control, and both live in an exclusive world under the guise of an all-encompassing, diverse, supernatural fantasy world.

4

Breaking Bad: Privilege and the Power of Choice

I am alive!—Walter White, season 1

I won.—Walter White, season 4

Paul MacInnes, in his 2012 article in the UK's *Guardian,* introduced readers to the *Breaking Bad* series and to Vince Gilligan.

> "I originally pitched it to the studio with one line," says Vince Gilligan, the creator of *Breaking Bad*. "I told them: 'This is a story about a man who transforms himself from Mr. Chips into Scarface.'" The line turned out to be a clincher, and it remains as good a description as any of a show that wins serial Emmy awards and is frequently described by fans as being the best drama on TV.[1]

As the article continued, Gilligan delved into his process of developing Walter White, the series protagonist: "I wondered why someone like us [he and a fellow writer]," he asks, "which is to say a basically law-abiding citizen, would suddenly do such a thing." Gilligan asks,

> why would someone make such a radical change in their lives if they were basically a good person, a non-criminal? I think of *Breaking Bad* as a bit of character study. It's really about this one man and this one particular set of circumstances, the fact he makes decisions that most of us, myself included, would not. We are telling a story of transformation in which a previously good man, through sheer force of will, decides to become a bad man.

Renegade Hero or Faux Rogue

The emphasis in all of the articles available about Gilligan and his series is on his singular desire to turn his protagonist into an antagonist. And, to many, by season 4 he had succeeded. Walter White, *Breaking Bad*'s everyman hero, becomes a vicious, morally contemptible man who keeps the audience guessing and on edge and the fictional characters who surround him walking on eggshells.

What, however, formulates the soul of the series? What has kept viewers faithful and reverent through five seasons, even after Walter surpasses the relatively innocuous term "anti-hero" into what his creator labels "a villain?" It is a complicated question. In order to fully analyze the series I must first argue that Walter is not a true villain in the show, but a confused man of white, middle-class privilege suddenly cast into a world he does not fully understand, but who is living on the high he gets by "winning" the strange game he is playing. His motivations may be different than Dexter's or Jax's or Eric's or Nucky's, but I still see him as a faux rogue. He is a man making choices that are criminal. And occasionally insane. He is not a good man, but he frequently does bad things for good reasons. But the same could be said of all the other anti-hero characters featured in this book.

Perhaps what makes Gilligan and critics argue that Walter truly has become the series villain instead of seeing him as a rogue hero is that he, unlike any of the other characters of this book, enters into the criminal arena purely by choice and with a lucid plan. He then continues to make calculated decisions. Unlike Dexter, early trauma and psychotic tendencies do not shape his plans. Unlike Eric or Bill, someone else did not turn him into a monster. Unlike Jax and Nucky, he was not raised in an environment where his actions and involvement in a criminal empire were part of his upbringing. *Breaking Bad* focuses from the very beginning on Walter's choices and their consequences. By season 4, however, he can be read as a character with the face of a villain, but one who is truly just another privileged citizen engaging in capitalist lust at the expense of others, depending on appearances and circumstances to hide his evil deeds. He is exploiting the chaos and devastation around him for his own benefit. He is not an everyman character climbing out of the wreckage of economic downturns and medical bills; he is using those negatives to excuse his malevolent acts.

4. Breaking Bad

At first glance, Walter White seems far from privileged as he scrubs down cars at a rundown car wash while trying not to cough up blood. Daily he faces a sea of blank and apathetic faces as the chemistry teacher of a local public high school; he tries to maintain a warm and happy home for his wife Skyler, his teenage son Walter Jr., who faces the challenges of cerebral palsy, and the unexpected, late-in-life baby he and his wife await. He also spends a good deal of time trying to suppress the coughing episodes that indicate his late-stage diagnosis of lung cancer. Yet though his life is not glamourous or easy, he is a middle-class white male in America. He is privileged in a very particular way. In Chapter 2, I discuss Dexter and how the privilege of "invisibility" affords the white race substantial benefit; the same argument applies to Walter White. Peggy McIntosh, speaking from her experiences in women's studies, argues that "whites are carefully taught not to recognize white privilege, as males are taught not to recognize male privilege."[2] Coming to grips with her own recognition of her white privilege, she colloquially compares it to an "invisible weightless knapsack" full of provisions that provide her with tools she needs daily to make life flow more smoothly.

Recognizing this beneficial carry-all of privilege is not something white people are taught to acknowledge or understand. It is "just there." As in Ross Chambers' discussion of invisibility from Chapter 1, being privileged as a member of a class to which others are compared has significant benefit. I mention this argument because, in all of the critical responses, blogs, and fan pages I have read about *Breaking Bad,* and in reading interviews with its creator Vince Gilligan, there is a distinct lack of discussion of race. Walter's privilege may seem a strange place to begin my discussion of a lowly high school teacher who turns to cooking methamphetamine. But as this chapter progresses, I argue how this privilege is the backbone of the character.

Walter is presented as a man downtrodden by life: teaching ungrateful, uninterested teenagers, scraping daily to support his family, and dealing with the diagnosis of his extremely progressed lung cancer. The setting of the show mimics Walter's presentation: Albuquerque, New Mexico, in the middle of the housing crisis, with drugs and crime running rampant in a city obviously short on funds as seen through its struggling schools and angst-ridden middle class. Premiering in America in 2008, just as the housing bubble burst was showing its full effect, *Breaking Bad* sets Walter up as an "everyman hero" who begins to slowly and surely rebuild his confidence and his financial livelihood. It's no wonder people fell for him: The first time he stands up for his son and physically confronts a bully or the time he manages to out "tough guy" Tuco, as I discuss later, shows a man coming into his full power, a man who is freer and more autonomous than many audience members might feel. The "swagger" of early TV heroes comes back through Walter as the series progresses. He loses more and more of his fears and gains a feeling of invincibility. Though Walter becomes increasingly despicable as a person, as a character he is easy to love because he embodies the American traits of toughness and brutality so loved in early Westerns without the internal turmoil that plagues the other anti-heroes of contemporary television.

In the pilot episode, during a ride-along with his DEA agent brother-in-law Hank, Walter learns that those in the meth trade make enough fast money to put both his kids through college and keep his wife comfortable for life. In season 2 he does the actual math:

> Adjusting for inflation—good state college—adjusting for inflation, say $45,000 a year, two kids, four years of college ... $360,000. Remaining mortgage on the home, $107,000. Home equity line, $30,000, that's $137,000. Cost of living, food, clothing, utilities, say two grand a month? I mean, that should put a dent in it, anyway. Twenty-four K a year provide for, say, ten years. That's $240,000, plus 360 plus 137 ... 737. $737,000, that's what I need. That is what I need. You and I both clear about 70 grand a week. That's only ten and a half more weeks. Call it eleven. Eleven more drug deals and always in a public place from now on. It's doable. Definitely doable.

Compared to his yearly income (approximately $43,000), the lucrative business is too much of a temptation for the Nobel Prize–winning chemist, and this ride-along proves to be the catalyst for his career in meth production.

Walter, on his ride-along, recognizes one of his former students escaping a DEA raid. Jesse Pinkman, a.k.a. Cap'n Crunch, had been doing fairly well in the meth trade with his partner Emilio until their lab was raided. Jesse's escape sparks Walter's interest, and he quickly finds Jesse's address in his school's database. He blackmails young Jesse

4. Breaking Bad

into partnering with him to cook and deal meth by threatening to turn Jesse over to Hank if he does not help.

Walter fronts the money for an RV so the two can have a movable lab, which they drive out into the desert and turn into a cooking station. They then proceed to cook their first batch of meth. The purchase of the RV and the particular choice of Jesse as a partner are the first indications that Walter is not simply a desperate man making a panicked decision to help his family. These small clues are the first pieces of the puzzle of Walter's true character, as I discuss further.

Walter and Jesse's first endeavor begins with animosity, Jesse mocking Walter's meticulousness as he strips to his jockey underwear so as to not get chemicals on his clothes. After an awkward moment of Jesse coming to terms with his new partially dressed partner, the two begin to work, yet their exchanges are tense. An example from the first episode:

> WALTER: Did you learn nothing from my chemistry class?
> JESSE: No. You flunked me, remember? You prick! Now let me tell you something else. This ain't chemistry—this is art. Cooking is art. And the shit I cook is the bomb, so don't be telling me.
> WALTER: The shit you cook is shit. I saw your set-up. Ridiculous. You and I will not make garbage. We will produce a chemically pure and stable product that performs as advertised. No adulterants. No baby formula. No chili powder.
> JESSE: No, no, chili P is my signature!
> WALTER: Not any more.

However, once Jesse sees the finished product, his attitude improves:

> JESSE [about Walter's meth]: This is glass grade. I mean, you got ... Jesus, you got crystals in here two inches, three inches long. This is pure glass. You're a damn artist! This is art, Mr. White!
> WALTER: Actually, it's just basic chemistry, but thank you, Jesse. I'm glad it's acceptable.
> JESSE: Acceptable? You're the goddamn Iron Chef! Every jibbhead from here to Timbuktu is going to want a taste!

Jesse's excitement is short-lived: Heading out to sell his new stash to some dealers, he is abducted as the dealers force him to return to the RV where they snare Walter and Jesse at gunpoint.

Walter, under the pretense of sharing his "recipe," poisons the two men. The disposal of the men becomes complicated when one of them wakes up. Walter and Jesse ultimately decide to dissolve the dead man's corpse in acid and they hold Krazy-8, the other dealer, prisoner in Jesse's basement.

What follows is a gruesome sequence of events. They have to get rid of the dead man and decide what to do with the live one, so they flip a coin. Walter is stuck with the live man in the basement. Jesse gets the body dump. Jesse, not following Walter's instructions to dissolve the body in plastic tubs, chooses the easier route of dissolving him in the bathtub. Walter and Jesse stare dumbfounded as bloody pieces of Emilio fall to the floor through a hole in the ceiling that was eaten away by hydrofluoric acid.

> WALTER: I'm sorry, what were you asking me? Oh, yes, that stupid plastic container I asked you to buy. You see, hydrofluoric acid won't eat through plastic. It will, however, dissolve metal, rock, glass, ceramic. So there's that.

In this instance the audience gains even more insight into Walter's true genius, but we also get to watch him as he is forced to decide what to do with Krazy-8 in the bathroom. He makes a list—cons on one side, pros on the other—with regard to killing the dealer. The "cons" side says, basically, "killing is wrong," while the "pros" side declares Krazy-8 will kill him and his entire family if Walter lets him go. Ultimately, when Walter realizes his prisoner intends to stab him with a piece of shattered plate, he gains the courage to strangle him to death. The pilot episode concludes with two murders and one perfect batch of meth completed.

Season 1 runs a complicated narrative slalom between Walter's cancer diagnosis, his family's reaction to the diagnosis, and his entry into the drug trade. When Walter is diagnosed, his prognosis is very poor. So in his mind, he has already decided he will die. Once he conceptualizes that, each decision he makes is based on the idea that he has nothing to lose. He does not fear death or arrest or scandal or pain because all he sees is his world ending. Though Walter never explicitly states it, it is assumed by the audience and Jesse and other characters, that Walter is "breaking bad" to leave behind money for his family. Things change between him and his young partner when Jesse, in season 1, episode 6, learns of his illness:

4. Breaking Bad

> JESSE: When were you going to tell me?
> WALTER: Tell you what?
> JESSE: Cancer. You got it, right?
> WALTER: How did you know?
> JESSE [*pointing to the chemo mark on Walter's chest*]: My aunt had one of those ... dots on her to target the radiation. What is it, in your lung? I'm your partner, man. You should have told me. That's not cool, okay? Not at all. What stage are you?
> WALTER: 3-A.
> JESSE: Gone to your lymph nodes.
> WALTER: Your aunt.... How bad was she when they caught it?
> JESSE: Bad enough. She didn't last long.
> WALTER: How long?
> JESSE: Seven months. I get it now. That's why you're doing all this. You want to make some cash for your people before you check out.
> WALTER: You got a problem with that?
> JESSE: You tell me. You're the one that looks like you just crawled out of a microwave.

This scene offers significantly more insight into Jesse's character than Walter's, and it, just slightly, changes the overtones of their relationship as Walter realizes Jesse lost his only loyal family member, and Jesse sees Walter no longer as an irritating schoolteacher but a dying man with a family.

Walter's family also begins to see him in a different light after he tells them of his condition. They are confused and angry when he says he will not be seeking treatment. Completely flabbergasted, Skyler calls a family meeting in season 1, episode 5, and she, Walter Jr., her sister Marie and her brother-in-law Hank take turns airing their concerns (and anger) about his decision.

> WALTER: Look, we all in this room, we love each other. We want what's best for each other and I know that, I am very thankful for that. What I want ... what I want, what I need ... is a choice.
> SKYLER: What does that mean?
> WALTER [*with tears in his eyes, very emotional*]: Sometimes I feel like I never actually make, any of my own ... choices. I mean, my entire life it just seems I never ... had a real say about any of it. This last one, cancer, all I have left is how I choose to approach this.
> SKYLER [*calmly*]: Well, make the right choice; you are not the only one it affects. What about your son? Don't you want to see your daughter grow up? I just....

Renegade Hero or Faux Rogue

> WALTER [*still emotional*]: Of course I do, Skyler. You've read the statistics sheet, these doctors talking about surviving, one year, two years, like it's the only thing that matters. But what good is it to survive if I'm too sick to work, to enjoy a meal, to make love. For what time I have left, I want to live in my own house, I want to sleep in my own bed. I don't want to choke down 40 or 50 pills every single day, and lose my hair, lie around, too tired to get up, and so nauseated that I can't even move my head. You cleaning up after me. Me ... me some ... um ... some dead man, some artificially alive, just marking time.... No. And that's how you would remember me. That's the worst part. So ... that is my thought process, Skyler.... I'm sorry, it's just I choose not to do it.

The emphasis for Walter is on his choice on how to live his final days. What his family does not know is that these final days also include his meth production and his adrenaline-filled life in the Albuquerque underworld. Though Walter ultimately does agree to treatment, I wonder how much of him simply wanted to go out in a blaze of glory—high on endorphins and adrenaline, living a life he would only have ever dreamed of, if only for a few months. Regardless, it becomes clear that his choice for treatment rather than a fast death is the key push in the change of Walter White.

In the episode prior to Walter's enforced family meeting, Jesse returns to his parents' house—his family home—in a wealthy suburb. It is revealed that Jesse has two upper-middle-class parents and a younger brother who is quite gifted, a spoiled preteen on whom his parents dote. As Jesse digs through his own childhood room and talks with his parents, it is obvious his drug problem started in high school and, after several attempts at helping him, his parents finally kicked him out of the house. But Jesse, disturbed by what he has recently endured, thanks to Walter, seems determined to behave under their roof and spend time with his family. However, when a maid discovers a joint in the house, Jesse's parents automatically assume it is his (it is his brother's) and tell him to leave. Jesse covers for his brother and heads out lonely and despondent. Ironically, these two episodes, though very different, both feature a family circle of discussion, tears at feared abandonment, and anger directed at both Walter and Jesse for the choices they have made.

I see two men, one fifty, one twenty-five, who walked away from lucrative, comfortable situations in which they could have potentially

4. Breaking Bad

succeeded well beyond their current lifestyles, through their own choices. Jesse turned to drugs, and Walter, for reasons that are never made entirely clear, walked away from his chemistry research corporation with $5,000 instead of the millions he could have made if he had stayed. He did not have to become a high school teacher, but he chose to. Walter and Jesse began their journey together in the series not because life was unfair to them or inexplicably cruel, but because of choices they made in their past.

Breaking Bad

The phrase "breaking bad" comes from the American Southwest slang phrase "to break bad," meaning to challenge conventions, to defy authority and to skirt the edges of the law. Regardless of how Jesse and Walter come to be partners, the show fuses them together from episode 1 and the two, henceforth, break bad together. Theirs is not an easy relationship, but it is ideal for both the show and the character study of Walter White himself. Jesse is a skinny, hapless kid who started making major mistakes and poor choices very early in life. Yet he has an innate compassion for people, especially children, and it is clear he has suffered from his parents' abandonment and scorn. His time with his sick aunt seems to have strengthened his resolve to persevere, as it would have had to. Caring for a terminally ill loved one can easily break the strongest of adults. Though he is by no means an intellectual, he has developed street smarts and learns quickly, often more quickly than Walter in dangerous situations. And as Walter hardens as the series progresses, Jesse softens. He feels more deeply than Walter, and he suffers from the emotional baggage the two acquire as they maneuver their way through their partnership.

In contrast, Walter, though the audience is left with very little to go on, seems to have had a stable enough background to get through school, earn his doctorate, and win a Nobel Prize. He is a caring father, having earned the devotion of Walter Jr., and has obviously spent at least fifteen years in a loving domestic relationship with Skyler. The only insight the audience is given into his past is his phone conversation (in season 2, episode 6) with Gretchen, his former lover and partner in the "empire" he and his friend Elliott were building:

> GRETCHEN: Let me just get this straight: Elliott and I offered to pay for your treatment, no strings attached—an offer which still stands, by the way—and you turn us down out of pride, whatever. And then you tell your wife that in fact we are paying for your treatment. Without our knowledge, against our will, you involve us in your lie, and you sit here and tell me that that is none of my business?
> *[long pause]*
> WALTER: Yeah. That's pretty much the size of it.
> GRETCHEN: What happened to you? Really, Walter? What happened? Because this isn't you.
> WALTER: What would you know about me, Gretchen? What would your presumption about me be exactly? That I should go begging for your charity, and you waving your checkbook around like some magic wand is going to make me forget how you and Elliott—how you and Elliott—cut me out?
> GRETCHEN: What? That can't be how you see it.
> WALTER: It was my hard work. My research. And you and Elliott made millions off it.
> GRETCHEN: That cannot be how you see it.
> WALTER: Oh God, that's beautifully done.
> GRETCHEN: You left.
> WALTER: You are always the picture of innocence.
> GRETCHEN: You left me.
> WALTER: The picture of innocence. Just sweetness and light.
> GRETCHEN: You left me. Fourth of July weekend, you and my father and my brothers. And I go up to our room and you are packing your bags. Barely talking. What, did I dream all that?
> WALTER: That's your excuse? To build your little empire on my work?
> GRETCHEN: How could you say that to me? You walked away, you abandoned us. Me, Elliott....
> WALTER: Little rich girl, just adding to your millions.
> GRETCHEN: I don't even know what to say to you. I don't even know where to begin. I feel so sorry for you, Walter.
> WALTER: Fuck you.

The ease with which Walter changes from downtrodden chemistry teacher to hardened criminal is perhaps explained somewhat by the ferocity in tone and the amount of scorn heard in this brief conversation. Scott Meslow, in his article "The Big Secret of *Breaking Bad*: Walter White Was Always a Bad Guy," argues that Walter's greediness comes

4. Breaking Bad

from his "subconscious attempt" to make back the millions of dollars he lost leaving Grey Matter so early, now that Gretchen and Elliott's company is worth over two billion dollars. But, Meslow argues, it also tells us something larger, that "the point at which Walter had the capacity to 'break bad' happened long before the series began. In chemistry terms, cancer was merely the catalyst for Walter's transformation; all the elements that have since turned him into a monster were already in place."[3] It seems as though Gilligan's desire to turn "Mr. Chips into Scarface" tripped over itself, investing a little bit too heavily in the roots of Scarface for him to appear out of nowhere.

In fact, the Scarface side of Walter shows up very early. As the hair loss from his chemo kicks in full force in episode 6 of the first season, Walter shaves his head. When he emerges from the bathroom, Skyler stifles a cry while Walter Jr. smiles and calls his dad a badass. Walter smirks self-effacingly, joining the others at the breakfast table with no words. It is in this episode that the first major explosion occurs in the series—both figuratively and literally. Jesse and Walter, not making enough money dealing with individuals, decide they need to find a bigger hitter. Walter wants more money per deal than he is getting. Jesse offers to look into his connections and, along with his friend Skinny Pete, goes to see Tuco, one of, if not *the* biggest dealer in their corner of Albuquerque. Jesse takes a pound of Walter's meth and asks for their cut of the profits up front. Tuco responds by beating him so badly that Jesse is in the hospital for days.

When Walter sees Jesse in the hospital, he decides to go and see Tuco himself. The terminally ill, downtrodden schoolteacher trudges into the den of a heavily armed, well-defended meth head, and the scene, needless to say, is tense. However, it is here that Walter surprises everyone as he puts a pound of meth on Tuco's desk.

> TUCO: What's your name?
> WALTER: Heisenberg.
> TUCO: Heisenberg. Okay, have a seat, Heisenberg.
> WALTER: I don't imagine I'll be here very long.
> TUCO: No? All right, be that way. It's your meeting. Why don't you start talking and tell me what you want?
> WALTER: $50,000.
> TUCO [*laughs*]: Oh man! Fifty Gs? How you figure that?

WALTER: Thirty-five for the pound of meth you stole and another fifteen for my partner's pain and suffering.
TUCO: Partner? *[puts a cigarette out on his tongue]* Oh yeah, I remember that little bitch! So you must be his daddy. Let me get this straight ... I steal your dope, hmm? I beat the piss out of your mule boy, and then you walk in here, and you bring me more meth? That's a brilliant plan, *ese*. Brilliant.
WALTER: You got one part of that wrong. *[Walter takes a small piece of meth from the bag.]* This is not meth.
[Walter throws the piece to the floor. The impact causes a tremendous explosion, which knocks everyone off their feet and blows out all the windows in Tuco's office. Walter grabs the bag in the midst of the smoke.]
TUCO: Are you nuts?!
WALTER *[threatening to drop entire bag]*: You want to find out?
[Tuco's men get to their feet and draw their guns.]
TUCO: No-Doze, Gonzo, *calma! Calma. Calma.* You got balls, I'll give you that. All right, all right. I'll give you your money. *[Tuco opens his safe and hands Walter a sack filled with $50,000.]* That crystal your partner brought me, it sold faster than ten-dollar ass in TJ. What you say you bring me another pound next week?
WALTER: Money up front.
TUCO: All right. Money up front. Sometimes you got to rob to keep your riches, just as long as we got an understanding.
WALTER: One pound is not going to cut it. You have to take two.
TUCO: Orale. *[points to Walter's bag]* Hey, what is that shit?
WALTER: Fulminated mercury. A little tweak of chemistry.

Walter the victorious stalks down the still-smoking street, blood trickling from his head, money and mercury in his hands. He climbs into his family car, and laughs, banging his steering wheel and cheering over his victory. The adrenaline is flowing and it is obvious that Walter's taste for adventure has deepened his hunger.

Mr. White

Though I admit to enjoying Walter's breakthrough and his initial triumph over Tuco, I must say that this is the point at which I began to think about his position of privilege. As an audience, we see him as an underdog in a world he does not understand, attempting to avenge his young partner and claim what is rightfully his. He uses his intellect and

4. Breaking Bad

bravely gets his way, against the odds. But looking at the scene again, I see that none of the other men are Caucasian, none are as well-spoken or obviously as affluent as Walter, and both the characters and the setting are dressed in a manner that suggests urban decay and poverty, criminality, and danger. Walter is actually at an advantage in this situation because of the white, male privilege he carries unacknowledged. He is not demarcated as Other as are Tuco and his criminal friends. And even though the scene is tense and also hilarious, it is underscored by a level of racism that goes unchecked in contemporary American culture.

The next episode makes a joke of Walter's inexperience in the criminal world and his obvious illiteracy concerning the urban drug scene. He lines up an exchange with Tuco at a junkyard and Jesse is irate, chastising Walter (who stands silently in an oversized hat and dark sunglasses):

> JESSE: A junkyard? Let me guess, you picked this place?
> *Walter*: What's wrong with it? It's private.
> JESSE: This is.... This is like a ... a non-criminal's idea of a drug meet. This is like, "Oh, I saw this in a movie. Ooh, look at me."
> WALTER: Yeah, so ... so where do you transact business? Enlighten me.
> JESSE: I don't know. How about Taco Cabeza? Half the deals I've ever done went down at Taco Cabeza. Nice and public. Open twenty-four hours. Nobody ever gets shot at Taco Cabeza. Hell, why not the mall? You know, wait at the Gap. "Hey! It's time for the meet!" You know, I'll put down the flat-front khakis, head on over, grab an Orange Julius. Skip the part where psycho lunatic Tuco, you know, comes and steals my drugs and leaves me bleeding to death.

Luckily for Jesse and Walter, their choice of odd meeting place, also mocked by Tuco ("the mall closed or something?" he asks), leads not to their demise but to that of one of Tuco's men who dared speak without consent of his boss. Though their exchange is successful and Walter and Jesse walk away unscathed, the pair's activities do not go unnoticed, particularly once they begin using Walter's new formula that produces meth without the need for large amounts of pseudoephedrine, a difficult ingredient to get. The new formula works, but it has a distinctive blue color, and thus attracts more attention from the DEA.

Renegade Hero or Faux Rogue

Becoming Tuco

In season 2, the DEA is hot on Tuco's trail. Jesse and Walter's attempts to poison Tuco fail, but he's taken out in a shootout by Hank during a raid. Eliminating the crazy Tuco creates more problems for Jesse and Walter, and Jesse insists they change course. In season 2, episode 5, Jesse lays it out for Walter:

> JESSE: We got to be Tuco. All right, cut out the middle man, run our own game.
> WALTER: So you're going to what? Snort meth off a Bowie knife? You're gonna beat your homies to death when they "dis" you?
> JESSE: Look, I know some guys, all right? I can create a network. Look, we control production and distribution. That way we stay off the front lines while moving some serious glass. I mean, the point here is to make money, right? Sky-high stacks!
> WALTER: No.
> JESSE: No? That's not the point?
> WALTER: No, I am not willing to do that!
> JESSE: Who said anything about you?
> WALTER: I don't vote for this plan. I'm not comfortable bringing in unknown entities into our operation.
> JESSE: Yeah? Well, you don't get to vote.
> WALTER: I beg your pardon? This is a partnership, remember?
> JESSE: I remember, oh, I remember—that you cook, I sell. That was the division of labor when we started all this. And that's exactly how we should have kept it! 'Cause I sure as hell didn't find myself locked in a trunk or on my knees with a gun to my head before your greedy old ass came along, all right?
> WALTER: All right, I will admit to a bit of a learning curve.
> JESSE: Oh-ho!
> WALTER: And perhaps I was overly ambitious. In any case, it's not gonna happen that way any more.
> JESSE: Yeah, damn straight. Know why? 'Cause we do things my way this time or I walk! You need me more than I need you, Walter.

This moment of clarity is the last time Walter and Jesse are playing the same game. If season 1 was an introduction to Walter and a complicated narrative interweaving his disease, family, and the drug trade, season 2 is the advanced course on "Who is Walter White?" Walter seems to have truly convinced himself that all his underground dealings truly were to

4. Breaking Bad

help his family. But when he finds that his condition is improving, his mood begins to sour and his personality warps more visibly. His internal struggle with his identity is at a crux as he faces a return to his previous life with the imminent addition of baby Holly. Jesse also moves on, developing a new romantic relationship but also sliding back into drugs. While Walter is pondering his next move, Skyler is becoming more suspicious of his erratic behavior. When Walter is introduced to a new distributor and the chance to move his large batch of meth, he jumps at the chance, missing the birth of his daughter in order to meet with his new distributor Gus instead. Walter goes in search of Jesse, whom he needs to fulfill another order, and intends to help him get sober. When he finds Jesse passed out from the aftereffects of heroin next to his new girlfriend Jane, he does his best to wake the young man up. His efforts bump Jane onto her back. Jane, who had been blackmailing Walter so he would leave Jesse alone, begins to asphyxiate on her own vomit. Rather than save her, Walter walks away. His new lawyer, Saul, and his "fixer," Mike, are left to tend to the mess.

Jane's death leads to a series of horrible secondary aftershocks, including the audience's need to re-evaluate who Walter actually is. From pathetic, cancer-ridden Walter in the series beginning to a man who missed the birth of his own daughter and allowed the death of someone else's, the transition is a brutal one for audiences. Yet fans remained loyal.

So loyal, in fact, that when Skyler learns of Walter's other side in season 3, they rallied around Walter on blogs, fan pages, and AMC's website, declaring her an irritating obstacle to their hero Walter. Skyler, horrified, tries every tactic she knows to stop Walter's new way of life—a very human, realistic reaction for a woman who has been cocooned in a middle-class domestic situation of part-time work and child-rearing her entire life. Yet she is demonized by many viewers who worry she will ruin all the fun!

Skyler tries everything she knows to help Walter or at least stop him. She files for divorce, she calls the cops to get him thrown out of the house, and she even has an affair. Walter remains steadfast in his own belief, constructed or true, that he is doing what he is doing for his family.

WALTER: I love you, Skyler. And I would do anything for you. Would you even consider, I mean ... Jesus! You come in here and you wave these papers in my face, when there's a whole other entire side to this thing. There's your side and there's my side and you haven't heard my side yet. You haven't heard any of it at all.
SKYLER: You're a drug dealer.
WALTER: No. How.... What?
SKYLER: Yeah. How else could you possibly make that kind of money? Marijuana. That Pinkman kid. *[Walter is silent.]* No? Oh my God, Walter. Cocaine?
WALTER: It's methamphetamine. But I'm a manufacturer, I'm not a dealer.
SKYLER *[shocked]*: Oh....
WALTER: Per se. I ... it doesn't mean.... *[Skyler gets up and heads to the door.]* No, Skyler! Listen to me, Skyler! *[Walter grabs her arm.]* Listen.
SKYLER: No!
WALTER: There are a lot of angles to this, okay? It's complicated, all right? So please listen. Please, let's just sit back down and we'll talk it through.
SKYLER: I'm going to make you a deal, Walter. I won't tell Hank and I won't tell your children or anybody else. Nobody will hear it from me, but only if you grant me this divorce and stay out of our lives.
WALTER: No, Skyler....
SKYLER: I mean it. Now let me the hell out of here before I throw up.

No matter how Walter tries to paint the picture for Skyler, she cannot join him in his positive outlook, nor can she deal with the new Heisenberg she is forced to live with. Walter figures out how to maintain his domain at home and, essentially, will not let Skyler or his children go. His position as protector has changed to that of threat, and Skyler knows this, but she finally decides to help him with the money aspect of his new career so that he won't go to jail. Working with his corrupt lawyer, the two attempt to launder money by buying the carwash at which Walter was working in the first episode.

The Ripple Effect

By the end of season 3, the ripples of Walter's life choices have lapped over his entire family and nearly drowned young Jesse. Nothing seems to scare Walter any more. He continues to outmaneuver and outwit his opponents, all of whom, with the exception of Hank and other

4. Breaking Bad

DEA agents, are men of color. Like the plane crash from the end of season 2, debris rains down around Walter as he moves forward, relentlessly garnering a fortune and amassing control of his own empire. When Gus, his former boss and the major player on the U.S. side of the cartel drug trade, decides to take him out, Walter forces Jesse to kill the innocent Gale, the young scientist being groomed to take over from Walter. Jesse comes unglued from what he has had to do, but Walter is steadfast in his own belief that what came to pass was necessary. In the season 4 opener, when he confronts Gus, he argues,

> All right, let's talk about Gale Boetticher. He was a good man and a good chemist. He didn't deserve what happened to him. He didn't deserve it at all. But I'd shoot him again tomorrow and the next day and the day after that. When you make it Gale versus me, or Gale versus Jesse, Gale loses! Simple as that. This is on you, Gus, not me, not Jesse. I mean, really, what'd you expect me to do? Just simply roll over and allow you to murder us? That I wouldn't take measures—extreme measures—to defend myself? Wrong! Think again.

Walter is a murderer, a manipulator, a greedy monster sitting on more money than he can launder or do anything with. His wife despises him, his son is confused and hurt, and his infant daughter is in the middle of everything. Even Jesse is traumatized, his life repeatedly ripped apart by Walter's various maneuvers. Yet as far as Walter is concerned, the only thing he needs to do is "win" each battle as it comes his way. He is playing a dangerous game, never giving one thought as to whom his drugs go to, who gets caught in the crossfire of the gunfights at his back, or whose worldview he has shattered forever. His own wife wishes him dead and the only emotion he can muster by the end of season 4 is joy that he has managed to murder Gus and can take control of his own empire. "I won," he tells Skyler. "It's over. We're safe."

Breaking Bad may have begun as simply a writer's attempt to turn a protagonist into an antagonist, but its convoluted, bizarre storylines go well beyond a character study. They present a privileged, white, middle-class male infiltrating and dominating the urban drug scene in a horrible era of economic crisis that has ripped families from their homes, destroyed lives, and changed the landscape of America. Yet the show celebrates Walter's debauchery and greed and allows viewers to

Renegade Hero or Faux Rogue

cheer as men of color are murdered in scores and urban junkies are painted as flotsam to be exploited, then kicked aside. It is a show that perpetuates the model of the strength and innate dominance of privilege and intelligence in the masculine male hero but no longer asks that the hero have any kind of moral compass or desire. The show has surpassed creating a Scarface and entered into a new game of how far Scarface can go and still hold a dedicated fan base. Of all the shows I have studied for this book, *Breaking Bad*'s faux rogue hero and the show itself are the most disturbing.

5

Boardwalk Empire: The Romantic Side of Crime and Capitalism

Boardwalk Empire, HBO's series about Atlantic City during Prohibition, was adapted by Emmy-winning writer-producer Terence Winter from Nelson Johnson's *Boardwalk Empire: The Birth, High Times, and Corruption of Atlantic City*, about historical criminal kingpin Enoch L. Johnson. The series is a beautifully scripted piece of historical fiction. In contrast to the muscle, dirt, and motorcycles of the gangs in *Sons of Anarchy*, *Boardwalk Empire* presents audiences with a much different vision of organized crime. The series begins in 1919 on the Atlantic City boardwalk on the eve of Prohibition. The protagonist, Enoch "Nucky" Thompson, is based loosely on the real-life Atlantic City politician Enoch L. Johnson. Nucky is Atlantic City's treasurer and master schemer, effectively ruling the city, tangled up in politics and corruption. The onset of Prohibition offers a new black market in the United States, and the ruling politicians and law enforcement agents of Atlantic City are eager for a piece of the pie, cheering as Nucky declares he will keep the city "wet as a mermaid's twat," despite the federal mandate. Nucky offers a unique vision of an American gangster with the aid of actor Steve Buscemi's skill at performing this complex character.

The Gangster

From the rise of the Mafia to the biker gangs of California, certain attributes have become associated with the archetype of "gangster": He swaggers, he is physically dominant, he is quick to anger, his emotions are on the surface, and confrontation is not something he avoids but often seeks out. Nucky offers a very different set of characteristics as well as a new definition of toughness.

Buscemi, typically a character actor with a litany of incredibly awkward, strange supporting roles in films on his résumé, seems an odd casting choice for the show's protagonist. However, audiences are first introduced to him in the title sequence, where he stands, in suit and wingtip shoes, on the shore as waves crash over his feet. Empty liquor bottles roll in with the tide and bounce around him as he calmly smokes and thoughtfully gazes out over the Atlantic. As a wave recedes and cleans his shoes of sand, he turns to head back to the boardwalk. His gaze is focused and determined, and the bizarre Buscemi roles of his past seem to dissipate as a new, focused leader emerges. But as he turns back toward the boardwalk, he *waddles* in that awkward way most of us do when trying to negotiate sand and a hill in inappropriate footwear. It is a very subtle waddle, but obvious enough, and a clear indicator that Nucky is a unique character who will continuously challenge audience expectations. And though he is the true protagonist of the series and a sympathetic rogue, his core desire for power and wealth render him not much more than a complicated Horatio Alger character, a champion of unbridled capitalism who makes political corruption seem not only a given, but somehow thrilling and romantic. Thus our humanist rogue proves, again, to be a faux rogue.

Steve Buscemi is 5'9" tall and slight in build. He stands in stark contrast to his HBO predecessor gangster Tony Soprano of the popular series *The Sopranos* (1999–2007). The character of Nucky is not outwardly intimidating and not outwardly bombastic, impetuous, or emotional. His emotions are very closely guarded. Buscemi's characterization of Nucky is not as a man who would resort first to his fists in a fight. He is always immaculately dressed in a formal, vested suit and tie with a trademark red carnation in his buttonhole. His most powerful weapon is his intelligence. Strategy, patience, and an incredible poker face are Nucky's main arsenal, and Terence Winter is able to challenge the tropes of the American gangster and twist the genre expectations in a way that is slight yet remarkable, particularly as it elevates intelligence as the

5. Boardwalk Empire

mark of a leader among the common mainstream message of anti-intellectualism on television.

Nucky is calculating, corrupt, and deadly when crossed, yet these traits are often balanced for the audience by his humanity. He is an anti-hero who is easy to root for, particularly in contrast to the characters he comes up against. He's the Prohibition rogue, maintaining a fun "getaway" as a place for an escape, which initially seems harmless. He is a businessman—organized, efficient, and smart enough to treat those in his city with kindness. And this kindness is often genuine. The fact that he is challenged again and again yet uses his intellect to come out on top makes him extremely likable and admirable. Though as a character he is unique, among popular gangster fictions he is reminiscent of Michael Corleone in that he is sympathetic, relatable, and at times easy to forgive (or at least understand) when he commits a particularly heinous act.

The *Godfather* tradition and the tropes of gangster entertainment run rampant through the series, but Nucky challenges this trend. While many of the traditional gang dramas highlight the negotiation between family and "the Family," as *The Sopranos* did so well, Nucky is negotiating politics with family. However there is no true Family in his world, as is discussed later. What is romanticized in *Boardwalk Empire* is not the gangster lifestyle as it has become typically fictionalized. In contrast, gangster life is shown as ugly, brutal, treacherous, and utterly devoid of any false notion of some kind of "brotherhood." With Nucky there are no second chances and no bonds that cannot be broken or people who cannot be used as pawns in his master plan. His wife, his only brother, even his surrogate son suffer because of Nucky's ambition and drive for self-preservation. What is glamorized is Nucky's opulent lifestyle and the opulence of the series' other criminal kingpins, such as Chalky White, whose family lives in a beautiful home and who has educated children despite the difficulties of being a black man in the early part of the twentieth century. Another kingpin, Arnold Rothstein, is consistently shown in billiard rooms, surrounded by silver tea trays and delicate china cups. The implication is that it is the power behind the criminals that truly matters, and he who can distance himself the furthest from actual wet work is the most skilled and the most masterful in the world of gangland Prohibition.

Though initially a seemingly innocuous, if corrupt, politician, Nucky inwardly deteriorates quickly as he morphs from dirty politician to full-on gangster. Yet this transformation is subtle. Winter makes no huge jumps and there are no character inconsistencies in his depiction of Nucky. The poker face remains, though he becomes deadlier and less stable as the show progresses. But, as stated earlier, this is not dramatically played out. He is not sociopathic or even out of control—he is not Scarface. Nucky's most obvious changes are played through Buscemi's facial expressions, his eye movements, and his jerky mobility. The times he loses control, when emotion is displayed, are shocking and extremely discomfiting to watch. For example, in season 1, episode 7, after his abusive father's stroke and the subsequent evacuation of the family home, Nucky offers his family homestead, in a gesture of goodwill, to one of his employees with young children. But when he takes a tour of the newly refurbished house, the memories of his childhood overwhelm him and he sets off an inferno that destroys the home. He walks casually away and a composed Nucky emerges from inside the burning home, handing money to the family to make up for the damage. Yet this demented act betrays the layers of grief and anger that lurk just below the surface of his façade of unflappability.

Sympathy for the Devil

Though he continues to instigate corruption and the detestability of his acts increases as the show progresses, Nucky remains a consistently sympathetic protagonist. This is largely due to Winter's writing and the way he weaves moments of honesty or tenderness into the fabric of Nucky's character at key moments. It also has a lot to do with the fact that few of the other characters are as fully developed and complex as the lead. Nucky's enemies, cronies, nemeses, and so forth are mostly two-dimensional and essentially loathsome. There is also no true "good guy" to serve as a contrast. There is no strong presence of purity in the show. With minor exceptions, the *Boardwalk Empire* characters are all twisted by the lives they lead, even the ones we find innocuous and lovable, such as Angela and Margaret. Arguably, besides Nucky, the women

5. Boardwalk Empire

of the show prove the most complex in their characterizations. And though I discuss them throughout the following chapter, a more thorough analysis of *Boardwalk Empire*'s women is offered in Chapter 6.

From Serial Killing to the Charleston

In many ways, *Boardwalk Empire* reflects similar attitudes to the black market, the trade in illegal intoxicants, and gangsters of the previous shows I have addressed thus far. Yet I have chosen to end my discussion of individual shows with this one that utilizes nostalgia to create a loss of historicity, enabling the romanticizing of criminal behavior and embedding corruption in politics as a given part of U.S. culture.

Atlantic City has a fascinating past and, really, any era chosen as the backdrop to *Boardwalk Empire* would have proven interesting. But Winter selected the 1920s because it was the era that "most struck [his] creative fancy."[1] Atlantic City in the twenties, he offers, "was a place of excess, glamor, and most of all, opportunity. Loud, brash, colorful, full of hope and promise—it was a real microcosm of America. A place of spectacle, shady politics, fast women, and backroom deals."[2] Inevitably, regardless of decade, using an iconic landscape such as Atlantic City allows nostalgia to be a conduit for audience connection. "Nostalgia" can be a contentious term, particularly for scholars. The connotations related to nostalgia range from a whimsical desire for a past unknown to a destructive homesickness.

Fredric Jameson stands out in his use of the term in his goliath *Postmodernism; or, The Cultural Logic of Late Capitalism* in which he introduces "nostalgia mode" to describe the way in which contemporary culture, through pastiche, detaches past style, icons, and images and imagines them through the lens of current culture, resulting in what he identifies as a "loss of historicity."[3] Hila Shachar argues that the

> idea that our modern culture functions via the flattening out of history as a marketable "image" or a commodified "style" is assumed as fact. And it is a fact that is applied to a whole host of contemporary historical and period films that utilize the appeal of the past through a type of museum aesthetic, where the cultural legacy of the past is displayed as a pleasing aesthetic, and nothing more.[4]

Renegade Hero or Faux Rogue

Of course, many critics, such as Linda Hutcheon, take issue with Jameson's theory of nostalgia and the loss of historicity, arguing that the use of past artifacts and their manipulation can be used self-critically, opening a space in the discourse on one's evaluation of the social past.[5] I, however, agree with Jameson's argument and, like Baudrillard, see the mediation of the past in particular as unable to produce anything more than simulacrum, as discussed in my introduction. Thus, placing the script of *Boardwalk Empire* within a simulated past allows a manipulation of fact and a loss of historicity.

Dylan Trigg argues in *The Aesthetics of Decay: Nothingness, Nostalgia, and the Absence of Reason* that

> the divergence between universality and the temporal present is compounded as ideas are mistaken to be intuitive, humanistic, or otherwise innate: terms which justifiably warrant suspicion. In the absence of such suspicion, the familiarity of reason prevents it from disbanding. The implications are twofold. Disillusionment and dogma are the likely consequence as a society adjusts to the void between a static principle and the mutable world in which that principle exists.[6]

A loss of historicity, consistently perpetuated by a culture that is mediated in a manner never before imagined, rather than offering opportunities of creativity and empowerment through art and entertainment, has blurred the line between reality and fiction to a moment of crisis. The more we lose of history, whether as a people, a nation, or a disenfranchised group, the more ground can be lost as the lessons we were supposed to have learned return, mutated and mediated. This is not self-reflexive, but a loss of the self. It is not ironic, but terrifying. Though Trigg's argument seems apocalyptic within the context I have placed it, to fear the new ideological notions that seem "intuitive, humanistic, or otherwise innate" seems entirely logical. I offer *Boardwalk Empire* as a simple, somewhat more mild example of this phenomena when I argue that presenting political corruption alongside brothels, speakeasies, and the fantasy playhouse of 1920s Atlantic City further perpetuates the underlying notion that corruption is already always present in U.S. politics. With messages such as the omnipotence and omnipresence of corruption in politics, I fear the apathy and discouragement that may be easily absorbed by audience members when such

5. Boardwalk Empire

messages are repeatedly shown on television. Shooting scenes in which scandalous political dealings are waged beside the bare breasts of giggling prostitutes emphasizes the spectacle of politics, reducing it to entertainment. In a world where politics has truly become a mediated spectacle, this is not shocking, but seemingly natural.

The Atlantic City location, particularly in the 1920s, most certainly helps perpetuate all of these ideas. Both Trigg and author Elizabeth Wilson discuss the issue of nostalgia in connection with place, cities in particular. This is, of course, covered extensively in European-based study of nostalgia and romanticism, or, in Trigg's case as with many others, tragedy. In the United States, nostalgia, as it pertains to cities or "place" in general, seems to inevitably harbor some form of decadence, some desire for debauchery and "freedom" that is longed for. The thong-bikini-lined South Beach along Ocean Drive in Miami; the roller-skating, bikinis, and weight-lifters of Venice Beach; the blinding lights of Times Square in New York City; and the gaudy indulgences of Los Vegas all come with connotations of desires fulfilled, fantasies indulged, and the everydayness of life truly escaped. Winter has reminded us of how Atlantic City fits in with these nostalgic dreams, even as it currently faces a steep decline in attraction. Within the series, the symbol of the boardwalk has come to stand for other American landmarks of excess and self-indulgence.

Self-indulgence, excess, debauchery, escape—all of these suggest a certain kind of freedom and autonomy. "What happens in Vegas, stays in Vegas," the latest catchphrase of Sin City, implies not only the discretion of a place one goes to indulge, but also says something about the very indulgence itself. To suggest that one must not speak about his/her behavior in Vegas outside the city suggests that the moral turpitude in which one must have engaged is so vile or so outside of what stands as normalized behavior that it must not be revealed in one's everyday life, for fear of some kind of repercussion. With this dichotomy established (fun in Vegas versus punishable offenses in Real Life), the notion that one is not truly free within the confines of one's day-to-day existence has been established. The quest for freedom, fun, and escape becomes a modern-day form of nostalgia in relation to place. There are certain places one can *go* to enjoy life, while normal existence means restriction, prohibition, and regulation. Outside of cities, vacation spots, fun parks, and resorts rely on the implication that a trip to their location will somehow change you, free you, and empower you. Parents are shown acting like teenagers to the dismay of their children in a popular cruise liner's advertisements. Theme parks show adults reverting back to children and experiencing the pleasures of the park as a child would. Resorts suggest that they can restore romance to a relationship. The ads and temptations to "escape reality" are endless, really. But again and again, what is unsaid is that life—real life, outside of a vacation—is restrictive and tedious. It appears as though the United States has drawn a clear line between the two that encourages a playful rebelliousness. It also appears that in order to have fun, one must consume and commodify the elements of one's escape, to perpetuate the materialist, late consumer culture in which the U.S. is so mired.

The Loss of Historicity

To set a series in the time of American Prohibition taps into that same rebelliousness. For a culture that assumes real adult life to be boring and constricting, looking back on the Volstead Act (the act that enforced Prohibition, the 18th Amendment) appears to show us a people who rose up against something intended to end their freedom of extracurricular fun. Flappers and speakeasies have become symbols of innocent mutiny. Trading in alcohol and challenging social morals, those involved in the 1920s liquor industry, it seems obvious, were simply paving the way for a celebration of personal liberty.

In reality the political and social violence of Prohibition touched the lives of the working class, immigrants, people of color, Jews, and Catholics in ways unmentioned in the series. Much of the discourse surrounding the debate between "wets" and "drys" was surprisingly ethnocentric. The "drys" in Congress fought for deportation of those found in violation of the Volstead Act. The Immigration Restriction Act was passed in 1924, severely limiting the number of immigrants, particularly those from non–Protestant, non–"Nordic" nations.[7] It was not actually a crime to consume alcohol, thus those with wealth and influence could maintain their private stocks, leaving the messiness of cooking new bottles of booze and selling them to those who needed money the most. This era in U.S. history was incredibly difficult for men and women of color, but also extremely difficult for Irish, Italian, and Jewish immigrants, a fact that *Boardwalk Empire* seems to either be ignoring or playing with, as its most powerful characters happen to be from the most oppressed groups. The Roaring Twenties was not a time of dancing and shorter hemlines, but a battlefield of years for women, immigrants, the working poor, people of color, and returning veterans of World War I.

To the Lost

Boardwalk Empire has received numerous accolades for its dedication to maintaining historical accuracy. The show is particularly notable for the nuances it includes, such as Arnold Rothstein's diet of cake and milk, and the subtle ambiguity of the relationship between Harry Daugherty and his accomplice Jess Smith. Even Luciano's gonorrhea, which he contracted to avoid going into battle during World War I, is explored in excruciating detail.[8] The detail of the architecture, the precision of the costuming, and the news of the time is beautiful and precise, and Winter and his team are proud of their accomplishments. This precision also helps the plot; the storylines are moved along and the characters are developed sometimes simply by the props around them or the events to which they refer. For example, season 3 features an Egyptian-themed New Year's Eve party at the Thompson residence. King Tut's tomb had only been discovered a few months prior, leading to an explosion of Egyptian references and themes throughout popular culture. This shows the audience that Margaret is on the cutting edge of culture, thriving as a "society" wife and hostess, demonstrating her transition over the fourteen-month gap between seasons 2 and 3.[9]

Beyond the superficial and the spectacular, what I find to be the most powerful historical component of the series is the ever-present ghost of World War I that lingers among the men, the families, and the violence of the series as a whole. The pilot episode introduces Jimmy Darmody, at age twenty-two a three-year veteran of the Great War. With

Renegade Hero or Faux Rogue

a damaged leg and a Pandora's box of memories he comes back from overseas to his fiancée and young son, his mother, and the man who had been his life-long father figure, Nucky Thompson. Jimmy expects to rise quickly within the ranks of Nucky's organization but is surprised to be relegated to driver and bodyguard with an offer of an assistant clerkship. Nucky gently but firmly rebuffs Jimmy's frustration, reminding him that had he stayed at Princeton instead of going to war, he'd be in a better position at this point. Outside of Nucky's celebratory dinner on the eve of Prohibition, he corners a sulking Jimmy:

> NUCKY: What's with you? And don't tell me it's your stomach.
> JIMMY: You wanna know what's with me? You expect me to go to work for Ryan, that mick?
> NUCKY: You'd rather be my driver?
> JIMMY: Of course not. You make Ryan clerk? I could run rings around that chump.
> NUCKY: Well, listen to Bonnie Prince Charlie....
> JIMMY: Come on, Nuck. You were assistant sheriff when you were my age.
> NUCKY: And for eight years prior to that I spent night and day kissing the commodore's ass.
> JIMMY: I've been kissin' your ass since I was twelve!
> NUCKY: Yeah? Well what about the past three years?
> JIMMY: I wanted to serve my country.
> NUCKY: And nearly get yourself killed.... You know who dies for their country? Fucking rubes.

This discussion plays out with Jimmy looking like an impetuous adolescent and Nucky an overly strict parent. But it is through Jimmy that the audience is able to bond more firmly with Nucky. He is introduced as a benign father figure despite his underhandedness and corrupt dealings in office. He is seen as parental not just with Jimmy, but also with his vapid showgirl mistress Lucy, playing the straight man to her impish ridiculousness. We see his tolerance and willingness to indulge her and a side of him that desires, enjoys, and escapes—a slice of wildness that he hides behind his normal façade of detached coldness.

Lucy is frivolous, excessive, outlandish, and brash. In essence she is the physical embodiment of Atlantic City. And she is Nucky's sexual plaything. And though he enjoys her wiles, he provides for her and treats her with a kind of paternal indifference, ensuring that she is pacified and taken care of without having to do any work. The quintessential "here's some money, go buy yourself…" line is used often between them. He treats the city the same way, ensuring it is cared for and happy as long as it offers its favors in return. Though sleazy and corrupt, Nucky manages to keep the city like a happy mistress.

In the pilot episode, when he first meets Margaret and listens to her story and grief, Lucy stumbles out of his bedroom into the meeting, leaving␣Nucky, who had the night before addressed the women's Temperance League, in an awkward position. Yet his generosity and warmth toward the then Mrs. Schroeder muffles the immoral audacity of the moment. Looking at the photo of his wife and then looking back at the heavily pregnant woman, his face softens as he listens to her plight. And she, knowing her place, ignores the broach in his moral conduct.

A Worthy Opponent

Margaret plays the final role in setting up Nucky as a benevolent anti-hero in the pilot episode. She comes to him as a beaten wife with two young children, scared for their well-being as winter is approaching and her husband lacks work. Nucky gives her a shoulder to cry on and enough money to tide them over until her husband returns to his job as a baker's assistant at the start of the busy season. He ensures that the heavily pregnant woman is safely driven home and then goes about his business. This seemingly uneventful moment unfolds into a series of life-changing events. Margaret's brutish husband finds the money for the children, punishes her with a beating, and then steals the money. When he and Nucky have a run-in at a casino and Nucky has Schroeder physically removed, the drunken man goes home and beats Margaret so severely that she suffers a miscarriage and ends up in the hospital. Nucky has the police pick up Schroeder, beat him to death, and dump him in the sea. His body is caught in a fishing net and thrown back onto the boardwalk the next day.

Nucky's order is an act driven by emotion. Here we see what many would identify as a kind of vigilante justice, the sort of act that makes a violent anti-hero seem a humanist hero, as is discussed throughout this book. Nucky's passions, glimpsed as they escape his cold, heartless persona, are flames that burn as brightly as the inferno he starts at his father's house, but they cut Nucky both ways. The ones to which audiences may be attracted—his struggles to overcome his childhood victimization, his desire for Margaret, his affection for Jimmy—are beautiful in their humanity and depth. His father was a brute, unforgiving and physically dangerous, leaving Nucky with plenty of scars. It's obvious that as the oldest boy he felt the need, even as a child, to protect his family and somehow protect those around him and it often leaks through his stone-faced demeanor that he has to try very hard not to become his father. However, his desire for control and power lead him to decisions that destroy those around him and chip away at his humanity. The Nucky of the pilot episode, who is patient with Jimmy, kind to Margaret, and pained by memories of his deceased wife, becomes a self-contained monster fueled by selfish desire by the end of season 2.

The complexity of his character, however, makes him fascinating. And though he is clearly the show's protagonist, the inner workings of his mind are still mostly hidden, unlike *Dexter* and similar shows that use a voice-over monologue to invite the audience into the character's mind, or a show with more simplistic writing, such as *True Blood*, in which most motivation and feelings are articulated through dialogue. *True Blood*'s protagonist, Sookie, even talks to herself frequently, externalizing her thought process for the audience. Even within the complex narrative of *The Sopranos*, Tony had his therapy sessions that helped reveal more of his inner world. With characters as complex as Nucky, what writers often do is posit them against a nemesis whose insights and dialogues with others help the audience understand the character. In Nucky's case, one would expect law enforcement officers or some kind of opponent of strong moral standing to offer these insights as they oppose him. Yet each time a character appears on the show who pursues Nucky in the name of law or "good," the character falls—if not under his spell, then to the corruption that surrounds them all, leaving audiences with only vague ideas of Nucky's scheming. He is never profiled and never truly challenged to the extent that he opens up or becomes vulnerable enough to reveal his inner workings.

The moral opposition of lawless or corrupt behavior is very slim,

5. Boardwalk Empire

almost nonexistent in the series narrative. The two main characters of moral order initially appear to be Mrs. McGarry, the president of the Atlantic City Women's Temperance League, and Father Brennan, Margaret's son Teddy's parochial schoolmaster and her priest. Both figures surround Margaret, but not Nucky. And their guidance, their ability to provide a moral compass for Margaret, becomes complicated as the series progresses. Mrs. McGarry is earnest in her desires to perpetuate the Temperance movement, and she seems a model of first-wave feminism: demure, domestic, and willing to work within the political system dominated by men to achieve her goals for women's rights. As the series progresses, the audience learns that Mrs. McGarry is much more of a radical than she is first presented as, telling Margaret that she uses her deceased husband's wealth to be a land-owning, independent woman intent on helping other women. So though she is strong, noble, and admirable, her position in Margaret's life becomes less of an oppressive source of feminine guidance and antiquated "morals" and more of a progressive source of wisdom as she teaches her about birth control and helps her navigate her understanding of her relationship with Nucky.

Father Brennan is also a complicated figure in Margaret's life. She first encounters him in discussions about her son and is essentially forced back into the church to help Teddy with his first communion. Father Brennan is the one to whom she confesses and the person she goes to for guidance when her daughter Emily is stricken with polio. His directive that she examine herself and her actions before she asks anything of God forces her to once again examine her relationship with Nucky, her fixation on monetary stability, and her affair with Nucky's young Irish bodyguard Owen. But after she ponders her sins and takes "action" in the form of donating a significant amount of money to her parish church, we see that Father Brennan might be slightly less concerned with her soul than he is with her money, as he guilts her into giving even more. Though we see the strikingly intelligent Margaret change and develop even very early in the series, her skills at manipulation and deception gain significant traction by the end of season 2, and the woman whom the audience may have used as a moral contrast to Nucky has simply become more like him.

Nucky does face jurisprudence to some degree, and there is tension at times between the legal system and his preferred way of doing things. In season 1 this comes in the form of Agent Van Alden, an overly earnest Prohibition officer. He develops an obsession with Nucky, recognizing that he is "running the show" in Atlantic City. All of his evidence falls on deaf (and corrupt) ears, and Van Alden realizes that he is more of a figurehead, a simulacrum of an enforcement officer when he recognizes that the extent of bootlegging in the city can barely be touched by the resources he is given. He flexes his muscles when he can, making example busts—some legal and some not. For example, when his long-suffering wife comes to visit, he attempts to show her the "good" side of Atlantic City as she is an extraordinarily devout Christian woman who would be appalled at the real world of Atlantic City. One evening, as they dine, she notices the presence of alcohol on the premises. To show off for her, Van Alden instigates a brawling, unsupported bust-up of the restaurant, issuing threats and throwing around orders.

The tightly wound agent, initially so strict in his religious code that he self-flagellates after having lustful thought, begins to unravel as he recognizes his position of weakness. To be clear, he does more than unravel. He explodes. He kills his deputy and he impregnates Nucky's ex-mistress and keeps her in an apartment during her pregnancy in the hopes that he can buy her baby for his infertile wife. His wife finds out and leaves him. His attempts at redeeming himself by helping the Assistant U.S. Attorney in her case against Nucky for election rigging backfire, and he shoots her clerk and flees Atlantic City with his daughter and her sexy Scandinavian nanny.

In season 2, Esther Randolph, the assistant U.S. attorney, comes to Atlantic City to build a case against Nucky for election rigging. She digs into all aspects of Nucky's dealings, finding scores of skeletons in his closets, unearthing his years of entertaining every crook and politician on the East Coast, his intimate knowledge of the flesh trade, and his multiple holdings and properties. Her pressure becomes a force of nature and her zealous desire for justice nearly matches Van Alden's, though it lacks the obsessive insanity. Nucky is forced into a very complicated kind of chess match with the legal system while he deals with strife in his city as many of his loyal followers have turned against him. Although Randolph is really on the side of good and attempting to stop a tidal

5. Boardwalk Empire

wave of corruption, her demeanor and manipulations make her an unsympathetic character. Father Brennan, Van Alden, and Randolph all underscore the weight of ever-present political corruption. We see how corruption perpetuates corruption, and we see it as an impenetrable force and as a goliath that cannot be tackled by ethical means. In *Boardwalk Empire*, our affection for Nucky puts us on the side of the corrupt. After having invested so much time in his development, we as an audience do not want Van Alden to succeed or Randolph to put Nucky in jail, and we certainly do not think too deeply about Father Brennan's methods of garnering funds for his parish.

Nucky, despite his misdeeds and the blood on his hands, remains the protagonist and the implied character for whom the audience is to root. It is his master plan that we follow as an audience and his intellect and calmness under pressure that come across as heroic. Even after the series' largest scene of bloodshed, which he instigates to free himself of vote-rigging charges and his disavowal of both his brother and young Jimmy, when he and Margaret discuss their life and a possible trip with the children, we are pulled into the domestic bliss, hoping for a happy outcome. His anti-hero status remains, despite the waves of destruction he has wrought simply to maintain his wealth and his position of power.

At the end of season 2, however, Winter throws the audience a narrative curve ball when Nucky kills an unarmed Jimmy by shooting him at point-blank range, all the while screaming *"I'm not looking for redemption!"* It is a frightening moment. All of Nucky's mannerisms change, his voice changes, and all of the rage that he pockets away lunges forth in a moment of violence intended to send audiences reeling. Jimmy, to whom Nucky had been a surrogate father and who had been a primary character on the show, dies violently for turning on Nucky, though he was prepared to atone for his betrayal. The twist ends season 2 and, perhaps, forces audiences to question their support of Nucky.

Thinking about the series' point of departure in contrast to the finale of season 2, in some regard Nucky has indeed changed. His character has become more aggressive, more bloodthirsty, and more of a stereotypical gangster. But the corruption and the things for which he fights never change. The audience is brought into the series with Nucky lying to a room full of women in order to garner their future vote and

Renegade Hero or Faux Rogue

then taking Jimmy to a dinner table surrounded by men already corrupted in their politics, plotting to squeeze more money out of the game. The corruption is there from the very beginning. And Nucky Thompson carries it through to the end (of season 2). He never lies to the audience, never pretends to be anything he is not. That he bloodies his own hands killing Jimmy is shocking, but the amount of bloodshed he instigated or that simply followed in his wake is enormous. Seeing him as anything other than a villain is frightening, yet the entire series enraptures the audience and encourages them to bond with the single-mindedness of a man who will do anything for wealth and power, a faux rogue who refuses to hide from himself or anyone else.

6

The Woman and the Faux Rogue

As all advocates of feminist politics know, most people do not understand sexism or if they do they think it is not a problem. Masses of people think that feminism is always and only about women seeking to be equal to men. And a huge majority of these folks think feminism is anti-male. Their misunderstanding of feminist politics reflects the reality that most folks learn about feminism from patriarchal mass media.
—bell hooks

We have to constantly critique imperialist white supremacist patriarchal culture because it is normalized by mass media and rendered unproblematic.
—bell hooks

I knew when I began this book that my focus would be on the men of contemporary U.S. television. I had to find limits and boundaries so as to not create a monster. And though current or recently aired shows feature female protagonists one might consider to be faux rogues, the men far outnumber the women, and thus I chose my focus. Yet as I watched each series, I made notes on the women closest to the main male characters, studying them to see if they, like the male anti-heroes of the shows, shared similar traits or behaviors. And they do. Debra from *Dexter*, Gemma and Tara from *Sons of Anarchy*, Sookie and Tara from *True Blood*, Skyler from *Breaking Bad*, and Margaret from *Boardwalk Empire* are strong, bold women with a clear sense of self and inner strength that moves them forward at even their darkest moments.[1] Yet like the men they perform alongside, these women ultimately betray themselves, specifically falling back on tropes of femininity that counter the strength and courage of the feminist fight. Though they may seem progressive or even rogue themselves, as their respective series progress the characters are written into submission in a way that reflects the public dialogue of the United States of the early 2000s, which is shockingly oppressive, signifying several steps backward for the rights of women, undoing what good had been won by the movements of women's rights advocates of previous decades. The women around the faux rogues in contemporary U.S. TV perpetuate a narrative of submission and subjugation detrimental to U.S. culture and the feminist fight of today.

Many feminisms exist, as do many theoretical standpoints from which to address the theories. For both the sake of brevity and in keeping with my own understanding and formulation of feminism, I define the term as that which theorizes a demand for equality for all despite gender, sexual difference, race, age, class, (dis)ability, ethnicity, religion, or any and all combinations of these. I believe in a feminist standpoint that aims to disassemble patriarchal rule and white, male privilege; however, I do not believe that feminism is anti-male or detrimental to masculinity, as such. Freeing ourselves from the shackles of powered or disempowered gender roles, standardized gender codes, and limited legitimization of sexual behavior means freedom for humans as a whole, opening up a world in which people can decide for themselves how to emote, whom to love, how to physically control their bodies, and how to use the power they possess as individuals, which ultimately means a world of more possibilities, more growth, and more self-awareness. I work within both intellectual-ideological feminism as well as materialist feminism, as I believe that feminist theory shapes and helps both the mind and the body.

Anti-feminist rhetoric and an internalization of anti-feminist discourse is a social issue. It is a lens through which we, as humans, see the world. It, like all ideologies, is created to perpetuate a particular kind of power. How culture "owns" feminism depends on what it collectively sees as important and what it privileges.[2] Studying the women of contemporary television shows that empower men masquerading as antiheroes is one way of studying how the United States popularizes and examines women and the tenets of feminism.

6. The Woman and the Faux Rogue

Debra

In Chapter 1 I discuss Debra, Lt. Maria LaGuerta, and Rita, the three recurring female characters in the *Dexter* series, addressing how their—what we in a heteronormative system would identify as "feminine"—traits lead to their inability to live up to Dexter's level of success as hero in the show. Debra is the series' most fully developed secondary character, so the following discussion features her, examining how she breaks traditional gender roles and succeeds in maintaining her core identity throughout the drama of the show. I also discuss how her female masculinity both helps and hurts her character's ability to be a potential role model for young women. I then address how her character flaws are stereotypically feminine failings and how these flaws overpower her successes and dominate her character.

As stated in Chapter 1, Debra modeled her career choice and demeanor after her father, a former policeman. She is determined and focused and rises quickly through the ranks of Miami Dade's homicide division through her skill and her work with Dexter, though she is unaware of the depth of his help. Debra is very tall, very thin, and carries herself in a slightly awkward way, with a barely noticeable stoop and propensity for perpetual motion. She compensates for her inner insecurities, given away only occasionally by her posture or awkwardness physically, with her external tenaciousness, her masculine swagger, her choice of clothing, and her incredibly foul mouth.

In J. Judith Halberstam's 1998 work *Female Masculinity*, she addresses the issue of the socially constructed gender dichotomy of male/female and masculine/feminine. Halberstam explores the qualities that constitute "masculinity" and explores why, when women take on such qualities, they become "threatening." She argues that as we evolve, so must our ability to identify differing genders, suggesting that a new taxonomy would help alleviate the terminology that demeans or Others men and women who fall outside of the very narrow, very rigid definitions of masculine and feminine that pervade our culture and our language.[3] Debra Morgan exudes female masculinity in her mannerisms, choice of wardrobe and makeup, and limited use of tact. She herself points this out in season 3, episode 12, when she, dressing to be Dexter's "best man," dons a dress and immediately says, "Ugh, a dress. I feel like a transvestite." As a forceful and complex character, Debra's masculine qualities seem, early in the series, put on or self-consciously acted out. But as the series progresses, Debra as a character grows more confident and comes into her persona quite strongly. It is also possible that Jennifer Carpenter, the actress who plays Deb, also began to feel more comfortable in her role, thus helping the performative aspect of her masculinity diminish as time goes by. The balance in the first few series between Debra's masculine demeanor and heterosexual sexuality work well together, offering a complex character with a multifaceted personality, one able to control and direct as well as give and care. Her relationship with her brother highlights this. They taunt each other as siblings do. For example:

> DEXTER: I remember your first words: shoes. You were very girly once upon a time.
> DEBRA: That's funny. I always remember my first words as being, "Hurry the fuck up."

Like any sister, she teases him about his relationship with his girlfriend:

> DEB: The wedding band has to match the engagement ring, so what does that look like?
> DEXTER: She said she didn't want one.
> DEB: Oh my God, you just get dumber every day! How do you survive in this world? Of course she wants one!
> DEXTER: How am I supposed to know that?
> DEB: You are such a Y-chromosome cliché! Just buy her a beautiful, romantic, "I love you with all of my heart" fucking engagement ring. And Dex, size matters!

They banter about work quite frequently. In season 1, for example, Deb asks Dexter why they never talk about any normal "brother-sister stuff," to which he responds, "Our dad was a cop, you're a cop, I work for the cops.... For us, this is brother-sister stuff." These types of exchanges underscore Deb's ability to embrace both masculine and feminine roles. Her "feminine" strengths of compassion, sexuality, and affection are not (initially) negated by her work role or her foul-mouthed, aggressive personality outside of the bedroom.

This is something to applaud. Many women who exude female

6. The Woman and the Faux Rogue

masculinity, such as the characters of Miranda Priestly in the film *The Devil Wears Prada* and Detective Kima Greggs from the television series *The Wire*, are limited or restricted as to how they can succeed. Their roles are often narrowed because of their gender. Miranda Priestly, the internationally successful editor of a fashion magazine, succeeds in terrifying most everyone around her. She is incredibly smart, but also underhanded, backstabbing, and entirely self-focused. In the film, though her career flourishes, it is made clear that her personal life is a disaster and she cannot maintain any sort of loving commitment, nor can she be a mother to her two daughters. Priestly is not allowed to embrace both sides of herself, a common theme in U.S. fictions of all kinds. Detective Kima Greggs is openly gay, making her female masculinity less threatening as she is demarcated as Other. But she, too, as a successful woman in a predominately masculine field, is plagued by relationship issues and issues of intimacy. Both characters offer insight into how female masculinity is typically handled in mainstream narratives. Thus Debra Morgan's character, who is able to balance friendships, sisterhood, and work, is a step in the right direction.

Despite the positive way that Debra's demeanor is handled and the strength of her character, over time the series inflicts more and more psychological damage upon Debra, all of which is related, in some way, to her intimate relationships. In season 1, her first boyfriend turns out to be married. She is then the victim of "The Ice Truck Killer," Dexter's previously unknown brother Brian (known to Deb as "Rudy"). He seduces Debra, forming what she begins to think of as an intimate relationship before he abducts and tries to kill her. Though she is traumatized, moving in with Dexter in season 2 and spending increasing amounts of time alone, she moves on as she becomes romantically involved with FBI Special Agent Lundy, in town to investigate the discovery of a massive grave of dismembered bodies (Dexter's victims). Lundy is able to bring Debra out of herself, allowing her to take things less seriously, to a degree, and bringing out a flirtatious, fun side of her character. Their initial introduction hints at such:

> DEBRA: What fucking asshole left this here? (*Stepping over a suitcase blocking her desk*)
> SPECIAL AGENT FRANK LUNDY: It's, uh, Special Agent Fucking Asshole.

Renegade Hero or Faux Rogue

In season 2, as the two become closer, this dynamic is underscored in an exchange in Lundy's kitchen:

> LUNDY: Start peeling potatoes.
> DEBRA: Oh, I like a man that takes control.
> LUNDY: Wash your hands first.
> DEBRA: You're so turning me on.
> LUNDY: You know, considering our age difference, you're not too old to spank.
> DEBRA: No, stop, please. I can't control myself....

Debra is able to release some of the tension and trauma she holds onto for so many months after her time as Brian's prisoner. Yet when she and Lundy are gunned down in season 4 and Lundy dies, Debra begins a downward spiral emotionally, though her work ethic and tenacity remain and she is promoted and well-respected at work. She misunderstands one lover's motives and breaks up with him in a hail of metaphorical bullets, and she loses Anton, her super-calm, "like valium" boyfriend, when she cheats on him with Lundy in season 4. In season 5 she crosses several boundaries and begins sleeping with her partner Quinn, despite the fact that he's investigating her own brother for murder. The two form a quick bond and are living together by season 6. But then Quinn proposes, Debra refuses, and Quinn becomes an irresponsible man-child while Deb is disgusted and indifferent.

In season 6 Debra is promoted to lieutenant and, though this is something she has aimed for her entire career, once she takes the job she feels ostracized, as though all the bonds she had formed with her brothers-in-arms have dissipated. As she struggles with the various traumatic incidents in her life and her adjustment to her new career, she begins therapy. It helps her discover the depths of her feelings for Dexter and, guided by her therapist, she realizes that she is in love with him in a romantic way. Traumatizing the audience, and leaving her last shred of personal respectability behind her, Debra leaves her session to declare her love, only to discover Dexter murdering Travis, the antagonist behind the Doomsday killings, in season 6's cliffhanger ending.

Though Deb is a solid, dynamic character with enormous potential, she is written into a submissive, slightly unstable version of the woman she was earlier in the series. She lets her romantic entanglements dictate

6. The Woman and the Faux Rogue

many of her life choices, she becomes weakened by the idea that she doesn't have many friends or close bonds, and the most important character whom she plays off of and gains significant strength from becomes a love interest, changing that relationship forever. The Dexter bond is crucial to Debra's character development throughout the entire series; as stated previously, it truly shows the way Debra manages to interweave her feminine and masculine traits in a positive way. Sexualizing this relationship, if only for a moment, undermines Debra's character, placing her in the role of a woman who begins to lose control until she discovers her "true love," a trite and unnecessary narrative for the show. She seems desperate and confused, and the impact of this realization, even though it is really only addressed for one scene in season 6 and discussed very briefly in season 7, changes both her temperament (she becomes a nagging, domineering taskmaster determined to fix Dexter in season 7) and her focus. Though work was her primary focus with a healthy balance of men throughout the series, in season 7 her focus is split between work and Dexter. She is less capable, less independent, and less able to challenge the traditional heteronormative paradigm as she does earlier in the series. The writing of the show's narrative arc begins to limit her role and her strength. The transition is a disappointing one, but it perpetuates longstanding ideological notions of womanhood, a trend that falls in line with the folly of the faux rogue stories discussed throughout this book.

Gemma and Tara

Sons of Anarchy is a fictional world of absolute patriarchal dominance. Both within and outside of the world of SAMCRO, *Sons* immerses its audience in hypermasculinity and a clear hierarchy of male authority. On a superficial level, one might think I should just skip this show, as any kind of analysis of its female characters would be clichéd. The women in the series are strippers, porn stars, hookers, victims, and/or "old ladies." Not much to say to that, is there?

The women on *Sons of Anarchy* are clearly surrounded by and a seemingly organic part of what bell hooks calls a "dominator culture":

Renegade Hero or Faux Rogue

Dominator culture teaches all of us that the core of our identity is defined by the will to dominate and control others. We are taught that this will to dominate is more biologically hardwired in males than in females. In actuality, dominator culture teaches us that we are all natural-born killers but that males are more able to realize the predator role. In the dominator model the pursuit of external power, the ability to manipulate and control others, is what matters most. When culture is based on a dominator model, not only will it be violent but it will frame all relationships as power struggles.[4]

Separating the two most developed female characters on the show, Gemma Teller Morrow and Tara Knowles, from this world of masculine dominance means that the following analysis of these two women is framed by the knowledge that the women are clearly living in a very particular kind of situation with regard to men and women, violence, and relationship dynamics, and that certain aspects of their "domination" or lack of power within the circle of the men with whom they are involved should be seen within such a context.

That said, the character of Tara, early in the series, is a liminal character, one who is neither exclusively outside nor inside the world of SAMCRO. At age nineteen, Tara left Charming to pursue her education. Over a decade later she returns a skilled surgeon. She and Jax shared a teenage love, and it is clear she was involved with him and the club at that point. But it is also obvious she has not been a part of his life or his club since she left. Presented as a thoughtful, intellectual woman, Tara struggles with her definitions of morality, love, and loyalty. Yet from the pilot episode, it is clear that a large portion of Tara's world has and always will revolve around Jax. The following exchange, from the opening episode of season 3, illustrates this:

> TARA: I didn't come back to Charming because I was afraid of Kohn. And I didn't stay because of what we did to him.
> JAX: Doesn't matter now.
> TARA: When Donna was killed, those things you said to me in the hospital about my life being a series of hit and runs, that my face was the only one you saw.
> JAX: I shouldn't have said that.
> TARA: It was the truth. I have created this very serious life for myself. And when I'm inside it, I barely know myself. I have these moments sometimes in the middle of my surgeries when suddenly I'm aware of my

6. The Woman and the Faux Rogue

> hands, you know, doing these extraordinary things. And I think, "Whose hands are these? What am I doing here?" When I'm with you, I never ask that question.
> JAX: I'm not the answer. Look at me, look at this.
> TARA: I'm always looking at it. My brain never stops. Why am I here? Should I be here? Am I afraid to stay, afraid to go, afraid to be a mother? It's endless. I drive myself crazy.
> JAX: None of that matters.
> TARA: I know. That's become so clear to me. The noise doesn't matter. We don't know who we are until we're connected to someone else. We're just better human beings when we're with the person we're supposed to be with. I wasn't supposed to leave. I belong here.

Tara represents a level of maturity and depth of self-exploration that seems lacking from the show's other characters. Though Jax begins the series contemplating himself, his future, and the entire philosophy of his lifestyle, as life comes at him, he reacts quickly and viscerally. Slowly the thoughtful, different Jax on the verge of an epistemological breakthrough disintegrates. He maintains his desire for ontological change, but it is Tara who maintains the ability to question and analyze. Ironically, however, her behavior—her ontology—changes as she is absorbed back into the world of SAMCRO. The first major sign of this is in season 2, episode 12, when Tara confronts her hospital's main administrator, Margaret, who has been making her working environment extraordinarily difficult, largely because she disapproves of Tara's involvement with the motorcycle club:

> TARA: I pity you. You walk around here with your little administrative degree, pretending like you know medicine. You're just a cheap suit too stupid and lazy to get into med school. So now you compensate by making the healers jump through hoops.
> MARGARET: Well, I guess someone's true colors have finally bled through. I guess you and that biker whore you travel with....
> TARA [grabs Margaret by the throat]: How dare you? You don't know her. You don't know any of them.
> MARGARET: Oh my God! You hit me. You're finished. I'm calling security. This is assault.
> TARA: No. [punches Margaret] That's assault.

Oddly, this scene does not end Tara's career, and over time she and Margaret establish a relationship that is both positive for her medical career and helpful for her personally. But after this scene, Tara is clearly no longer liminal—she is different, but very much a part of the SAMCRO world. This act of violence was precipitated by a discussion she had with Gemma, when Gemma told her that she didn't have to take "shit from anyone any more" because she was now the old lady of the vice-president of SAMCRO. In a way, her ability to exude physical toughness during a time of threat is a positive. Like Debra, Tara's female masculinity works well from season 2 until season 4. She is well balanced as a human, loving and family-focused but also tough and determined, successful at work, and devoted to her friends and family. She becomes a mother to Abel basically from his time in the NICU in season 1 and bears another son, Thomas. She is able to handle all the turmoil that a life with Jax offers with minimal grief. Yet after she punches Margaret, she shifts from someone who has a clear mind-body separation to someone willing to act physically out of emotion, a shift that makes her more like Gemma and the women of SAMCRO than an outsider.

As the seasons progress, Tara's physical appearance changes: She dresses differently and is more sexualized. From her clothing to her hair, makeup, and posturing, she has gone from a doctor-girlfriend of a gangster to the old lady of a gangster. The emphasis in the plotlines that involve Tara from season 3 on focus on her relationship with the club and with her new family. At the end of season 2, Abel is physically taken from her and she is powerless to stop the man who kidnapped him. She, too, is kidnapped in season 2, though she does all she can to end the situation herself but is forced to rely on Jax to save her. Though she works with him, she is as dependent on him as she was with Kohn and continues to be so through the end of season 4. Though Tara's character has the most potential to be liminal, dynamic, and complex, she, like Debra, is written into a role much different from the one in which she began. At the end of season 4, she stands by Jax's side at the head of SAMCRO's table, posing in her black leathers as the old lady by his side, not as the independent, cautious, skilled surgeon she was in season 1.

In contrast to Tara's somewhat slow warm-up to force on the show, Gemma Morrow blows into the series like a hurricane. The reverberations of her power are felt through the bones of nearly every character on *Sons of Anarchy*. She is queen of a kingdom, matriarch of the über

6. The Woman and the Faux Rogue

macho Sons, and as intertwined within the roots and shoots of SAMCRO as its bikes. Gemma makes a powerful first impression in the series pilot. She discovers Wendy who, having taken too much methamphetamine, lies prone on her kitchen floor, nearly losing her unborn child. Gemma handles that situation while simultaneously trying to scare Tara (whom she sees for the first time at the hospital since her teenage departure) away from Jax, force Jax to accept his role as Abel's father, and threaten Wendy, giving her a dose of drugs and the opportunity of an overdose while telling her that Abel will never call "his murderous, junkie mom who cared more about a $40 fix than she did her own flesh-and-blood 'mommy.'" She also warns Clay about Jax's emotional instability and, using her sexuality, "encourages" Clay to get Jax back into the club whole-heartedly. She is funny and sharp, but also cunning and manipulative. Gemma is a sexy, scary, complex woman, an incredibly strong female lead able to stand out in a show that *Rolling Stone* referred to as the manliest of man shows.[5]

Gemma was married to John Teller, marrying Clay Morrow after John's death. As the club president's old lady, what she says goes. She is not involved directly in club politics but wields considerable influence among the men and their families. She runs the office of the legitimate mechanic's shop the club operates but still has time to be a mother, grandmother, surrogate mother, enforcer, community organizer, and general badass in her own right. Unlike Tara's initial separation of body and mind, Gemma's actions and reactions are typically as violent and immediate as many of the men's. In season 1, episode 6, when she sees a young woman her husband recently slept with walking the streets of Charming, she beats her with a skateboard. There is no discussion, no crying or wails of betrayal, just a simple beat-down and warning that young Cherry should stay away from Clay. She then confronts Clay directly as she sits in police custody:

> CLAY: What did you do?
> GEMMA: Same thing you did. Nailed some little tart from Nevada.
> CLAY: All the shit I got coming outta my ears and you go and do this.
> GEMMA: You should have thought of that before your dick went on a cheerleader hunt.
> CLAY: I didn't ask her to come here.

Renegade Hero or Faux Rogue

GEMMA: But she's here.
CLAY: Well, that's not my fault.
GEMMA: And it's not my pussy.

Clay and Gemma have what begins as a loving relationship. It is strained, at times, by the club's activities and Clay's less-than-chivalrous behavior, but their shared history and shared desires for the club bring them together. Gemma is brash and bold, but given her role, those qualities make her strong—*frightening*, but definitely strong. She is shown as both fearless and ruthless throughout season 1, ruling the world around her. She is also valued and necessary to the world around her, not merely an accessory. As one writer puts it,

> One of the things I appreciate most about *Sons of Anarchy* is the way Gemma is allowed to have specifically female problems, and to have those problems treated as if they're on a level with the hurts and angers of Jax, Clay, and the other members of the club.[6]

In addition to her toughness and her power, she also possesses a strong maternal streak when it comes to Jax and the men of SAMCRO. Her female masculinity is actually bolstered by the "women's" roles she plays in the show. She is not just Clay's old lady, but someone people share their secrets with, commiserate with, and want to be close to. At the close of the pilot episode, after she has threatened Tara, tried to kill Wendy, and worked her magic on Clay, Gemma is seen hosting a large "family" dinner with the SAMCRO men and families gathered around the table. Even the club's young prospective member is invited, though not without hassle from Gemma. Her extended invitation to the gathering shows her humor, strength, and masculine character assessment:

GEMMA: You coming to dinner tomorrow night? I'm picking up steaks from the German.
JAX: Oh, you know it.
GEMMA: You should bring Chibs and that new kid.
JAX: New kid doesn't eat meat.
GEMMA: Don't patch him in; can't trust anyone who doesn't eat meat.

Gemma's humor is an insight into her self-awareness. Her quips and gallows humor often are typically ironic. Sometimes they hide her pain, and other times they show her ability to make fun of herself. One light-hearted exchange with Tara shows her respect for Tara's abilities

6. The Woman and the Faux Rogue

as a doctor and her growing, albeit grudging, acceptance of the young woman's presence. Tara discusses Abel's need for soy formula instead of milk-based. Gemma agrees but says she doesn't want him to turn into "some pussy vegetarian." Tara suggests he wear a "wife-beater" onesie while he drinks it. Gemma's intellect and strength make her a standout female character on U.S. television, and the first season perfected her character as one who bucked the oppressive writing for female characters in most shows. Which is why the opening of season 2 was such a shock.

In the season 2 premiere, Gemma is brutally, horrifically raped by three men in a very long, very graphic scene. The League of American Nationalists, a white supremacy gang intent on bringing drug and business interests to Charming, are determined to be rid of SAMCRO. During Gemma's assault she is told that she will be attacked again unless she tells Clay to end his collaboration with gangs of color (a way of ensuring L.O.A.N.'s monopoly of the area's drug trade). Discovered by Unser, who rushes her to the hospital, Gemma tells no one but him and Tara, who cares for her. She is determined to withhold her horrendous ordeal from the men of SAMCRO because she knows they will retaliate their way into a trap.

Gemma's rape and beating was horrific for obvious reasons, but I found it troubling for another reason: I could not understand why the show's matriarch, a new kind of character who could change the shape of female narratives on television, had to be subjected to the trope of sexual victimization. In no way, of course, does her victimization make her any less powerful or unique. But it, for a moment anyway, objectifies her, making her a tool for one group of men and a possession of another. The men who rape her assume that if they damage Clay's prized possession, he will react in a certain way. She goes from a puppet master in season 1 to a chess piece in the opening of season 2. According to Sarah Projansky's book *Watching Rape: Film and Television in Postfeminist Culture,*

> In many ... contexts, rape functions as the narrative event that brings out a latent feminism in the woman (or a man) who experiences rape; thus the texts make rape necessary for the articulation of feminism.[7]

Renegade Hero or Faux Rogue

It is possible that the use of sexual assault is used, in some way, to counter the misogynistic undertones of the show. I offer this argument because of the way the aftermath of the assault is handled. Writer Alyssa Rosenburg seems to agree with this line of thought, arguing:

> [A]fter Gemma is raped (a plot that I think is handled better than almost anything else in the series), *Sons of Anarchy* deals with her sexual anxieties respectfully and in a way that insists that rape victims shouldn't be treated as marked by their experiences. It's terribly, terribly sad to hear Gemma tell Tara that "Clay's never gonna ... want to be inside something that's been ripped up like me.... Love don't mean shit. Men need to own their pussy. His has been violated. He'll find another. It's what they do." But the show insists she's still wanted, first in Tig's advances towards her in the wake of the attack—*Sons of Anarchy* probably spends more dialogue insisting that Gemma is attractive than any other individual character—and in her eventual reconciliation with Clay.
>
> It's tremendously moving to see Clay exceed her expectations of him, not just having sex with her again but seducing her, clearing off her office desk and declaring as only Ron Perlman can, "I want my wife." Her hurt and recovery are couched in the language of ownership: Neither Charming nor the MC are exactly feminist paradises. But even when Gemma puts off telling Clay and Jax about the fact that she was attacked to avoid hurting them and destabilizing the club, both of the men in her life make her recovery a priority when she finally does tell them.

Gemma is not a damsel in distress after the rape. She is tortured mentally, damaged physically, and traumatized in general, but she handles it remarkably well, seeking the appropriate health care she needs (right down to a snippet of her getting an HIV test and the necessary follow-up test) and opening up to Tara about her fears and feelings. When she finally does tell the men, it is in a measured, straightforward manner with calculated reasoning. The assault does not change her character in any way, but I argue that the use of rape as a narrative trope unnecessarily brings attention to what the world typically sees as a threat to women, a weakness they cannot control. The discourse in the United States about women soldiers on the frontlines mirrors this. Many people seem to feel that because more women are raped than men, women are uniquely vulnerable to this particular form of violence and should be hidden from it at all costs, even though rape is about power and control, not sex. But just like soldiers on the front lines regardless of their gender,

6. The Woman and the Faux Rogue

Gemma is a warrior. Though she may be traumatized and suffer, she, like all warriors, carries on. Someone's attempt to debase her does not make her any weaker or any less powerful.

Making Gemma a victim does not fit her character. My concern is that the use of the event at the beginning of the series was used to assuage whatever threat her female masculinity offered an audience searching for the manliest of man shows. I was relieved, however, to see that this event does not change her. She remains independent, focused, determined, and mistress of her domain. She remains a force to be reckoned with and an excellent female lead after which many could be modeled, until, that is, the series progresses through season 4. In season 4, as Clay loses control, he turns on her, beating her, overpowering her, and throwing her away. Her manipulation of Jax shows her as power-hungry and selfish, not motherly. When it is revealed that she and Clay worked together to have Jax's father murdered, she is no longer a woman of balanced feminine and masculine powers but a manipulative schemer who uses her feminine wiles to get her way. At the end of season 4 she tries to manipulate Jax to kill Clay, thereby hiding her guilt in John's death and ensuring Jax's loyalty when he comes to power as president. Jax instead pulls away and Gemma is left in the cold as Tara stands with Jax at the end of season 4. Gemma, written as a stellar example of female power throughout the season, is gradually written into the corner as a duplicitous, self-serving manipulator, perpetuating the image of the "powerful woman as back-stabbing bitch" and undermining her strength as a woman.

Tara and Sookie

Tara Thornton, Sookie's best friend since childhood, is my favorite character of the *True Blood* series. In a show that attempts yet often fails to subvert stereotypes and create a fantastical world in which viewers can get lost and engage with alternative visions of sexuality, morality, and power, Tara is one character who, at least early in the series, manages to play with and subvert the stereotype of "the angry black woman." In the pilot episode, Tara is seen working at the Sav-a-Bunch, a store one can assume is much like a Wal-Mart. In her blue work vest, Tara lounges in a camping chair reading Naomi Klein's book *Shock Doctrine*,[8] the first contradictory image and indication of the complexity of her character. She is presented as a frustrated young, poor black woman working in a dead-end job, yet she is reading a work of enormous political implication about "disaster capitalism." She begrudgingly has to put her book down to help a customer who, at the conclusion of their exchange, proclaims her to be a very rude young woman, to which Tara replies, "Oh, this ain't rude. This is uppity." Her manager, hearing the exchange, chastises her for her constant inappropriate conduct. The following exchange occurs:

> TARA [slaps manager]: That's for pattin' my ass too much! I'mmo get my baby daddy who just got outta prison to come and kick your teeth in!
> SAV-A-BUNCH MANAGER: Jesus, Tara. Please don't do anything like—
> TARA: Oh, my God! I'm not serious, you pathetic racist! I don't have a baby! Damn! I know y'all have to be stupid, but do you have to be that stupid? Shit, fuck this job.

Here we see the quintessential Tara: a woman very clearly aware of her situation as a poor black woman in a small Southern town, aware of the prejudice that surrounds her and the battles she has had to and will have to deal with throughout her life, but who uses humor and intelligence to distance herself from what could be a soul-crushing existence. Her frustration gives her an edge and lends to her "stereotypical" behavior as an angry black woman, but the gleam in her eye and her ability to win the upper hand in verbal duals subverts this negative identity and shows how dynamic and complex she truly is. After she quits her Sav-a-Bunch job, she calls on Sookie, who, exasperated, talks to her even though she is busy at her own job at Merlotte's bar. The lifelong friends' quick chat is insightful:

> TARA: My life sucks.
> SOOKIE: Tara, don't you be feelin' sorry for yourself. That's just lazy.
> TARA: But why can't I keep a job?
> SOOKIE: Maybe because you can't keep your mouth shut.
> TARA: Bitch, who asked you?
> [Tara winks at Sookie, and Sookie smiles.]

6. The Woman and the Faux Rogue

Here we get an insight into Sookie's work ethic and outlook on life as well as her relationship with Tara. The two are like sisters and their relationship is a stellar example of positive female relationships until the show's narrative twists and mutilates it late in the series. In season 1, Tara, out of work and needing a new job, tries to get one from Sam, Sookie's boss and friend and an obvious long-term acquaintance if not friend of Tara's. He is direct in his response:

> SAM: It would only be a matter of time 'fore you went off on somebody. I don't wanna drive my customers away.
> TARA: I only go off on stupid people.
> SAM: Most of my customers *are* stupid people.
> TARA: Yeah, but ... I could help you keep an eye on Sookie. You see the way she was looking at that vampire? That is just trouble looking for a place to happen.

When Sam finally relents and Tara shows up for her first shift, her cousin Lafayette, the bar's cook, expresses his disbelief in his unique way:

> LAFAYETTE: Hey, hooker. How you doin'? What are you doin' here?
> TARA: I work here.
> LAFAYETTE [*not believing*]: Oh no, the hell you don't.
> TARA: Oh yes, the hell I do too, you ugly bitch! You need to make peace with that.
> LAFAYETTE: Shit. Sam must've lost his damned mind 'cause you should not be allowed to work in no situation where you actually gotta interact with people.

But again, despite the text itself, the exchange is funny and light-hearted and, in its own way, quite loving. The bonds Tara forms with nearly all of the characters in Bon Temps portray a soft-hearted, protective woman who loves her friends and family dearly. As the series progresses, Tara's life story is revealed. She grew up with no father present and an extremely drunk, abusive mother Lettie Mae. Tara, from a very tender age, was responsible for both herself and her mother, with whom she has an incredibly complicated relationship. Understanding what it means to be bullied, Tara saved a very young Sookie from schoolyard bullies, and the two became friends for life. Tara became a part of the Stackhouse family, running to Sookie, Jason, and their grandmother Adele in her times of need.

Renegade Hero or Faux Rogue

Though Tara despises her mother for the life she was put through and the years of mental and physical abuse and neglect, Tara loves her, unable to officially break free until her mother begins an intimate relationship with her married pastor. Finally pushed over the edge, Tara leaves her behind.

Tara is deeply wounded and her anger is most definitely not an affectation. She is easy prey for Maryann, the monstrous maenad masquerading as a "social worker." She takes Tara in and both through magic and simple affection turns Tara into a very subservient and willing member of her hypnotized cult following. It is through Maryann that Tara meets Eggs, with whom she begins a relationship, one that ends tragically when Eggs is gunned down by Deputy Sheriff Jason in a complicated scene following his realization of the evil he had committed under Maryann's influence. Tara's grief at this loss and her feelings of betrayal at her sometimes lover Sam's revelation that he is a shapeshifter, push her out of Bon Temps. Unbeknownst to her friends and family, Tara lives a brief life as a cage fighter in New Orleans with her new love, a woman named Naomi.

Her brief relationship with Naomi is loving and tender and, as I discussed in Chapter 3, the only truly positive depiction of homosexual relations in the series. Tara sacrifices her own happiness to save Naomi, who had followed Tara to Bon Temps, when she sends her away and back to New Orleans for her own safety, ending their affair.

Tara's human character is a complicated one and a very positive representation of a person struggling with her demons while maintaining healthy, positive relationships. Tara gives and receives help, and her humanity leads her through all the pleasure, pain, darkness, and light that a young woman could endure. She also offers insight into the many facets of womanhood. She is funny and smart. She is a sister to Sookie, a lover to Eggs and Sam, a friend to most, a defender to those who need it, and a strong, independent individual. In one of Tara's best scenes, she encounters a strung-out Jason, fearful that the side effects of the drug V (vampire blood) are affecting him:

JASON [*really worried*]: I think I mighta ODed.
TARA: Oh, my God. On what?
JASON: V.

6. The Woman and the Faux Rogue

TARA: You're doin' V now?
JASON: It was my first time.
TARA: Where on earth did you come across V in this town?
JASON: Lafayette.
TARA: My cousin is dealin' vampire blood now? God damn idiot. Well, at least that explains why I walked in on you dancin' around in that Laura Bush mask yesterday, 'cause I gotta tell you, without a reason, that was some fucked-up shit! All right, let me see it.
JASON: Huh?
TARA: How long have you had the erection?
JASON: Well, how do you know?
TARA: Um, I read. You're not the first vain-ass, body-conscious ex-jock to overdo the V and wind up with an acute case of priapism!

She is a mother figure, a disciplinarian, and a woman strong enough to watch the man she's had a crush on since childhood have a needle of extreme length shoved into his penis in the emergency room.

Her female masculinity is only seen as threatening in a comic manner, and though she is subjected to some of the typical tropes of black female subjugation, such as Maryann's machinations and her sexual and mental torture by the vampire Franklin Mott, she emerges from both ordeals stronger and more resilient. She is also faithful to her loved ones literally until her death. Despite her own trauma and fears after her time with Franklin and her part in the witch and vampire war, at the end of season 4, Tara, who had been fighting with Sookie over the nature of vampires, sacrifices herself by jumping in the way of a shotgun's kill shot aimed at Sookie.

The character of Tara, however, is changed forever when she is brought back to "life" as a vampire by Pam. Sookie and Lafayette, unable to accept the loss of the valiant woman, bribe Pam to make her a vampire. When Tara emerges in her new form, she is no longer a part of the civilized norm.

She is now a monstrous fledgling vampire, hating both herself and her "saviors" for turning her into that which she hates. She is vicious, hateful, and ultimately suicidal until she is brought into line by her maker, Pam. Though she may be less insane as the series progresses after her rebirth, she becomes more Othered. Her female masculinity is no longer comic; it is threatening. Her sexuality is no longer flexible and loving; it is Othered, and it intermingles with blood, hunger, anger, and power. The Tara who stood out as a funny, caring, compassionate woman able to balance her female masculinity with her wit, intellect, and devotion is an Othered vampire, unpredictable, lustful, and clearly demarcated as monstrous by the end of season 5.

Sookie is an odd counterpoint to Tara. Sookie was born a telepath, but she is unable to understand or control her powers and suffers years of torment from a town that thinks she is a lunatic and from the agony of trying to shut out the cacophony of voices in her head. Despite her struggles, Sookie is self-assured, independent, and quietly insightful. She was raised, from the age of eight, by her Gran Adele who instilled in her the manners, religion, and integrity of a Southern belle. However, Sookie is not a belle. She works full time as a waitress at Sam Merlotte's bar and holds her own against drunks, bigots, and a town of condescending masculine powers. Sookie begins the series as a naïve, sweet young woman whose inner strength has been solidly constructed through her struggle with her telepathy and the early loss of her parents. Though strong and independent in the sense that she works hard, takes care of herself, and does not allow herself to be cowed by ignorant locals, she lacks experience and often seems childish in her fearlessness rather than brave. She inspires a fierce protectiveness from those close to her. For example, after Sookie saves Bill from blood drainers in the series' opening episode, rather than laud her heroics her friends chastise and warn her of the recklessness of her actions. At work, Sam is particularly upset:

> SAM [*hauling her into his office*]: Sookie, you're being a very stupid girl!
> SOOKIE: Who asked you? I—I can take care of myself.
> SAM [*yelling*]: I don't think so! Mac could have seriously cut you up last night!
> SOOKIE: How do you know what Mac would have done?
> SAM: Now you're setting up a date with a vampire. What do you have, a death wish?
> SOOKIE: No I don't have a death wish. I just happen to think that judging an entire group of people based on the actions of a few individuals within that group is morally wrong!
> SAM: Well, I will not let you put yourself or this bar in danger. I won't!
> SOOKIE: Am … am I fired?

6. The Woman and the Faux Rogue

SAM: No! But next time you think somebody's being harmed in the parking lot, pick up the phone and call the police. Do not go out there alone like a goddamn vigilante!

Sookie lacks the kind of female masculinity seen in the characters discussed earlier. Her femininity is emphasized both through her physical appearance and her thought processes. Even after she has saved Bill with an odd, surprisingly violent counterattack against those torturing him, she plays the role of a well-behaved girl:

BILL: Aren't you afraid to be out here alone with a hungry vampire?
SOOKIE: No.
BILL: Vampires often turn on those who trust them, you know. We don't have human values like you.
SOOKIE: A lot of humans turn on those who trust them, too. [*She wraps a silver chain around her neck.*] I'm not a total fool.
BILL: Oh, but you have other very juicy arteries. There is one in the groin that's a particular favorite of mine.
SOOKIE: Hey, you just shut your nasty mouth, mister! You might be a vampire, but when you talk to me, you will talk to me like the lady that I am!

Sookie is blond with a very womanly figure, soft features, and gentle coloring. She has ample breasts and a curvy, toned figure yet she is rarely dressed immodestly. Before she meets Bill, her first vampire, she is a virgin and almost completely inexperienced with men.

Sookie's first sexual experience (with Bill) occurs the night after her Grandmother's funeral. She makes the decision, leaving her house and running, barefoot with her gothic white nightgown flowing behind her, to his arms. Though she initiates this and is, in a sense empowered, it is an oddly childlike moment. Sookie, grieving and lost without her parental figure, enters into the adult world completely unprepared and completely defenseless.

As much as she champions the cause of the newly "liberated" vampire community, she knows truly nothing about them and yet willingly gives herself over to the first vamp she meets. And from that point forward, Sookie is always "claimed"—she is "his" or "mine" or, though it doesn't necessarily denote ownership, she becomes a friend of a werewolf pack which marks her as "theirs." Sookie, though she remains sarcastic, strong-willed, and self-assured, is a pawn in the

Renegade Hero or Faux Rogue

supernatural. And not just a pawn, but often a sexualized pawn. She is made aware of this when Bill introduces her to the wider world of vampires at Fangtasia:

> BILL *[arriving at Fangtasia]*: You said you wanted to go out tonight.
> SOOKIE *[clearly upset]*: I did not mean Fangtasia! I mean, really, all those pathetic people who come here looking for sex with vampires.
> BILL: I know. It's despicable.
> SOOKIE: You know what I mean. So what? Five, ten minutes?
> BILL: As long as Eric requires us.
> SOOKIE: You mean as long as he requires me! Didn't even have the decency to ask me himself.
> BILL: You are mine. He didn't need to ask your permission.
> SOOKIE: He cannot check me out like a library book!
> BILL: Unfortunately, Sookie, he can. Eric is sheriff of Area 5.
> SOOKIE: Sheriff?
> BILL: It's a position of great power among our kind. We do not wanna anger him. As long as the requests are reasonable, we should accede to his wishes.

As the series progresses and Sookie becomes more a part of the supernatural world, she is regularly a consistent damsel in distress though she always *attempts* to settle matters for herself. The show attempts to present her as an empowered protagonist, but she plays a rescued victim more often than not and the center of sexual desire for supernatural men, not an independent hero. Though she is not "domesticated," in the sense that she stays home and plays a supporting role for those fighting, she frequently takes on the roles of nursemaid, confidant, welcoming lover, and counselor. She embodies those characteristics that the dichotomous heteronormative system identifies as feminine and, though this does not make her less powerful, it does not make her any *more* powerful.

She may be the central character, but the action happens around her and to her. Even given her super fairy light–flinging power, she is not an action hero. She is a symbolic leader rather than an actual one. Sookie has the façade of a female heroic protagonist, but actually offers audiences a sweet little troublemaker who does her best to help everyone else save the world.

6. The Woman and the Faux Rogue

Skyler

Skyler White, devoted mother to a teenage son and infant daughter, learns in season 1 that her loving husband has been diagnosed with aggressive lung cancer. Devastated by the news, she responds how most people would: She decides to try to save the man she loves by any means necessary. When she becomes despondent and angry at Walter's seeming desire to just let the cancer take him, she comes across as harpy, demanding, and controlling—even though the same emotions are expressed by her son, her sister, her brother-in-law, Walter's former best friend, as well as his former lover.

In season 1, episode 5, a heavily pregnant Skyler gathers her son and family together to discuss Walter's reluctance to seek medical intervention (see Chapter 4 for an excerpt of the discussion), Walter emphasizes his desire to choose how he spends his final days. He says, "sometimes I feel like I never actually make any of my own ... choices." Walter's words, his desire for "a choice," are what underscore the entire premise of *Breaking Bad,* as discussed in Chapter 4. Walter feels beaten by life, a life that has been hard on him and left him with little dignity or self-respect. When he sees that his life may end soon, he embraces a desire to finally take control of something and die with dignity—not sick, weak, or helpless. To a degree, it is very easy to understand that. And, in a fictional tale based on a male hero, it is easy to ignore the pain and shock of a woman who has bound her life to his. Her fears and sense of devastating loss are muted by the dialogue of the show, which portrays her anger rather than her pain. Many people lash out in anger when faced with devastation. It is a common reaction. But for fans of Walter White, Skyler becomes "a bitch" early on, a victim of the writing of a very masculine show focused on a male anti-hero. The presence of anti–Skyler White commentary from fans has led to something now referred to by media writers such as Marion Johnson, who blogs for the *Huffington Post,* as "The Skyler White Effect": "It goes like this: a female character judges the male protagonist's bad behavior in a completely rational way, and the audience hates her for it."[9] In Alyssa Rosenberg's July 16, 2012, *Slate* post, she describes Skyler as "one of many TV wives who …

Renegade Hero or Faux Rogue

fans turn on rather than visiting moral judgment on the anti-hero men themselves."[10]

Just as Walter White proved to be a much more complex character to fit into my discussions of television's new faux rogues than I had originally imagined, Skyler also proved to be more difficult to conceptualize than I had anticipated. I, too, must admit that I was struck initially by her coldness and what I originally judged as ineffectiveness as a character. I found her immersion in the realm of domesticity inconsequential to Walter's development. I found her vanilla, a mere reference to the dullness and claustrophobia of suburbia emphasized in the show. Yet she, just like Tara and Gemma, who are framed and contextualized by the world in which they inhabit, must to some degree follow, as a character, the rules of the world in which *she* inhabits and has been a part of for what one can assume has been her entire life. Of course she would be angry with her husband for threatening to leave her—which is what she hears when he first declines treatment. And as the show progresses and Skyler becomes aware of Walter's criminal acts, she responds as any sheltered, law-abiding citizen probably would: with shock and revulsion. Skyler White is not a bitch; she is a loving housewife who finds herself propelled into a Twilight Zone reality.

After initially trying to leave Walter, she instead decides to help him. But this is through no selfish drive to become a drug kingpin's partner or some kind of Mafia wife. Her change of heart is the same reaction as the one she has to the news of Walter's cancer. She vows to help him, to do what she can to keep him safe. She, more than Walter, does what she does to protect her family. Yet regardless of what she does in the early half of the series, fans and critics could not leave her alone. The Skyler White effect had taken hold. Stephen Silver, writing for TechnologyTell.com, argues that

> [t]he past decade of prestige cable dramas, from *The Sopranos* to *The Shield* to *Mad Men* to *Sons of Anarchy* to *Breaking Bad*, have all focused at least in part on a male anti-hero protagonist. Therefore, despite all the numerous bad acts committed by the main character, the instinct of many audience members is to root for him and see the world through his eyes. As a result, a certain segment of fans of these shows end up adopting an adversarial attitude towards the wives or other female characters, who often end up the way of his sometimes-nefarious plans.[11]

6. The Woman and the Faux Rogue

Johnson is more direct in her assessment of the continued assault on Skyler and her ilk: "The Skyler White effect is a pretty warped set-up. It speaks to the overwhelming preference for a male perspective over a female one, and for a male hero free from any woman's 'interference.'"[12]

As the series progresses and Walter truly becomes Heisenberg, Skyler is limited in what she can do to stop him. Again, her context is domestic and her ability to negotiate her reactions to Walter's atrocious acts is rooted in what she knows. Thus her affair with Ted, which seems trivial and even petty, is, for Skyler, an ultimate betrayal and a way of attempting to shock the Walter she *used* to know. She has no way of understanding how to handle the Walter he has become. As the Ted affair continues and unravels, Skyler finds she is out of her depth. According to Rosenberg,

> Skyler has experimented with the kind of power that Walter is addicted to in her dealings with Ted.... But seeing Ted crippled as a result of her actions was a comedown for Skyler, not a rush, and it clarified her horror that Walter is both willing to do the things he does and takes a perverse kind of joy in them.[13]

Skyler's machinations and dealings with Walter, Saul, and Ted as the series progresses, particularly in season 4, are not those of a harpy trying to end Walter's fun. They are of a woman desperate to save her family. As her situation grows worse, her manipulations become more impactful yet they remain within her domestic realm of knowledge. Though she ventures into the money-laundering business to support Walter, she finds herself once again out of her depth. Some may read this is an anti-feminist narrative of a woman incapable of succeeding in contrast to Walter's many "triumphs"; yet it is more realistic than most of the other storylines in the show. I do not read it as a narrative of oppression, but one of honesty and truth.

When Skyler realizes she cannot save Walter, she refuses to give up and desperately tries to save the rest of her family. She is not swayed by money or power or Walter's subversion of a system that nearly crushed him. She stands up to him, ultimately, for her children. In season 4, episode 6, she finally admits, more to herself than to Walter, "someone has to protect this family from the man who protects this family." While many see her as an obstacle to Walter's success, no one talks about the power she wields to protect four innocent members of her family, risking her life to save theirs. In contrast to the rest of the women in this chapter, it is not the narrative of the series that writes her power away or places her, ultimately, in a position of submission. It is the audience that does this. As Rosenberg argues,

> Skyler sees Walter as we're meant to see him: a self-deluding, pathetic man, but a dangerous one. She punctures the fantasy that there's anything admirable left about Walter White, that we should still root for the man who fought back against illness and emasculation with a pork pie hat and chemistry. But even if Skyler has a moral clarity that those of us who want to identify with Walter as a badass would like to deny, she can't easily act on it. She has an infant daughter and an ill son to protect, and her husband is a man who boasts of killing legends, who's used physical force to establish his dominance over her before. It's hard enough for women who aren't married to evil geniuses to leave abusive relationships. Skyler is attempting to negotiate a livable existence for herself in highly unusual circumstances.[14]

Skyler White does not perpetuate a narrative of female oppression. She exposes the reality of this oppression in the world outside of fictional television.

Margaret

Throughout this chapter I have attempted to discuss how the women closest to the faux rogue characters of U.S. television between 2008 and 2012 in many ways reflect the state of feminism in the country and how the narratives of the shows discussed in this book ultimately write most of the initially strong female characters into a position that is subordinate, not subversive, to patriarchy. To write about *Boardwalk Empire*'s Margaret adds a level of complexity to my discussion, as the show is set in the 1920s and thus Margaret's character is written and filmed in a historical period through a contemporary lens. Though the series attempts to maintain a serious level of historical accuracy, in many ways the bias of contemporary mediation is everpresent, resulting in a certain loss of historicity. This is particularly important to remember when exploring the character of Margaret. The series does a remarkable

6. The Woman and the Faux Rogue

job of illustrating the role women played in Prohibition, the limitations of their sex during the period of the newly dawning U.S. Women's Suffrage movement, and many of the common obstructions to their personal liberty, but it is still a series about gangsters, a show about tough guys, with an emphasis on the anti-hero Nucky Thompson. It is a series directed and written primarily by men aimed primarily, at least in the first season, at a heterosexual male audience. Thus, approaching Margaret presents unique challenges in separating the superficial narrative of her 1920s-based character from the underlying narrative of contemporary U.S. culture. In order to fully explore Margaret, the following section offers a significant explanation of plot as a way to show how her character is developed and molded before discussing the current implications of her portrayal in the series.

Margaret makes her first appearance as a young, pregnant mother of two who, after hearing Atlantic City's treasurer Nucky Thompson speak at a Women's Temperance meeting, steels herself to head to his office and ask for his help. Her husband Hans, she tells him, is out of work and "has a weakness for the tables." She is facing a fast-approaching winter with two bootless children and no money to care for them, let alone her coming third. Her heavily accented Irish voice breaks with humility as she tells Nucky how moved she was by his story of his own impoverished childhood. Her goal in meeting with him is to ask for a job for Hans. Nucky instead offers her a large amount of money to get her through the winter with a somewhat flippant "I'll see what I can do" regarding a job for her husband. He arranges for her to be driven home by his personal driver, decrying that she is in no condition to walk anywhere.

Nucky is as full of shit as a politician can get, yet his tenderness toward Margaret seems sincere and, after we learn of his own wife's death and the loss of his newborn son later in the series, we can assume that in many ways there is sincerity there. However, his good intentions don't have the desired effects: A drunken Hans discovers Margaret's stash of money, which he subsequently steals for his gambling habit after beating her brutally in front of their children. When he is discovered by Nucky and manhandled out of the casino, his rage is aimed again at Margaret, who is hospitalized after another brutal beating and subsequent miscarriage.

Renegade Hero or Faux Rogue

The depth of Nucky's sincerity toward Margaret's plight is seen in full as he orders Hans beaten to death and dumped at sea at the end of the pilot episode. His connection to Margaret is formed from this point forward. Despite the loss of her husband and her unborn child, her inner strength shines as she seeks work on her own to support her children, a difficult feat for a young immigrant woman with no family, no child care, and few skills. Nucky, however, intervenes, and she is "offered" a job as an assistant in Atlantic City's most affluent women's store, housed in the Ritz Carlton Hotel.

From here, the dance of wills between the two contrasting characters begins with a simple loaf of soda bread. Margaret, humbled and thrilled to have her new job, offers "Mr. Thompson" a loaf of homemade soda bread with her deepest thank-yous for his help. Nucky, distracted and self-involved, accepts the bread willingly but brushes off Margaret's grateful attentions. She later sees him throwing the bread in a trash bin. The next morning, young Margaret catches a distracted Nucky and asks him how he enjoyed her bread. When he declares it delicious, a new light sparks in her eyes and her insightfulness and dangerous intelligence gleams. She has seen through the beloved treasurer's thick layer of b.s., and her personal war begins. The two struggle back and forth in an unspoken, unacknowledged battle of wills. The final showdown is precipitated by barrels of green beer being stored in a garage behind Margaret's home. Margaret's staunch belief in Prohibition leads her to bring it to a supposedly shocked Nucky's attention, and he assures her he will break up the illegality immediately. When he does not, Margaret turns to the city's overly enthusiastic Prohibition agent, giving him the proof he needs to make a very public, very embarrassing arrest at one of the city's biggest political events on St. Patrick's Day. As Nucky and the rest of the city's elite are led out of their party by law officers, he catches Margaret's eye as she sings with the petitioning Women's Temperance group outside.

The spark of recognition of a true challenge ignites in Nucky's eyes, and the two become lovers and sparring partners that night, quickly forming a bond of wit and attraction. Margaret is easily able to replace Nucky's flighty showgirl girlfriend and soon has a lover, a benefactor, a nice home and schooling for her children. Though she struggles with

6. The Woman and the Faux Rogue

the morality of her position, her practical nature wins out and she settles in as a kept woman. But her intellect makes her much more than a concubine, and she and Nucky soon form a kind of power couple. He uses her to gain votes and she moves up in the world in both a material sense as well as in her own position of power. She is no longer pushed around by shopkeepers or treated as a mere mistress, but stands alongside Nucky and gains from the experience of learning his finely tuned art of political manipulation.

As the series progresses, Nucky becomes more of a bootlegging gangster and Margaret pays more attention to his puppet mastery, helping him when necessary but growing wary of him as things move forward. Margaret is an ideological feminist, a surprisingly well-read and educated woman who follows world events, women's achievements, and the plights of the women of her time. She takes control of her body, using the crude methods of birth control available to her. It is obvious she understands that having Nucky's child would give him leverage she is unwilling to let him hold over her. When he discovers her use of contraception and calls her a common whore for denying him a child, she states clearly that she will have no more children. And she wins.

The two grow further apart, but marry in order to keep Margaret from testifying against Nucky in court. Margaret is also coping with her young daughter's fallout from polio and sees the positives in having Nucky as a stepfather. But as season 2 ends and Margaret discovers the depths of Nucky's depravity and his role in Jimmy's death, she punishes him by signing over a deed to a highway, worth millions, to her church rather than back to Nucky as they had agreed. This dissolves their relationship in all but name, yet they remain together.

By the beginning of season 3, the two despise one another. Margaret maintains her role as social benefactor, working with the local Catholic hospital and eventually involving herself in women's reproduction education. The consistent barriers placed in her way as she attempts, with the help of an eager young doctor, to educate women about their bodies are very well written, with the overseeing nun requesting that the two refrain from using terms such as "menstruation" and "vagina" in their courses, and of course any reference to sex is taboo. It is obvious that the Church still maintains an iron grip on women's reproductive rights, and the trials of women forced to have too many children or unable to understand their own health are brought to light in a very graphic, realistic way. This is a shining light in a series that tosses naked showgirls about episodes as scenery and uses brothels as a mainstay for scene location shoots.

In addition to her social work, Margaret begins a relationship with Nucky's young Irish bodyguard Owen, as Nucky takes up with beloved actress Billie Kent. Though Margaret discovers Nucky's infidelity when he flaunts it in Atlantic City, she remains discreet as her love for Owen grows. The two plot their escape from Nucky and Atlantic City and Margaret is soon pregnant with their child. This plan is thwarted when Owen's dead body is sent to their hotel suite, a victim of the war raging around Nucky. Margaret's secret is finally revealed as she breaks down over the discovery, and she quickly leaves Nucky. She also wants to get an abortion, deciding not to bear Owen's child without him. After his battles are over, Nucky seeks Margaret out, asking her to come home (he lost his lover in a deadly blast on the boardwalk). When she refuses, he offers her money to tide her over until she makes her decision. She rebuffs him, and seemingly makes the decision to live in poverty with her children rather than return to a life of dependence.

As stated earlier, *Boardwalk Empire* is a very "masculine" show, emphasizing graphic violence, male political intrigue, and the fantasy of illicit sex and naked women as a staple of Atlantic City. Season 1, the first few episodes in particular, are awkwardly awash with what I candidly call "excessive boobage"—bare breasts lining scenes almost like wallpaper, often fragmented from faces or the whole of a body in general. The appeal of the show is obviously geared at a particular audience, most likely those who felt a vacuum in programming after the ending of *The Sopranos* in HBO's line-up. So for Margaret to be such an integral part of the series is a major coup. She is brilliant, self-protective, and capable of surviving without men. Her decisions are her own, even when she chooses to rely on Nucky for support. The context of her decisions is always couched in the time period of the show, yet her strength of will and desire to champion the cause of women make her a very modern character.

I believe Margaret largely to be a positive character. She is complex,

6. The Woman and the Faux Rogue

dynamic, and believable. The damage to her character, however, is still severe enough for contemporary repercussions. For example, her decision to turn over Nucky's land deed to the church as a method of punishment is awkward. It was clearly a move so powerful she knew it would end her relationship with Nucky, yet she chose to stay with him. It is a rare moment when she seems impulsive in anger. It is also a move that seems overly aggressive for someone who plans things meticulously and rarely makes a move without considering future complications. It is a decision that perpetuates the notion of women as irrational in anger. It is also a shortsighted move that does not just punish her lover but damages her own lifestyle and the lives of her children. It does not fit with the rest of her characterization.

The end of season 3 is also odd. Prior to Owen's death, even though she despised Nucky, she still served as a kind of military support when Nucky, concussed and confused, needed to be told how to rally support. She attempts to help him. He fails himself, but Margaret was willing to help him in his battles. There is a steeliness to her, despite how badly she had been treated. She was willing to help Nucky protect his empire. So for her to go from that woman to one who completely falls apart at Owen's death in a very public, visceral way, is inconsistent with her character. This leaves her destitute and alone at the end of season 3 which, though realistic to a degree, is not smart and is not planned or well focused. In the end of the season she is helpless and groundless without a man. And until season 4, that is the last the audience sees of her. For a woman willing to seek help for an abusive husband, stand by the side of someone who murdered his surrogate son, and meticulously plan each of her important moves, leaving her alone in a dirty tenement simply because she fled Nucky undermines every act of strength and insightful move she had made in the entire series run. It is a weak ending for a strong woman and one that suggests more about what, perhaps, audiences have come to expect from gangland shows than the reality of what a woman such as Margaret truly would be capable of.

Though I have spent well over a year contemplating and studying the men of U.S. TV and the crazy worlds of serial killers, vampires, and gangsters, I fell in love with the women in their lives. To grant them only a chapter in this book has been difficult, and I hope they will get the research, attention, and focus they deserve in the form of a larger project, particularly as studying how they are handled by writers and producers and received by audiences may have much to teach us all about not only the state of feminism in contemporary U.S. culture, but perhaps also about socio-cultural issues unique to women.

Conclusion

> *The media's the most powerful entity on Earth. They have the power to make the innocent guilty and to make the guilty innocent, and that's power. Because they control the minds of the masses.*
> —Malcolm X

This Doesn't Apply to Me

One of the biggest issues I confronted as I wrote this book was wording my concern of how the latent messages of the various series I discussed actually presented a problem for contemporary consumers of U.S. television. As I attempted to stress in my introduction, there is, I know, no such thing as true hegemony in an audience, in a medium, in a culture, or even within a singular series. But television, as I argue, is produced so uniquely and mediated so precisely that the overriding messages it offers are as close to hegemonic as one can get in a media-saturated world. However, the audiences who view these shows are by no means hegemonic. Even the notion of an audience being "American" is illusory. The idea of a U.S. ideology is a myth. Our nation is so diverse and our population comprised of such a complicated mix of histories, experiences, and influences that to argue even for an "audience" in a fixed sense of identity is unreasonable. I have been using the term "audience" as a way of addressing the consuming group of mediated fictions. What the "audience" of my book has as a common bond is merely that it is consuming, by whatever medium it chooses, a series narrative that, in conjunction with the similar narratives that dominate mainstream television, becomes a large dose of narratives with similar messages. My

Conclusion

concern is the cumulative effect of this large dose of the frighteningly analogous and well-composed stories that television offers over and over again. Regardless of the particular "public" that consumes the message, and whatever lens through which those who make up this public filter these messages, when the same messages are repeatedly conveyed, uncensored and at rapid speed, is it possible for them *not* to have an effect?

Even the most cynical of critics will concur that television at least helps identify "norms" in a culture, that it helps articulate what is acceptable, unacceptable, funny, harmful, trendy, or outmoded. More importantly, television shows us what "can" be seen, and leaves out what should "not" be seen. Inclusion and exclusion are by far two of the most powerful tools of persuasion in mediated fictions, fictions that, merely through repetition, have an effect on mainstream culture and thus on consumers.

Yet I know, from previous experiences in the classroom, at conferences, and through published works, that there are always members of U.S. culture insistent that my arguments about popular culture do not apply to *them*, that *they* are somehow immune to the effects of repeated narratives, advertisements, or stories directly about ideology. In class this is an easy thing to respond to: I offer an exercise in "cumulative" message reception involving a vulgar word and an imaginary experience of seeing this surprising term popping up suddenly on newspaper front pages, main street billboards, TV show titles, movie blurbs, and workplace conversations. The exercise attempts to show how we slowly become immune to that which was previously startling or even Othered through its constant, unprotested appearance in our everyday lives.

The most surprising criticism and that which is more complicated to respond to stems from fellow scholars, particularly those involved in the related fields of communication studies or even U.S. cultural studies, who view popular culture criticism based in theory to be somehow less important than work of a qualitative, investigative nature. This divide most likely can be explained by the argumentative split between how rhetoric is studied in the humanities versus how it is studied in the social sciences, one favoring theory and qualitative engagement, the other preferring quantitative engagement. However, there have been many crossover

Conclusion

points where both camps were able to dive into the repercussions of fictionalized narratives in mainstream media. These points revolved heavily around issues such as, for example, the politics of representation.

The Politics of Popular Culture

As a media scholar I believe fully that there are no innocent texts. From studying the Frankfort School to Laura Mulvey's first analysis of Le Gaze[1] in feminist film theory to the wild world of Baudrillard's mediation and simulacrum,[2] I embrace the idea that produced texts, particularly mediated texts, are as complicated and interwoven into a culture's politics, identity, and ideological self-awareness as are its laws and definitions of its self-identity.

> The idea that all cultural representations are political is one of the major themes of media and cultural theory over the past several decades. In the 1960s, feminist, African American, Latino, gay and lesbian, and diverse oppositional movements attacked the stereotyped and biased images of cultural representations of their groups. These critiques of sexism, racism, homophobia, and biases made it clear that cultural representations are never innocent or pure, that they can contain positive, negative, or ambiguous representations of diverse social groups, that they can serve pernicious interests of cultural oppression by positioning certain groups as inferior, thus pointing to the superiority of dominant social groups. Studies of representations of women or blacks on American television, for instance, would catalogue negative representations and show how they produce sexism or racism, or would champion more positive representations.[3]

Though many scholars across academic disciplines have proven quite dedicated, focused, and even united on issues of representation in popular media in both qualitative and quantitative studies, discussions of politics, ethics, and other sociopolitical- and socioeconomic-related issues are currently often excluded from qualitative analyses of popular culture in what have become the "established" forums of discussion of mainstream American culture. However, just as we study the political rhetoric of the House of Representatives and the discourse of news dissemination from various networks, I believe, as many do, that it is

Conclusion

imperative to engage popular culture in all its forms as a way of understanding the political messages that exist both implicitly and explicitly in the world around us. I find with each year more and more college students getting their news from social networks rather than traditional media, should they choose to seek out headlines at all. Apathy, arising from a callous awareness of disingenuous rhetoric from talking head panels to politicians alike has turned many citizens away from an engagement with civil discourse.

Thus, fictions—entertainment—exist as a primary vehicle for the distribution of both news and political voices. Most importantly, mass-produced culture contains the building blocks of ideological beliefs: the politics of representation, the politics of empowerment, messages about political and economic systems, gender, race, age, sexuality, disability, and every other component that completes the body politic. What we, as citizens, take for granted in our popular culture, such as standards of beauty or the presentation of casual violence, shapes the ideals of a consuming audience from a very early age. A 2010 study logged children and adolescents' (aged eight to eighteen) media consumption at an average of ten hours and forty-five minutes per day.[4] Another Kaiser Family Foundation study (2006) looked at the media consumption of children ages six months to six years old:

> In a typical day, 83 percent of children ages 6 months to 6 years use some form of screen media, including 75 percent who watch television, 32 percent who watch videos or DVDs, 16 percent who use a computer, and 11 percent who play either console or handheld video games. The percent of children who watch TV in a typical day is somewhat smaller than the share who spend any time reading or being read to (83 percent) and listening to music (82 percent).[5]

From their earliest years, young minds, so easily molded and so easily corrupted, are learning about their societies' ideas of what is right and wrong, privileged or oppressed, and valued or debased. This highlights the immense power of fictional entertainment, particularly television, as it remains the most visible access point for young viewers within a household. I hope this also draws attention to one of the many ways that popular television can shape a nation.

Conclusion

Not a Mirror

Jason Mittell, in his book *Television and American Culture*, writes:

> Television is a mirror of our world, offering an often-distorted vision of national identity, as well as shaping our perceptions of various groups of people.... Television is a part of our lives, as viewing and talking about it plays a central albeit underexamined role in our everyday routines.[6]

Though his book is insightful and clear and offers a good discussion of the state of American TV, this quote, taken from two bullet points on the second page of his introduction, startled me. I cringe whenever I hear someone use the phrase "a mirror of our world" in reference to any mediated artifact. As the above quote states, the reflection often is distorted *and* it helps shape perceptions, actions, attitudes, and ideals. Mirrors are not that powerful. Mediated information, entertainment, and art are much more powerful because consumers of media have conceived the idea that vehicles of information such as television and film can play the roles of both reflectors and creators of cultural ideals. I began this book as a way of exploring the rise of the new rogue protagonist hero on U.S. television; the intensity of my focus on television as a medium has grown obsessively, and my fear of it has grown in parallel. I know this sounds odd, and I should clarify: I am not scared of actual televisions. While I have lost certain degrees of sanity in the push to finish this manuscript, I have yet to run screaming from Best Buy when all the TVs are turned on at once. The electronic boxes that lurk around every corner are not themselves the threat. But, like weapons, the power they possess to do harm when wielded with dark intentions or simple indifference is what frightens me. The power of the mediated image, particularly on television, is greater than I had ever given it credit for, and it must be treated with respect.

Where We Stand

After September 11, 2001, President George W. Bush's neoconservative administration was allowed to flourish in a way that unleashed a

Conclusion

fervor of ethnocentrism, jingoism, and bloodlust in American culture costumed as patriotism. The second Bush's presidency became a war presidency, and the former playboy son of an ex-president and oil baron soon got to play the role of the cowboy leading the charge for "freedom," taking an unprecedented amount of liberties with the Geneva Convention and abusing the fundamental rights of American citizens to a degree unseen in decades. His Texas machismo, though grating to many, proved an inspiration to a generation ready to recapture a two-dimensional ideal of masculinity, a simulacrum of maleness that formed from images of cowboys, folk tales, war stories, and a past of heteronormative dominance. From John Wayne to G.I. Joe, Bush took his cues, dressed the part, mimicked the walk and talk, and did his best to recapture the glamor of our past national icons' simple logic of black-and-white ethics.

"If you're not for us, you're against us," citizens were told when an unpopular war raged on and on. An attack on U.S. soil was used as a fire to burn away autonomous citizenry and the progression of secular work in science, international relations, women's rights, and the rights of other oppressed groups in favor of resources and political focus funneled toward defense, foreign engagement in the Middle East, and projects that benefitted the wealthy, white ruling class of the country. Bush made a lot of his friends very happy during his eight years as president. War-related contracts were given to private companies, a national economic crisis was growing due to the costs of foreign wars, and the United States was becoming more and more isolated in its narrow scope of attack. Illegal detainees in Guantanamo Bay caused both national and international outrage, and, for the first time, images of American soldiers torturing prisoners of war were caught and distributed around the globe. It became increasingly difficult for citizens to easily defend our military actions without significant use of cognitive dissonance, and slowly the country became more divided, more uncomfortable, and more ideologically at war with itself.

Rather than address the issues or in any way change course, Bush defended his administration's decisions, his troops, and his country's missteps with verve. Religion was brought into the political rhetoric of Bush's administration in shocking and blatant ways that undermined the very basic tenets of the separation of church and state. Yet Bush did

Conclusion

not back down to detractors. He stood in front of world leaders and declared, "I am driven with a mission from God. God would tell me, 'George, go and fight these terrorists in Afghanistan.' And I did. And then God would tell me, 'George, go and end the tyranny in Iraq.' And I did." Mr. Bush went on: "And now, again, I feel God's words coming to me, 'Go get the Palestinians their state and get the Israelis their security, and get peace in the Middle East.' And, by God, I'm gonna do it."[7]

As a nation, we were publicly manifesting a "whatever it takes" mantra, becoming a muscle-flexing, self-focused nation, learning creative ways to self-congratulate and sublimate facts that horrified us about our own military and our own government. One of the ways we did this was through the mediation of our conflicts. Heroes from comic books came out in droves in cinema, characters like Dexter were forming an elegant tongue in popular literature, and television was shaping characters such as Jack Bauer from *24* into Christ-like figures, men who sacrificed their happiness and their conscience to do "whatever it takes" to save the lives of many. Torture, murder, even sacrificing friends were all part of the morality plays that popular narratives became as, consciously and unconsciously, U.S. writers of popular mainstream fictions dealt with the horrors of the world around them. The 2000s *Batman* film series is an excellent example of the resurgence of vigilante narratives in U.S. culture during the 2000–2008 Bush era. Rationalized violence became an important theme in American fictions as citizens dealt with the fallout from all they had had to deal with emotionally after 9/11 and throughout the raging wars in the Middle East.

A new cultural attitude was being formed, shifting from the grunge era of the early to mid-1990s to a complicated mix of a revisit to 1980s soap opera decadence and escapism, with simplistic cop serial dramas, and the new, complicated dramas that featured rogue heroes or monstrous anti-heroes in the early 2000s. Shows such as the renewed *90210*, *Gossip Girl*, and *The OC* allowed guilty-pleasure viewing of wealth and debauchery. The *CSI* franchise took its cues from the *Law and Order* franchise and offered intriguing yet straightforward crime drama that solved crimes and exterminated Others in less than sixty minutes. *Nip/Tuck* (2003–10, FX), *Smallville* (2001–11, The CW), *Heroes* (2006–10, NBC), and *Entourage* (2004–11, HBO) offered complicated protagonists—

Conclusion

some we love and some we love to hate—but all who present a challenge to an audience's ability to rationalize character behavior, and enjoy the antics of the "bad guys."

Though TV is still consistently offering such a wide variety of genres and demographic-specific programming, an emphasis on a complicated protagonist remains. However hard we try as a nation to go back to our Western roots of black-and-white narratives and good-and-evil tales, U.S. narratives have become increasingly complicated and the flawed hero—a favorite in literary fictions from our earliest national writers, a staple in American cinema since its humble beginnings, and everpresent in television narratives as early as he 1960s—today remains a feature of much mainstream entertainment in U.S. culture.

Mid–2012, while *Dexter* offers a unique challenge for viewers, and vampires Bill and Eric still struggle both within themselves and with a world far more complicated than many of the fictional worlds of our favorite characters, other shows have crept into the mainstream and are changing the landscape of contemporary television ever so slightly. Jax Teller is mired in criminality still, as is Nucky. Walter White is on the verge of some kind of implosion, yet viewers remain hooked. But new shows are drawing large fan bases as the faux rogue shows I have discussed draw to a close. Shows such as *The Walking Dead* (2010–present, AMC), *Game of Thrones* (2011–present, HBO), *Person of Interest* (2011–present, CBS), *Leverage* (2008–12, TNT), *White Collar* (2009–present, USA), *Arrow* (2012–present, The CW), *The Following* (2013–present, Fox), and *The Killing* (2011–present, AMC) are adding something (or taking something away) from the series most influenced by the Bush era. Now, in our second term of President Obama's administration, as the world changes, so do our fictions.

The shows I have examined between 2008 and 2012, represent a time between the sharp antagonism of the Bush era and the optimism of the election of President Obama. The moral ambiguity and permissive nature of the shows that ask viewers to abandon prior ideals of black-and-white ethics and revel in the danger and darkness of lovable villains serve as a way for people to engage with the darkness of the times since 9/11 when vengeance and vigilantism have taken on different meanings for average citizens. Being able to root for the bad guy because he is trying

Conclusion

to serve some kind of justice or establish some kind of order on chaos is freeing; to abandon the restrictions of moral order in favor of a more flexible, moral relativism can easily appeal to people struggling to understand the state of a global world that seems more complicated and frightening than ever before. Though the world may always have been as brutal, scary, and nonsensical as it is now, with twenty-four–hour access to information, unmitigated hours of misinformation, and a lack of real public, educated discourse, it certainly can seem more confusing and more daunting to the average person. Thus, I believe the shows featuring the faux rogue allow viewers to feel as though there is hope that someone can help restore order in a new, humane way, a way more suited to the world as we see it in all its shades of gray. And though these new heroes, as I conclude, are offering order, they also are bringing with them a renewal of oppression, narrow-mindedness, and jingoistic, displaced fervor for a broken system.

The new shows emerging, like the shows mentioned in the above paragraph, are different from the faux rogue dramas I discuss throughout this book for a variety of reasons. They all feature dangerous worlds and present ethical conflicts for viewers, but they also have developed boundaries of good and evil that had blurred in the shows I explore that aired between 2008 and 2012. Boundaries within the newer series seem to be setting up distinct lines between the hunter and the hunted or between camps of people. Yet each show features a main character or even a small cast of lead characters who are fighting for the side of good and are, clearly, "good" people—yet they are flawed, damaged, or somehow traumatized. For example, *The Walking Dead* takes place in a dystopian, post-apocalyptic world, featuring a small band of humans facing the odds to survive in a world full of "walkers" (flesh-eating zombies). The humans, diverse and surprisingly dynamic, help shape the series into more of a drama than a simple zombie show as they work, fight, and love among one another. The demons they fight outside of themselves clearly are marked as Other. The demons they fight within themselves, usually connected to their pasts, are less easily demarcated as Other. These characters, though they are significantly less "gray" than the faux rogues of my book, are battling within themselves. In *The Killing* and *The Following*, the agents on the side of jurisprudence are (typically)

Conclusion

the good guys, the white hats facing deranged murderers, cult fascinations, and demented human natures, all while trying to maintain their own humanity and remain on the side of good. The challenge in these narratives seems to have shifted from forcing the viewer to determine the moral or ethical code of the lead character, back to the writers and producers who are once again placing their creations in tidier worlds with clearly defined heroes and villains, with significantly less moral chaos than that of the faux rogue's world.

Arrow, the new CW superhero adventure-crime series, is based on the comic book character Green Arrow and features billionaire vigilante Oliver Queen (played by Stephen Arnell). Oliver, the victim of a sabotaged yacht voyage, is given a list of people by his now deceased father that he confessed, before his death, to having supported in "ruining" their home of Starling City. Queen's father admits his own guilt before killing himself to save his son. Oliver spends five years on an island near China learning to fight and developing his alternative ego as the "Hood." Upon his rescue, he, like Batman, hides behind the face of an average billionaire while at night dressing in a green hood and vanquishing his city's foes with his overly developed muscles and senses and a killer bow-and-arrow set. The voice of the father, as in many of the faux rogue shows I explore, dominates the show and serves as the motivational device for Oliver to right the wrongs of the generation that preceded him. It is a classic good-versus-evil tale straight from standard comic book lore. Oliver kills when necessary but avoids it when he can. He is the benevolent rich man, serving as jurisprudence in conjunction with the city's police force and attempting to help the poorer parts of town through land purchases and other monetary methods of assistance. Oliver is haunted by his time on the island, the ghost of his father, and the wasted years of his life as a hard-partying playboy before his ill-fated yacht trip. *Arrow* stretches no narrative boundaries nor is it innovative, but it stands as a clear example of the return to the black-and-white boundaries of ethics with a focus on the tortured hero.

Such new shows present a challenge for me. The faux rogue heroes, I argue, were perpetuating antiquated messages of oppression capable of presenting a hegemonic narrative of white power, male domination, class warfare, and the continued push for a capitalist regime with a desire for economic global imperialism under the guise of renegade, humanist heroes. These tales are powerful with a destructive edge. So what does it mean that they are losing traction and the traditional good-versus-evil worlds of fictions past are reemerging with characters, however flawed, clearly crowned as kings (and queens)? Perhaps it means simply that it is impossible to hide monsters behind masks of heroism for more than a few seasons. Or, it could mean that people are tired of examining morality and ethical codes and want their entertainment to be more succinct rather than didactic and challenging. What I would like it to mean and hope it might mean is that by dispensing with the guise of the humanist anti-hero we can once again have fictions that poke holes in narratives of oppression and false promises that crime can truly pay.

In my introduction I discuss my choice to explore the medium of television, as it offers a unique insight into particular time periods as it evolves and must be produced so quickly. Unlike films, which can be constructed from beginning to ending with a very particular image or metaphor used as its framework, television serials are often tacked together by a collection of writers, none knowing exactly how long their series will last or remain popular, meaning, therefore, that the overarching storyline of any series could be significantly longer or shorter than the series creator had originally imagined. Thus, characters have more room for development, plots can become either more convoluted or eloquently complex, and an audience can attach and adapt to the program in different ways from one year to the next. This ongoing evolution can be helpful for writers, directors, and actors, allowing them to flourish in their particular role and bring depth, insight, and meaning to the show. So as always, the new round of shows premiering and gaining in popularity as I write will have to be re-evaluated within a couple of years to see where the new trends are leading viewers ideologically.

Where We Can Go

There are new series that show promise of something new in the world of TV, a world where it is often argued that there will never be anything truly new. One of the most positive examples is *Person of Interest,*

Conclusion

which first aired on CBS in September 2011. In the first season, the brief opening sequence features the following voiceover monologue as a series of time stamps; frames of faces and a blur of activity are screened as though through a security camera:

> You are being watched. The government has a secret system: a machine that spies on you every hour of every day. I know because I built it. I designed the machine to detect acts of terror, but it sees everything. Violent crimes involving ordinary people, people like you. Crimes the government considered irrelevant. They wouldn't act, so I decided I would. But I needed a partner, someone with the skills to intervene. Hunted by the authorities, we work in secret. You'll never find us, but victim or perpetrator; if your number's up … we'll find you[8] [season 1 opening sequence].

The series features Harold Finch (played by Michael Emerson), a reclusive, security-conscious, and intensely private billionaire software engineer. Finch (his real name is unknown and he has many aliases) developed a machine that can isolate the Social Security numbers of people either with premeditated homicidal intent or who will be homicide victims, based on its analysis of surveillance data. He originally designed it for defense purposes following the events of 9/11. The machine is subsequently dismantled, but Finch is able to maintain contact with it, feeling it his duty to try to use the data it provides to make a difference. After a traumatic event in his own life that led to the death of his business partner and close friend Nathan Ingram, he recruits John Reese to help him deal with the people the Machine identifies. Finch lives and works in an abandoned library and shows the results of severe physical injuries, including the inability to turn his head, a rigid posture, and a limp. The details of his past are sparse and ambiguous, but with each episode, more about the expanse of his financial empire is revealed, as are small details of his past.

John Reese (played by Jim Caviezel), a former member of the U.S. Army Special Forces and a CIA field officer, is presumed dead following a mission in China during which he and his then-partner were separately given orders to kill one another; though both attempted, both survived. Following Reese's subsequent abandonment of his position, he appears in New York, seemingly homeless, injured and bloodied. He is unarmed when he is attacked by several thugs on a subway train, but manages to

Conclusion

viciously beat them down. His actions attract the police and also Finch, who helps him recover and offers him a job. Little is known about Reese's background, and his name is one of several aliases he uses. The betrayal he felt at his partner's assassination attempt, his disillusionment with his career after nearly being taken out despite all he had sacrificed for his country, and losing the woman he loved while he was deployed—all of these things have marked him deeply, and he seems damaged, continually struggling with the demons of the past. Reese demonstrates skill in the use of a range of weapons, hand-to-hand combat, and surveillance tactics. He is Finch's muscle but also becomes more of a teammate as the two men, both haunted in their own ways, struggle to make the United States a better place and move forward in a world that thinks them both dead.

They are helped by various entities at various times, but they rely heavily on the help of NYPD homicide detective Jocelyn "Joss" Carter (Taraji P. Henson). Carter is a former U.S. Army interrogator who passed the bar exam in 2004, but gave up practicing the law to return to police work. She first crosses paths with Reese following the subway attack and then subsequently as the mysterious "man in a suit" whom she kept catching sight of in and around her crime scenes. Carter is initially determined to apprehend Reese, but eventually forms an alliance with him and Finch, though she is not entirely sure who they are or what, exactly, they do.

Joss's partner, Detective Lionel Fusco (played by Kevin Chapman), is a formerly corrupt cop; Reese blackmails him into being a source inside the police department. He struggles to get out of his entanglement with "HR," the group of corrupt cops in the department, while simultaneously helping Finch, Reese, and Carter and keeping his own life together. At first, neither detective is aware of the other's "extracurricular" activities, but that eventually changes.

I have chosen to discuss *Person of Interest* because it shakes convention in that it is a cop-crime drama before the crime occurs, bringing in contemporary issues of surveillance post–9/11, as well as the complicated themes of vigilante justice and redemption. Unlike the faux rogues of the series this book explores, all of the main characters seem to be seeking redemption and a new start and their actions are clearly those

Conclusion

of good people doing their best to do good things. Though they fight with and against figures with questionable moral codes, the four main characters want to shake their demons and do what they must to reestablish their own moral codes. Though Carter and Fusco are outlaws within the realm of civility, Reese and Finch are Others trying to salvage the civilization they live without. It is a complicated show with multifaceted characters and is as oddly patriotic and humane as it is critical of big government and the ills of society. I argue that it serves as a good template for the kind of television that could potentially be used as an emancipatory tool in popular culture. It forces viewers to ask themselves questions about ethics, laws, rules, and morality without forcing anyone to slip into a morally ambiguous mindset. We are not asked to root for the villain in order to understand why that "bad guy" (or woman) is motivated to do what he or she does. It is a show that highlights big, frightening questions about human nature without the need to break its humanity.

To exemplify my point, season 1, episode 21, "Many Happy Returns," features Finch trying to keep Reese away from a new "number" that has come up. He gives Reese the day off, as it is his birthday, and tells him there is no one of consequence to fight that day. The person of interest, however, is Sarah Jennings, a woman on the run from her U.S. Marshal husband. Finch is worried that Reese will overreact and do something rash, given the similarities between this case and what happened to Reese's lover Jessica years ago. Finch enlists Fusco to tail Sarah, only to be forced to do it himself when Fusco loses her. Sarah's husband, Brad Jennings, catches Finch looking for his wife and corners him, but Reese appears in the nick of time to bail him out and keep him off of Jennings's radar. It becomes clear that Jennings is a formidable threat, using his contacts as a marshal to force Sarah to run constantly for her own safety. Finch reluctantly lets Reese join the case, but when he does, it is too late: Jennings finds Sarah and attempts to take her out of town. Finch tracks down his car and Reese pursues him, willing to do whatever is necessary to save Sarah. Reese finds them, subdues Jennings, and tells Sarah she is free to go. When Carter tells Finch that the FBI have a lead on Reese in New Rochelle, he encourages her to join the FBI in their investigation so she can learn a little more about their mutual friend.

Conclusion

While there, she finds out that Reese may have killed Peter Arndt, Jessica's abusive husband and eventual murderer, and fully understands why Finch wanted Reese to stay away from Sarah. Carter stops Reese on her way back from New Rochelle and asks him what he did with Jennings, but he is evasive and tells her to trust him; he is going to do the right thing. Convinced and deeply disturbed that Reese killed Jennings, a few days later a surprised Carter gets a call from a prison warden in Mexico, letting her know that Jennings was delivered to their jail with ten kilos of heroin on his person. Curious, Carter asks if there are other Americans in this jail, and the warden lets slip that there might be one or two more, the implication clear that this is not the first mysterious American to be delivered like a present to his prison. Reese, it seems, is not only more intelligently complex than first imagined, but also more dedicated to his own reformation than one might have been able to imagine.

What Has to Change

Series creators can continue to come up with amazing ideas for new television serials, writers can produce smart, creative scripts, and directors can bring together any number of fabulous, cinema-quality shows. But the fact remains that if media conglomerates continue to dominate mainstream American media, what we as audience members will see on our screens are shows that ultimately produce narratives that include vastly white, heterosexual characters in either comfortable, unrealistic suburban settings or overly exaggerated settings of urban decay. The narratives produced will privilege those who already are privileged in our culture and, with few exceptions, continue to oppress those who face oppression and resistance every day of their lives in reality. Problematized narratives taken from an unrealized American mythology will continue to be presented as real, and consumerism, violence, and an utter lack of global concern all will remain acceptable components of mainstream TV.

No matter the good intentions of individuals—viewers and producers of products alike—it is impossible right now to garner the kind

Conclusion

of audience numbers needed to sustain any show without the backing of large corporate systems. Fledgling webisodes, attempting to fight the good fight, are popping up in increasing volume and with increasing quality. Ironically, the best Web shows, however, end up either getting television "deals" with large companies and going mainstream or collecting advertising deals online, both avenues that end up touching the narrative ideology in some way.

There are also new series being bought by cable stations that are refreshing and surprising, shows such as Lena Dunham's HBO series, *Girls*, written for and produced by a "normal woman," dealing with the awkward, everyday issues women face in contemporary culture. There is also Mindy Kaling's *The Mindy Project*, which premiered on Fox in 2012, featuring Kaling as Mindy Lahiri, a South Asian American female lead who plays a single OB/GYN practitioner in a comedy about the life of a socially awkward but brilliant young woman. Both series have excelled in a medium that never has been kind to strong women. The problem in their cases, it seems, is not the shows themselves or their narrative ideologies, but the culture into which they have been released. Critics have jumped all over the women's non-perfect bodies, their "crossing of lines" with regard to sex scenes and sexual innuendo, and the general idea that shows about "normal" women must somehow be subversive or intentionally ridiculous. *Girls* continuously garners criticism for having "gone too far" or for "showing too much," criticism seemingly specifically saved for shows that show less-than-perfect female bodies, while shows featuring men or airbrushed, underweight female characters are spared such criticism.

Is there a solution to the problems I have outlined? Yes. But it is complicated. It will take time. And it may not be actually possible. But I am going to talk about it anyway, because I promised I would in my introduction. It is not enough to discuss the problems of our mediated culture; we need to offer solutions as well. Obviously the key to media awareness is education. We cannot have people able to challenge what they see as being portrayed as "normal" on television unless they realize it is not normal. Critical thinking skills, interrogations of the state of race, class, gender, sexuality, age, and (dis)ability in U.S. culture, and an understanding of what privilege means are basic concepts that need to

Conclusion

be addressed in general education. An educated audience is an audience able to say "no" to programs they find offensive, to say "what about...," and ask for different kinds of voices, and one that simply can choose to turn off programs they find insulting or harmful. But how we educate this giant, hypothetical "audience" is the issue. Who teaches? How do cultures learn? Who says "enough is enough" loud enough to free popular culture from the grasp of corporate domination and oppressive ideologies?

As the world develops, it seems the answer to "who teaches" is, ironically, media and technology. Schools and universities are concerned about getting more computers, bigger screens, and Internet access for their students. Content, it seems, is secondary. Inner-connectivity is a false ideal of some kind of public discourse. It mocks the "public sphere," Habermas' "Öffentlichkeit" ideal, a bourgeois public sphere that is rational-critical, disinterested debate among diverse peoples who, although occupying unequal positions in society, are able to function—in this sphere—as relative equals; "it is grounded in Enlightenment values of civility, rationality, neutrality, and autonomy"[9] or "rationality, equality, openness, democracy."[10] Access to mediated discussions and mediated fictions are not educational if they are not grounded in an education that promotes rational thought, independent thought, and subversive thought. Argument is not possible without some kind of equality of education about issues across races, genders, and classes. Yet, as a nation we continue to promote inequality, offering the spectacle of difference, the emphasis on the Other as inclusion of the Other in our fictional narratives, knowing full well the embarrassing inequality of our educational system. There is a void of difference in the hegemonic world of television that then spreads across various mediums of entertainment and information, unnoticed by a social system that never is taught to seek out and challenge the constructs of the ideologies that surround its education, work places, economy, or political leaders.

For a nation that so quickly grasped the "whatever it takes" mantra of a military presidency, we are indefensibly slow to grasp a "whatever it takes" mantra to support a unified social system of equality, justice, and true liberation. All one needs is a television to see the flaws of the United States. If the public could take back this ubiquitous medium and,

Conclusion

with an educated populace, use it as a forum to portray the diverse, complex, dynamic, and fascinating world of the real "audience" to whom our television currently plays, I do believe that not only could TV be used as an emancipatory tool for U.S. citizens, but it could be used as a way for the world to unite in a global system of positive symbiotic relationships that are within our grasp, a system that could benefit humanity as a whole. The simple television, dismissed and disused for decades, possesses the power to bring the world together.

Chapter Notes

Introduction

1. For more information, visit http://www.bls.gov/news.release/atus.nr0.html.
2. Show information: number 1: *American Idol*'s Wednesday show; number 2: *Dancing with the Stars*; number 3: *Dancing with the Stars* results show; number 4: *American Idol*'s Tuesday show; and number 5 (tie): *Dancing with the Stars*'s Tuesday show and *Glee*.
3. For more information, visit http://www.nielsen.com/us/en/insights/top10s/television.html.
4. For more information, visit http://www.csun.edu/science/health/docs/tv&health.html#tv_stats.
5. Those citizens with access to electricity and basic television, for example.
6. Jonathan Gray and Amanda D. Lotz, *Television Studies* (Cambridge: Polity, 2012), 2.
7. Slavoj Žižek, *Looking Awry: An Introduction to Lacan through Popular Culture* (Boston: MIT Press, 1992).
8. PBS, *America in Primetime*, episodes 1–4, first aired November 20, 2011, prod. The Documentary Group, dir. Lloyd Kramer, http://video.pbs.org/video/2167756796.
9. Ibid.
10. Roger D. Abrahams, "Some Varieties of Hero in America," *Journal of Folklore Institute* 3, no. 3 (1966): 341–62, 341.
11. D. Holt and C. Thompson, "Man-of-Action Heroes: The Pursuit of Heroic Masculinity in Everyday Consumption," *Journal of Consumer Research* 31, no. 2 (2004): 425–40, 429.
12. Ibid.
13. Ibid.
14. Ibid.
15. Harry Castleman and Walter J. Padrazik, *Watching TV: Six Decades of American Television*, 2d ed. (Syracuse: Syracuse University Press, 2003), 50.
16. Roger B. Rollin, "Beowulf to Batman: The Epic Hero and Pop Culture," *College English* 31, no. 5 (February 1970): 431–49, 432.
17. Jacob Zubler, master's student, Ball State University, December 2011.
18. *America in Primetime*, episode 1: "The Crusader."
19. Ibid.
20. Hal Hemmelstein, *Television Myth and the American Mind*, 2d ed. (Westport, CT: Praeger, 1994), 210.

Notes—Introduction

21. Ibid., 212.
22. Ibid.
23. Ibid., 215.
24. Ella Taylor, "From the Nelsons to the Huxtables: Genre and Family Imagery in American Network Television," *Qualitative Sociology* 12, no. 1 (Spring 1989): 13–28, 22.
25. Ibid., 16.
26. Kristin Lee, "The FCC and Media Democcracy [sic]," Women's Institute for Freedom of the Press, May 2003, accessed June 18, 2013 http://www.wifp.org/FCCandMediaDemocracy.html.
27. Ibid.
28. Though the "United States" and "America" are not precisely synonymous, I use them interchangeably in the text for style reasons.
29. M. Keith Booker, *Superpower: Heroes, Ghosts, and the Paranormal in American Culture* (Lincoln: University of Nebraska Press, 2010), 172.
30. See http://www.freepress.net/ownership/chart/main for specific information on the "big 6" media conglomerates and other issues of monopoly and the media as well as the 2012 article posted online at BusinessInsider.com: http://www.businessinsider.com/these-6-corporations-control-90-of-the-media-in-america-2012-6.
31. Joe Biden social networking committee, e-mail message to author, August 27, 2012.
32. For further discussion of independent versus corporate media, see the film *Independent Media in a Time of War,* featuring Amy Goodman.
33. Douglas Kellner, "TV, Ideology, and Emancipatory Popular Culture," *Socialist Review* 45 (May–June 1979): 386–421, 405.
34. Ibid.
35. Jean Baudrillard, *Simulacra et Simulation,* trans. Sheila Faria Glaser (Ann Arbor: University of Michigan Press, 1994), 22.
36. Raman Selden and Peter Widdowson, *A Reader's Guide to Contemporary Literary Theory,* 3d ed. (Lexington: University Press of Kentucky, 1993), 209.
37. There is no precise definition of "modernism" or "postmodernism" on which all theorists agree. My assertion that the lack of metanarratives is central postmodern theory is grounded in my belief of a clear split between modernism and postmodernism in timeframe, theoretical ideologies, and artistic formats. This is not a globally accepted or hegemonic argument in what has become a more and more convoluted realm of theoretical debate.
38. Fredric Jameson, *Postmodernism; Or, the Cultural Logic of Late Capitalism* (London: Verso, 1991), 49.
39. Jean-François Lyotard, *The Postmodern Condition* (Manchester: Manchester University Press, 1984).
40. Adam Roberts, *Fredric Jameson* (New York: Routledge, 2000), 115–16.
41. Slavoj Žižek, "Jameson as a Theorist of Revolutionary Philately," in *Fredric Jameson: A Critical Reader,* ed. Sean Homer and Douglas Kellner (New York: Palgrave Macmillan, 2004), 112. Precisely, the absence of any common language between them. Jameson says, "to put it briefly, the East wishes to talk in terms of power and oppression; the West in terms of culture and commodification" (*Fredric Jameson: A Critical Reader*, 112).

Notes—Chapter 1

42. Ibid., 112–13.
43. Some critics argue that the strength of the "fundamentalist" voice of various groups suggests a re-emergence of actual metanarratives, perhaps ushering in a time we must consider as separate from what many call "postmodernism."
44. Bill Osgerby, "Sleazy Rider: Exploitation, 'Otherness,' and Transgression in the 1960s Biker Movie," *Journal of Popular Film and Television* (Autumn 2003): 107.

Chapter 1

1. The following discussion of *Dexter* focuses specifically on the television show and not on Jeff Lindsay's books. Though a good deal of similarities exist between the two, a full discussion of the adaptation from book to show is needed. Many of the issues I address as I discuss the show are handled quite differently in the books. Even the character of Dexter is different in many ways from the original texts, thus I am treating the show as a different entity entirely for the purposes of this article.
2. Michel Foucault, *The History of Sexuality: Volume 1: An Introduction* (New York: Vintage, 1978; repr. 1990), 93.
3. Adam Roberts, *Fredric Jameson* (New York: Routledge, 2000), 19.
4. Ibid., 16.
5. Ibid., 36.
6. Fredric Jameson, *The Geopolitical Aesthetic* (Bloomington: University of Indiana Press, 1992), 2.
7. Chris Horrocks and Zoran Jevtic, *Introducing Baudrillard* (Cambridge: Icon, 1999), 61.
8. Michel Foucault, *Discipline and Punish: The Birth of the Prison*, trans. Alan Sheridan (London: Allen Lane, 1977), 136.
9. Ibid.
10. Ibid., 141.
11. Michele Byers, "Neoliberal *Dexter*?" in *Reading Dexter*, ed. Douglas L. Howard (London: I.B. Tauris, 2010), 146.
12. Ibid., 155.
13. There are, of course, those who take offense to both the violence and the tone of the show. The Parents Television Council, in particular, was extremely vocal in their concern when the show was aired on CBS.
14. David Schmid, "The Devil You Know: *Dexter* and the 'Goodness' of American Serial Killing," in *Dexter: Investigating Cutting Edge Television*, ed. Douglas L. Howard (London, England: I.B. Tauris, 2010), 133.
15. Michele Byers argues that the figures of the secondary serial killers in the series, such as Lila, Miguel Prado, and the Trinity Killer, serve as Dexter's foils in that they are truly Other, while he is not ("Neoliberal *Dexter*?" 153). My use of the term "foil" for the purpose of this chapter, however, is intended to represent that which is considered civilized or "normal" within the realm of law.
16. Philip L. Simpson, *Psycho Paths: Tracking the Serial Killer Through Contemporary American Film and Fiction* (Carbondale: Southern Illinois University Press, 2000), 9.
17. Ruth Helyer, "Parodied to Death: The Postmodern Gothic of *American Psycho*," *Modern Fiction Studies* 46, no. 3 (Fall 2000): 726.

18. My use of the masculine pronoun throughout this chapter is representative of the overwhelming male characters in such fictions. Female figures are a part of the narrative, but the issue of the female anti-hero deserves significantly more time, space, and consideration than can be offered within the scope of these pages.
19. Byers, "Neoliberal *Dexter*?" 149.
20. Season 4, episode 1.
21. Ross Chambers, "The Unexamined," in *Whiteness: A Critical Reader*, ed. Mike Hill (New York: New York University Press, 1997), 197.
22. Nicola Rehling, "Everyman and No Man: White, Heterosexual Masculinity in Contemporary Serial Killer Movies," *Jump Cut: A Review of Contemporary Media* 49 (Spring 2007), http://www.ejumpcut.org/archive/jc49.2007/Rehling/text.html.

Chapter 2

1. Bill Osgerby, "Sleazy Rider: Exploitation, 'Otherness,' and Transgression in the 1960s Biker Movie," *Journal of Popular Film and Television* (Autumn 2003): 102.
2. Ibid.
3. Ibid., 107.
4. James F. Quinn and Craig J. Forsyth, "Leathers and Rolexs: The Symbolism and Values of the Motorcycle Club," *Deviant Behavior* 30, no. 3 (2009): 235–65.
5. In a *Rolling Stone* article, Charlie Hunnam, who plays Jax, was quoted as saying, "So much television is geared toward women now.... So I'm doing my best to explore the darkest sides of society with some real shitkickin' boys." M.M., "The Manliest of Man Shows," *Rolling Stone,* September 17, 2009, issue 1087, p. 71.
6. Lilia Melani, "The Other," CUNY Brooklyn Department of English webpage, last modified February 5, 2009, accessed March 6, 2013, http://academic.brooklyn.cuny.edu/english/melani/cs6/other.html.
7. Matt Goldberg, "Ron Perlman Interview—*Sons of Anarchy*," Colliderwww, August 31, 2008, http://collider.com/entertainment/interviews/article.asp?aid=9017&tcid=1.
8. Quinn and Forsyth, 244.
9. Ibid.
10. Christopher E. Forth, *Masculinity in the Modern West: Gender, Civilization, and the Body* (Houndmills: Palgrave Macmillan, 2008), 114.
11. Ibid., 115.
12. Gemma's rape is discussed in detail in Chapter 5.
13. Racketeer Influenced and Corrupt Organizations Act, commonly referred to as the RICO Act or simply RICO, is a U.S. federal law that provides for extended criminal penalties and a civil cause of action for acts performed as part of an ongoing criminal organization.

Chapter 3

1. Meenakshi Gigi Durham and Douglas Kellner, eds., *Media and Cultural Studies: Keyworks* (Malden, MA: Blackwell, 2001), xiv.
2. Ibid., xxxv.
3. Ibid., xxix.

Notes—Chapters 4, 5

4. Rob Latham, *Consuming Youth: Vampires, Cyborgs, and the Culture of Consumption* (Chicago: University of Chicago Press, 2002), 11.
5. Dick Hebdige, "Subculture and Style," in *The Cultural Studies Reader*, 3d ed., ed. Simon During (London: Routledge, 2007), 438.
6. Julia Kristeva, *Powers of Horror: An Essay on Abjection*, trans. Leon S. Roudiez (New York: Columbia University Press, 1982), 2–3.
7. Hebridge, "Subculture and Style," 439.
8. John Hartley, *Television Truths* (Malden, MA: Blackwell, 2008), 76.
9. Lyn Gorman and David Mclean, *Media and Society into the 21st Century: A Historical Introduction*, 2d ed. (West Sussex: Wiley Blackwell, 2007), 160–61.
10. Ibid.
11. More information is available at http://www.nypost.com/p/entertainment/tv/item_WKvyfOFvvONjfWj5S1xa8N#ixzz20oGjjMtr.
12. Such degradation as a means of empowerment is problematic, and I address this issue in detail in Chapter 6.
13. More information is available at http://www.nypost.com/p/entertainment/tv/item_WKvyfOFvvONjfWj5S1xa8N#ixzz20tpmSRvI.
14. Ibid.
15. Alan Ball, quoted in "*True Blood* Sinks Its Teeth into Religion and Politics," by Bill Keveney, *Huffington Post*, June 9, 2012, accessed November 11, 2012, http://www.huffingtonpost.com/2012/06/09/true-blood-religion-politics_n_1582512.html.

Chapter 4

1. "*Breaking Bad* Creator Vince Gilligan: The Man Who Turned Walter White from Mr. Chips into Scarface: How a Joke About a Meth Lab Grew Into One of the Best TV Dramas of All Time," *The Guardian*, May 18, 2012, 16, "The Guide" section.
2. Peggy McIntosh, "White Privilege and Male Privilege: A Personal Account of Coming to See Correspondences through Work in Women's Studies," in *Privilege: A Reader*, 2d ed., ed. Michael S. Kimmel and Abby L. Ferber (Boulder: Westview Press, 2009), 13–26, 14.
3. Scott Meslow, "The Big Secret of *Breaking Bad*: Walter White Was Always a Bad Guy," *The Atlantic*, August 31, 2012, http://www.theatlantic.com/entertainment/archive/2012/08/the-big-secret-of-breaking-bad-walter-white-was-always-a-bad-guy/261833/.

Chapter 5

1. Nelson Johnson, *Boardwalk Empire: The Birth, High Times, and Corruption of Atlantic City* (Medford, NJ: Plexus, 2010), xii.
2. Ibid.
3. Fredric Jameson, *Postmodernism; Or, The Cultural Logic of Late Capitalism* (London: Verso, 1991).
4. Hila Shachar, "Seeking Substance in Historical Costume Films," *Notes on Metamodernism*, October 24, 2011, http://www.metamodernism.com/2011/10/24/seeking-substance-in-historical-costume-films/.
5. See Linda Hutcheon, *The Politics of Postmodernism* (New Accents) (Lon-

Notes—Chapter 6

don: Routledge, 1989), and *A Poetics of Postmodernism: History, Theory, Fiction* (New York: Routledge, 1988).

6. Dylan Trigg, *The Aesthetics of Decay: Nothingness, Nostalgia, and the Absence of Reason* (New York: Peter Lang, 2006), xxi.

7. Daniel Orkent, *Last Call: The Rise and Fall of Prohibition* (New York: Simon & Schuster, 2010), 238–39.

8. Angela Watercutter, "TV Fact-Checkers: Ginning Up *Boardwalk Empire*'s Boozy Gangster Paradise," Underwire: A Cybernetic Finger on the Pulse of Pop Culture, *Wired*, September 14, 2012, accessed February 18, 2013, http://www.wired.com/underwire/2012/09/tv-fact-checkers-boardwalk-empire/all/.

9. Ibid.

Chapter 6

1. I will refer to and discuss other female characters from these various shows, but the women listed above are my primary focus for this chapter.

2. Obviously, this differs for different segments of society and even among every individual. But, as a collective, generalized look at what is popularized by television, I hope to garner an idea of what the dominant pulse of feminist thought is that runs through U.S. mainstream culture.

3. J. Judith Halberstam, *Female Masculinity* (Durham: Duke University Press, 1998).

4. bell hooks, *Teaching Community: A Pedagogy of Hope* (New York: Routledge, 2003), 115.

5. M.M, "The Manliest of Man Shows," *Rolling Stone,* September 17, 2009, issue 1087, p. 71.

6. Alyssa Rosenberg, "Week of Anarchy: Consider Gemma," ThinkProgress.org, February 21, 2012, http://thinkprogress.org/alyssa/2012/02/21/429257/week-of-anarchy-consider-gemma/?mobile=nc.

7. Sarah Projansky, *Watching Rape: Film and Television in Postfeminist Culture* (New York: New York University Press, 2001), 21.

8. Naomi Klein, *Shock Doctrine: The Rise of Disaster Capitalism* (New York: Picador, 2007).

9. Marion Johnson, "*Mad Men*, Megan Draper, and the Skyler White Effect," Huff Post TV, TheHuffingtonPost.com, posted April 3, 2013, accessed April 24, 2013, http://www.huffingtonpost.com/marion-johnson/mad-men-feminism_b_3005489.html.

10. Alyssa Rosenberg, "Stop Hating the Wives: In Praise of *Breaking Bad*'s Skyler White," Slate.com, July 16, 2012, http://www.slate.com/blogs/xx_factor/2012/07/16/skyler_white_and_breaking_bad_stop_hating_tv_wives.html.

11. Stephen Silver, "Essay: 'Skyler Is Such a Bitch!,' And Other Unfair *Breaking Bad* Observations," Technologytell.com, July 13, 2012, http://www.technologytell.com/entertainment/3659/essay-skyler-is-such-a-bitch-and-other-unfair-breaking-bad-observations/.

12. Johnson, "*Mad Men*, Megan Draper, and the Skyler White Effect."

13. Rosenberg, "Stop Hating the Wives."

14. Ibid.

Conclusion

1. Laura Mulvey, "Visual Pleasure and Narrative Cinema," *Screen* 16, no. 3 (1975): 6–18.

2. Jean Baudrillard, *Simulacrum et Simulacra*, trans. Sheila Faria Glaser (Ann Arbor: University of Michigan Press, 1994).

3. Douglas M. Kellner and Meenakshi Gigi Durham, "Adventures in Media and Cultural Studies," in *Media and Cultural Studies: Keyworks*, rev. ed., ed. Douglas M. Kellner and Meenakshi Gigi Durham (Malden, MA: Blackwell, 2006), xxxii.

4. Victoria J. Rideout, Ulla G. Foehr, and Donald F. Roberts, *Generation M: Media in the Lives of 8- to 18-Year-Olds* (Menlo Park, CA: Henry J. Kaiser Family Foundation, 2010), 1–85, 3.

5. Victoria Rideout and Elizabeth Hamel, *The Media Family: Electronic Media in the Lives of Infants, Toddlers, Preschoolers and Their Parents* (Menlo Park, CA: Henry J. Kaiser Family Foundation, 2010), 1–35, 7.

6. Jason Mittell, *Television and American Culture* (New York: Oxford University Press, 2010), 2.

7. Quote attributed to Nabil Shaath, who was Palestinian foreign minister at the time when Bush delivered this speech during a meeting with a Palestinian delegation during the Israeli-Palestinian summit at the Egyptian resort of Sharm el-Sheikh, four months after the U.S.-led invasion of Iraq in 2003.

8. Interestingly, but for reasons I am unable to discover, in the second season this voiceover is modified to say, "People the government considers irrelevant" from "Crimes the government considered irrelevant."

9. Trish Roberts-Miller, "Habermas' Rational-Critical Sphere and the Problem of Criteria," in *The Role of Rhetoric in an Anti-Foundational World,* ed. Michael Bernard-Donals and Richard Glejzer (New Haven: Yale University Press, 1998), 170–194, 18.

10. Lloyd Kramer, "Habermas, History, and Critical Theory," in *Habermas and the Public Sphere*, ed. Craig Calhoun (Cambridge: MIT Press, 1992), 251.

Bibliography

Abrahams, Roger D. "Some Varieties of Hero in America." *Journal of Folklore Institute* 3, no. 3 (1966): 341–62.
Alaimo, Stacy, and Susan Heckman, eds. *Material Feminisms*. Bloomington: Indiana University Press, 2008.
Arnett, Robert. "Eighties Noir: The Dissenting Voice in Reagan's America." *Journal of Popular Film and Television* 34, 3 (2007): 123.
Ball, Alan. Quoted in "'True Blood' Sinks Its Teeth into Religion and Politics," by Bill Keveney, *Huffington Post*, June 9, 2012, accessed November 11, 2012, http://www.huffingtonpost.com/2012/06/09/true-blood-religion-politics_n_1582512.html.
Baudrillard, Jean. *Simulacrum et Simulacra*. Translated by Sheila Faria Glaser. Ann Arbor: University of Michigan Press, 1994.
Best, Steven, and Douglas Kellner. *Postmodern Theory: Critical Interrogations*. New York: Guildford Press, 1991.
Boddy, William. *Fifties Television: The Industry and Its Critics*. Urbana: University of Illinois Press, 1990.
Booker, M. Keith. *Superpower: Heroes, Ghosts, and the Paranormal in American Culture*. Lincoln: University of Nebraska Press, 2010.
Butler, Judith. *Bodies That Matter: On the Discursive Limits of "Sex."* New York: Routledge, 1993.
Byers, Michele. "Neoliberal *Dexter*?" In *Reading Dexter*, edited by D. Howard. London: I.B. Tauris, 2010. 143–56.
Byers, Thomas B. "Terminating the Postmodern: Masculinity and Pomophobia." *Modern Fiction Studies* 41, 1 (1995): 5–33.
Calhoun, Craig, ed. *Habermas and the Public Sphere*. Cambridge: MIT Press, 1992.
Carroll, Hamilton. "Vampire Capitalism: Globalization, Race, and the Postnational Body in *Blade*." *Genre* XXXVIII (Winter 2005): 371.
Castleman, Harry, and Walter J. Padrazik. *Watching TV: Six Decades of American Television*, 2d ed. Syracuse: Syracuse University Press, 2003.
Chai, Sun-Ki. *Choosing an Identity: A General Model of Preference and Belief Formation*. Ann Arbor: University of Michigan Press, 2001.
Chambers, Ross. "The Unexamined." In *Whiteness: A Critical Reader*, edited by Mike Hill. New York: New York University Press, 1997.
Donovan, Josephine. *Feminist Theory: Intellectual Traditions*, 4th ed. New York: Continuum, 2012.
Durham, Meenakshi Gigi, and Douglas Kellner, eds. *Media and Cultural Studies: Keyworks*. Malden, MA: Blackwell, 2001.

Bibliography

Eagleton, Terry. *Why Marx Was Right*. New Haven: Yale University Press, 2011.
Forth, Christopher E. *Masculinity in the Modern West: Gender, Civilization, and the Body*. Houndmills: Palgrave Macmillan, 2008.
Foucault, Michel. *Discipline and Punish: The Birth of the Prison*. Translated by Alan Sheridan. London: Allen Lane, 1977.
_____. *The History of Sexuality: Volume 1: An Introduction*. New York: Vintage, 1978; repr. 1990.
Gitlin, Todd. "Prime Time Ideology: The Hegemonic Process in Television Entertainment." *Social Problems*, 26, no. 3 (February 1979): 251.
Goldberg, Matt. "Ron Perlman Interview—SONS OF ANARCHY." Colliderwww, August 31, 2008, http://collider.com/entertainment/interviews/article.asp?aid=9017&tcid=1.
Gorman, Lyn, and David Mclean. *Media and Society into the 21st Century: A Historical Introduction*, 2d ed. West Sussex: Wiley Blackwell, 2007.
Gray, Jonathan, and Amanda D. Lotz. *Television Studies*. Cambridge: Polity, 2012.
Halberstam, Judith. *Female Masculinity*. Durham: Duke University Press, 1998.
Hantke, Steffen. "Bush's America and the Return of Cold War Science Fiction: Alien Invasion in Invasion, Threshold, and Surface." *Journal of Popular Film and Television* 38, no. 3 (2010): 143.
Hartley, John. *Television Truths*. Malden, MA: Blackwell, 2008.
Harvey, David. *The Enigma of Capital and the Crisis of Capitalism*. Oxford: Oxford University Press, 2010.
Hebdige, Dick. "Subculture and Style." In *The Cultural Studies Reader*, 3d ed., edited by Simon During. London: Routledge, 2007. 429.
Helyer, Ruth. "Parodied to Death: The Postmodern Gothic of *American Psycho*." *Modern Fiction Studies* 46, no. 3 (Fall 2000): 726.
Hemmelstein, Hal. *Television Myth and the American Mind*, 2d ed. Westport, CT: Praeger, 1994.
Hill, Mike, ed. *Whiteness: A Critical Reader*. New York: New York University Press, 1997.
Hipsky, Martin. "Post-Cold War Paranoia in The Corrections and The Sopranos." *Postmodern Culture* 16, 2 (2006): 1–45. http://muse.jhu.edu/journals/postmodern_culture/v016/16.2hipsky.html.
Holt, Douglas B., and Craig J. Thompson. "Man-of-Action Heroes: The Pursuit of Heroic Masculinity in Everyday Consumption." *Journal of Consumer Research* 31, no. 2 (2004): 425–40.
hooks, bell. *Teaching Community: A Pedagogy of Hope*. New York: Routledge, 2003.
Horkheimer, Max, and Theodor W. Adorno. *Dialectic of Enlightenment: Philosophical Fragments*. Edited by Gunzelin Schmid Noerr. Translated by Edmund Jephcott. Stanford: Stanford University Press, 2002.
Horrocks, Chris, and Zoran Jevtic. *Introducing Baudrillard*. Cambridge: Icon, 1999.
Hutcheon, Linda. *A Poetics of Postmodernism: History, Theory, Fiction*. New York: Routledge, 1988.
_____. *The Politics of Postmodernism (New Accents)*. London: Routledge, 1989.
Hyatt, Wesley. *Emmy Award Winning Nighttime Television Shows 1948–2004*. Jefferson, NC: McFarland, 2006.
Jackson, Kevin, and James Bell. "The Vampire Next Door." *Sight and Sound* 19, no. 11 (2009): 40.

Bibliography

Jameson, Fredric. *The Geopolitical Aesthetic.* Bloomington: University of Indiana Press, 1992.

———. *Postmodernism; Or, the Cultural Logic of Late Capitalism.* London: Verso, 1991.

Johnson, Marion. "*Mad Men*, Megan Draper, and the Skyler White Effect." Huff Post TV, TheHuffingtonPost.com, posted April 3, 2013, accessed April 24, 2013, http://www.huffingtonpost.com/marion-johnson/mad-men-feminism_b_3005489.html.

Johnson, Nelson. *Boardwalk Empire: The Birth, High Times, and Corruption of Atlantic City.* Medford, NJ: Plexus, 2010.

Jones, Jeffrey P., and Geoffrey Baym. "A Dialogue on Satire News and the Crisis of Truth in Postmodern Political Television." *Journal of Communication Inquiry* 34, 3 (2010): 278.

Kellner, Douglas. *Cinema Wars: Hollywood Film and Politics in the Bush-Cheney Era.* Chichester: Wiley-Blackwell, 2010.

———. "TV, Ideology, and Emancipatory Popular Culture." *Socialist Review* 45 (May-June 1979): 386.

———, and Sean Homer, eds. *Fredric Jameson: A Critical Reader.* New York: Palgrave Macmillan, 2004.

Keveny, Bill. "'True Blood' Sinks Its Teeth into Religion and Politics." *The Huffington Post*, November 11, 2012, http://www.huffingtonpost.com/2012/06/09/true-blood-religion.

Kimmel, Michael S., and Abby L. Ferber, eds. *Privilege: A Reader,* 2d ed. Boulder: Westview Press, 2009.

Klein, Naomi. *Shock Doctrine: The Rise of Disaster Capitalism.* New York: Picador, 2007.

Kramer, Lloyd. "Habermas, History, and Critical Theory." In *Habermas and the Public Sphere*, ed. Craig Calhoun. Cambridge: MIT Press. 236.

Kristeva, Julia. *Powers of Horror: An Essay on Abjection.* Translated by Leon S. Roudiez. New York: Columbia University Press, 1982.

Kroes, Rob. "Advertising: The Commodification of American Icons of Freedom." In *Here, There, and Everywhere: The Foreign Politics of American Popular Culture*, edited by Reinhold Wagnleitner and Elaine Tyler May. Hanover: University Press of New England, 2000.

Latham, Rob. *Consuming Youth: Vampires, Cyborgs, and the Culture of Consumption.* Chicago: University of Chicago Press, 2002.

Lee, Kristin. "The FCC and Media Democcracy [sic]." Women's Institute for Freedom of the Press, May 2003, accessed June 18, 2013, http://www.wifp.org/FCCandMediaDemocracy.html.

Lyotard, Jean-François. *The Postmodern Condition.* Manchester: Manchester University Press, 1984.

MacInnes, Paul. "*Breaking Bad* Creator Vince Gilligan: The Man Who Turned Walter White from Mr Chips into Scarface: How a Joke About a Meth Lab Grew into One of the Best TV Dramas of All Time." *The Guardian*, May 18, 2012, "The Guide" section, 16.

McIntosh, Peggy. "White Privilege and Male Privilege: A Personal Account of Coming to See Correspondences through Work in Women's Studies." In *Privilege: A Reader,* 2d ed., edited by Michael S. Kimmel and Abby L. Ferber. Boulder: Westview Press, 2009.

Bibliography

Melani, Lilia. "The Other." CUNY Brooklyn Department of English webpage, last modified February 5, 2009, accessed March 6, 2013, http://academic.brooklyn.cuny.edu/english/melani/cs6/other.html.

Meslow, Scott. "The Big Secret of *Breaking Bad*: Walter White Was Always a Bad Guy." *The Atlantic,* August 31, 2012, http://www.theatlantic.com/entertainment/archive/2012/08/the-big-secret-of-breaking-bad-walter-white-was-always-a-bad-guy/261833/.

Mittell, Jason. *Television and American Culture.* Oxford: Oxford University Press, 2010.

M.M. "The Manliest of Man Shows." *Rolling Stone,* September 17, 2009, issue 1087.

Newitz, Annalee. *Pretend We're Dead: Capitalist Monsters in American Pop Culture.* Durham: Duke University Press, 2006.

Ollman, Bertell. *Alienation: Marx's Conception of Man in Capitalist Society.* Cambridge: Cambridge University Press, 1971.

Orkent, Daniel. *Last Call: The Rise and Fall of Prohibition.* New York: Simon & Schuster, 2010.

Osgerby, Bill. "Sleazy Riders: Exploitation, 'Otherness' and Transgression in the 1960s Biker Movie." *Journal of Popular Film and Television* (Autumn 2003): 98–108.

Parks, Rita. *The Western Hero in Film and Television: Mass Media Mythology.* Ann Arbor: University of Michigan Research Press, 1982.

PBS. *America in Primetime,* episodes 1–4. First aired November 20, 2011. Produced by The Documentary Group. Directed by Lloyd Kramer. http://video.pbs.org/video/2167756796.

Phillips, Lily. "Blue Jeans, Black Leather Jackets, and a Sneer: The Iconography of the 1950s Biker and Its Translation Abroad." *International Journal of Motorcycle Studies* 1 no. 1 (March 2005). http://ijms.nova.edu/March2005/IJMS_ArtclPhilips0305.html.

Porter, Lynnette. *Tarnished Heroes, Charming Villains, and Modern Monsters: Science Fiction and Shades of Gray on 21st Century Television.* Jefferson, NC: McFarland, 2010.

Projansky, Sarah. *Watching Rape: Film and Television in Postfeminist Culture.* New York: New York University Press, 2001.

Quinn, James F., and Craig J. Forsyth. "Leathers and Rolexs: The Symbolism and Values of the Motorcycle Club." *Deviant Behavior* 30, no. 3 (2009): 235–65.

Rehling, Nicola. "Everyman and No Man: White, Heterosexual Masculinity in Contemporary Serial Killer Movies." *Jump Cut: A Review of Contemporary Media* 49 (Spring 2007), http://www.ejumpcut.org/archive/jc49.2007/Rehling/text.html.

Roberts, Adam. *Fredric Jameson.* New York: Routledge, 2000.

Roberts-Miller, Trish. "Habermas' Rational-Critical Sphere and The Problem of Criteria." In *The Role of Rhetoric in an Anti-Foundational World,* ed. Michael Bernard-Donals and Richard Glejzer. New Haven: Yale University Press, 1998. 170.

Rollin, Roger B. "Beowulf to Batman: The Epic Hero and Pop Culture." *College English* 31, no. 5 (February 1970): 431–49.

Rosenberg, Alyssa. "Stop Hating the Wives: In Praise of *Breaking Bad*'s Skyler White."

Bibliography

Slate.com, July 16, 2012, http://www.slate.com/blogs/xx_factor/2012/07/16/skyler_white_and_breaking_bad_stop_hating_tv_wives.html.

———. "Week of Anarchy: Consider Gemma." ThinkProgress.org, February 21, 2012, http://thinkprogress.org/alyssa/2012/02/21/429257/week-of-anarchy-consider-gemma/?mobile=nc.

Schilling, Chris. *The Body and Social Theory*, 3d ed. Los Angeles: Sage, 2012.

Schmid, David. "The Devil You Know: *Dexter* and the 'Goodness' of American Serial Killing." In *Dexter: Investigating Cutting Edge Television*, edited by Douglas L. Howard. London: I. B. Tauris, 2010.

Schmitt, Richard. *Alienation and Freedom*. Boulder: Westview Press, 2003.

Selden, Raman, and Peter Widdowson. *A Reader's Guide to Contemporary Literary Theory*, 3d ed. Lexington: University Press of Kentucky, 1993.

Shachar, Hila. "Seeking Substance in Historical Costume Films." *Notes on Metamodernism*, October 24, 2011, http://www.metamodernism.com/2011/10/24/seeking-substance-in-historical-costume-films/.

Silver, Stephen. "Essay: 'Skyler Is Such a Bitch!,' And Other Unfair *Breaking Bad* Observations." Technologytell.com, July 13, 2012, http://www.technologytell.com/entertainment/3659/essay-skyler-is-such-a-bitch-and-other-unfair-breaking-bad-observations/.

Simpson, Philip L. *Psycho Paths: Tracking the Serial Killer Through Contemporary American Film and Fiction*. Carbondale: Southern Illinois University Press, 2000.

Swann, William B. "The Self and Identity Negotiation." *Interaction Studies* 6, 1 (2005): 69–83.

Taylor, Ella. "From the Nelsons to the Huxtables: Genre and Family Imagery in American Network Television." *Qualitative Sociology* 12, no. 1 (Spring 1989): 13–28.

Thompson, Graham. *American Culture in the 1980s*. Edinburgh: Edinburgh University Press, 2007.

Tietchen, Todd F. "Samples and Copycats: The Cultural Implications of the Postmodern Slasher in Contemporary American Film." *Journal of Popular Film and Television* 26, no. 3 (Fall 1998): 98–107.

Treat, Shaun. "How America Learned to Stop Worrying and Cynically ENJOY! The Post-9/11 Superhero Zeitgeist." *Communication and Critical/Cultural Studies* 6, no. 1 (March 2009): 103.

Trigg, Dylan. *The Aesthetics of Decay: Nothingness, Nostalgia, and the Absence of Reason*. New York: Peter Lang, 2006.

Watercutter, Angela. "TV Fact-Checkers: Ginning Up *Boardwalk Empire*'s Boozy Gangster Paradise." Underwire: A Cybernetic Finger on the Pulse of Pop Culture, *Wired*, September 14, 2012, accessed February 18, 2013, http://www.wired.com/underwire/2012/09/tv-fact-checkers-boardwalk-empire/all/.

Žižek, Slavoj. "Jameson as a Theorist of Revolutionary Philately." In *Fredric Jameson: A Critical Reader*, edited by Sean Homer and Douglas Kellner. New York: Palgrave Macmillan, 2004.

———. *Looking Awry: An Introduction to Jacques Lacan through Popular Culture*. Boston: MIT Press, 1992.

Index

Abu Ghraib 9
Adorno, Theodor W. 1-2, 36-37, 71, 184
Afghanistan 163
alcohol 116, 122
America 1, 5-7, 9-17, 19-22, 24, 26-29, 38, 41-43, 48-49, 51-55, 63, 70-73, 78, 83, 86-87, 90, 93-94, 99, 103, 107, 109-110, 113, 115-116, 137, 157, 159, 161-164, 171-172
anti-hero 2, 7, 13, 16, 19, 20-21, 27, 29, 30, 33-34, 42, 55, 56, 69, 71, 75, 86, 92, 94, 119, 123, 125, 147, 148, 151, 163, 167

Baudrillard, Jean 23-24, 35-37, 39, 114, 159
The Big Six 1, 17
Boardwalk Empire 30, 109, 111-115, 117, 119, 121, 123, 125, 150, 154
Breaking Bad 20, 29-30, 91-97, 99-101, 103, 105, 107-108, 125, 147-148
Bush, George W. 17, 41, 143, 161-164

Capitalism 23, 24, 26, 29-30, 35, 38, 53, 55-56, 71-73, 77, 83, 109-110, 113, 140
Compton, Bill 24, 79-82, 87-88, 90, 92, 144-146, 164
cowboy 10-13, 17-20, 162

Darmody, Jimmy 117-118, 120, 123-124, 153
democracy 1, 22, 52, 73, 87
deregulation 17
Dexter 2, 27, 30, 33, 37, 40-42, 48, 49, 52, 58, 73, 120, 125, 127, 164
drama 2-3, 12, 14-19, 22, 27, 30, 50, 70-71, 75, 91, 111-112, 127, 148, 163, 165, 169
drugs 28, 54, 93, 99, 103, 105, 107, 135

emancipation 22-23, 30-31, 170, 174
exploitation 3, 7, 27, 30, 53, 108

faux rogue 2, 5, 24-26, 30, 33, 52, 60-61, 69, 71, 82, 92, 108, 110, 124-126, 131, 148, 150, 164-166, 169
femininity 50, 85, 89, 121, 126-128, 131, 139, 145-146
feminism 30, 121, 125-126, 137, 150, 156
Foucault, Michel 34-35, 38-40
The Frankfurt School 2, 71

gang 20, 24, 27-28, 53-57, 61, 63, 109-113, 123, 134, 137, 151, 153, 155
Guantanamo Bay 9, 162

Habermas, Jurgen 173
Harris, Charlaine 28, 70, 84
hero 2-3, 7-21, 24-30, 33-34, 40-42, 44, 52, 56, 59-60, 62, 69, 74-75, 79, 82, 86, 88, 90, 92, 94, 105, 108, 119, 123, 127, 146-147, 149, 161, 163-168
heteronormative 9, 24, 59, 85, 127, 131, 146, 162

ideology 1, 3, 5, 7, 9-10, 12, 14-16, 22-23, 25, 27, 29-30, 34-38, 42, 44, 47, 52, 54-56, 65, 69, 71, 73-75, 83-84, 86, 114, 126, 131, 153, 157-160, 162, 167, 172
Iraq War 163

Jameson, Fredric 23, 25-26, 30, 35-37, 114

Index

Knowles, Tara 60–62, 64, 66–69, 125, 131–139, 148

Late Capitalism 23, 26, 29–30, 73, 77, 83, 113
LGBTQ 21, 79, 84–86, 129, 159
Lyotard, Jean-François 24–26

Marx, Karl 23–24, 26, 35–37, 76–77, 79
masculinity 3, 9–10, 12, 14, 24–25, 41–42, 47–49, 52, 54, 59, 62–65, 69, 82, 108, 126–129, 131–132, 134, 136, 139, 143–145, 147, 154, 162
metanarratives 23–27, 34, 52, 73, 176–177
Morgan, Debra 44, 49–50, 125, 127–131, 134
Morgan, Dexter 2, 8, 13, 20–21, 24, 27, 30, 33–34, 40–52, 92–93, 127–131, 162
Morgan, Harry 41, 44–45, 48; Harry's Code 44, 45, 46
Morrow, Clay 56–60, 62, 65–68, 135–139
Morrow, Gemma Teller 56, 61, 64–66, 68–69, 125, 134–139, 148
motorcycle 27–28, 54, 56, 58–59, 62–63, 109, 133
murder 19, 39–47, 56, 61, 64, 78, 86, 96, 107–108, 130, 135, 139, 155, 163, 165, 171

narrative 1–3, 7, 9–12, 14, 17, 20–21, 23–28, 34, 36–37, 41–44, 49–52, 54–55, 59, 72–75, 77, 82–83, 86–88, 96, 104, 120–121, 123, 126, 131, 137–138, 131, 149–151, 157, 159, 163–164, 166–167, 171–173
normalization 55, 69, 86, 115, 125
Northman, Eric 78–82, 87–88, 90, 92, 146, 164
nostalgia 30, 113–115

Obama, Barack 164
Oppressed 30, 48, 117, 160, 162
Other 26, 28, 40, 43, 45–46, 51, 55–56, 65, 68–69, 71, 85–86, 103, 129, 165, 173

patriarchy 10, 21, 40–41, 44–45, 50, 52, 55, 58–59, 69, 88, 125–126, 131, 150

Pinkman, Jesse 94–99, 101, 103–107
postmodern 22–27, 30, 36, 43, 71–72, 113
Prohibition 30, 109, 111, 116, 118, 122, 151–152

Reagan, Ronald 17

SAMCRO 58, 62, 65–69, 131–137
serial killer 24, 27, 30, 33, 40–44, 46, 48, 51, 155
Sons of Anarchy 2, 20, 27–30, 53–59, 62–63, 73, 109, 125, 131, 134, 136, 138, 148
Stackhouse, Sookie 70, 79–80, 82, 84–85, 90, 120, 125, 139–146

television 1–3, 5–17, 20–23, 25–27, 29–31, 34, 37, 39, 42, 52, 64, 71–72, 75–76, 83, 94, 111, 115, 125–126, 129, 137, 148, 150, 157, 161, 163–164, 167, 170–175
Teller, Jackson "Jax" 20, 28, 54–69, 92, 132–136, 138–139, 164
Teller, John 57–59, 61–62, 68–69, 135, 139
Thompson, Enoch "Nucky" 92, 109–112, 118–124, 151–155, 164
Thompson, Margaret Schroeder 112, 117, 119–121, 123, 150–155
Thornton, Tara 85, 88, 139–144
torture 9, 75, 78, 80, 85, 87, 138, 143, 163, 166
True Blood 20, 24, 28–30, 70–79, 83, 86–89, 120, 125, 139

violence 9, 14, 18, 28, 30, 33–34, 37–42, 47–50, 53–56, 58–59, 61, 63–64, 67, 69, 72, 83, 87, 116–117, 123, 134, 138, 154, 160, 163, 171

White, Skyler 93, 97–99, 101, 105–107, 125, 147–150, 164
White, Walter 20, 29, 91–107, 147–150, 164
whiteness 41, 47–48, 52

Žižek, Slavoj 7, 23, 26

www.ingramcontent.com/pod-product-compliance
Ingram Content Group UK Ltd.
Pitfield, Milton Keynes, MK11 3LW, UK
UKHW042011140426
5217IPUK00015B/1117